"Invaluable"

"A compilation of invaluable insights for those seeking to be successful inventors."
–Eric P. Rose, NPDP, MBA
Inventor with 70+ patents, consultant, and MBA Professor of Product Innovation

---

"Words of Wisdom"

"For an inventor travelling down the path from the 'I've got an idea' stage to successful invention development, it can be a long and lonely journey without help. Here are some words of wisdom and guidance from those who have 'been there and done that.' Read this book and take their advice with you on your journey. It won't be so lonely, you'll increase your chances of success, and the path may be shorter."
–John Rau
President/CEO of Ultra-Research, Inc.

"Accumulated Expertise"

"Edie has identified a terrific list of topics to help stimulate any aspiring inventor. She has also assembled a strong cast of industry experts to help guide the way. I strongly suggest taking advantage of their hands-on experience and accumulated expertise. Happy Inventing."
–Warren Tuttle
President, United Inventors Association
President, Monashee Marketing and Power Tool Innovation

SECRETS OF SUCCESSFUL INVENTING

FROM CONCEPT TO COMMERCE

EDITH G. TOLCHIN, Editor

SQUAREONE
PUBLISHERS

COVER DESIGNER: Jeannie Tudor
EDITORS: Edith G. Tolchin and Michael Weatherhead
TYPESETTER: Gary A. Rosenberg

Square One Publishers
115 Herricks Road
Garden City Park, NY 11040
516-535-2010 • 877-900-BOOK
www.squareonepublishers.com

Library of Congress Cataloging-in-Publication Data
  Secrets of successful inventing / Edith G. Tolchin, editor.
    pages cm
    ISBN 978-0-7570-0407-0
  1. Inventions. 2. New products. 3. Engineering—Vocational guidance.
I. Tolchin, Edith G.
  T47.S444   2015
  600—dc23
                                          2014020743

Printed in the United States of America

10   9   8   7   6   5   4   3   2   1

Contents

Acknowledgments

I am in awe of all of my contributors and would like to acknowledge these colleagues and friends here alphabetically, as there is no way to order them by preference. I would like to thank Don Debelak, Marsha Friedman, Andy Gibbs, Gary Greenberg, Steve Greenberg, Deb Hess, Maureen Howard, Bonnie Griffin Kaake, Jack Lander, Joan Lefkowitz, Leo Mazur, Gil Tatarsky, Eddie Vélez, Karen Waksman, and Josh Wallace. They have all taught me so much more about inventing than I'd ever even considered before, kindly raising me above my niche know-how of editing, product safety, Chinese manufacturing, and US importing. I am indebted to each of them for their graciousness and patience in the face of my occasionally obsessive-compulsive habits.

For their photo contributions to the book, I would like to thank CambridgeBayWeather, Billy Hathorn, Lars Karlsson, Roger McLassus, Adrian Pingstone, Matthieu Riegler, and Sparkla.

As always, I send all my love to Ken, Dori, and Dr. Max.

An especially big thank you goes out to Rudy Shur and Square One Publishers for believing in me, and in this book. My editor, Michael Weatherhead, has been a particularly talented teacher, and I thank him for helping to put the finishing touches on this work.

Finally, I must write a few extra words of special gratitude to Don Debelak, who gave me the additional boost of confidence I needed to write my first book back in 2007. Having experienced serious personal tribulations that year, I asked Don, "Where do I go from here?" His three magical words were, "Write a book!" I'd never pictured myself as an author, even though I had written numerous trade publications and articles over the years. Since then, I've written three books (two with the invaluable co-authorship of Don himself), served as a business columnist for an upstate New York newspaper, freelanced with *Orange Magazine,* and continue to work as a contributing editor for *Inventors Digest.* Thank you for empowering me, Don.

Introduction

So you want to be a rock star? Well, this is not quite the book for you, but I did get your attention, didn't I? The truth is many of you who are reading this book may really want to be the next rock star of inventors. But creating and developing an invention is in no way a walk in the park, unless you have bottomless resources, unlimited patience, and consistent rejection only fuels your determination. You'll need help. And I have assembled a team to give it to you.

This book's contributors are the cream of the crop in the invention industry. They have been working with customers, consumers, and clients for a long time. If you were to combine their collective years of experience helping inventors, you would have to pause at 100, catch your breath, and then continue counting. In organizing the work of this collection of experts, I have attempted to create a logical flow—an order that I feel will be the most helpful way for a beginning inventor to learn to navigate the waters of product development. If you follow the steps outlined herein and heed the advice of these seasoned professionals—many of whom have been in your shoes, whether they started out as inventors or "invented" their businesses—you will stand a better chance of avoiding the predators of the service provider world along your long journey.

As editor, I have done my best to leave each contributor's original material completely intact. I feel it is important for you to get the real words of these contributors, to hear their own distinctive voices as they relate their experiences and knowledge. They will teach you all about inventors' groups, prototyping, packaging, financing, manufacturing, patenting, marketing, sales, licensing, and more. While you are welcome to jump directly to a chapter that explains a particular aspect of the process of inventing, I nevertheless recommend that you go back and read the book from beginning to end as soon as you are done. Even though you might have passed a particular stage of development, the experts in this book may bring a new and fresh perspective to your work, and possibly a more beneficial way of accomplishing a particular task. I urge you to be completely open-minded and analyze all possibilities and suggestions found in this text. Take notes on a notepad, computer, or mobile device and have them nearby as you go through the material. It may take you a while to digest all the sound ideas provided in this guide, and having a quick reference sheet may be helpful. Always keep your notes handy.

Should you be particularly impressed with this book's contributors (and I am confident you will be), you will find contact information for each contributor on the first page of his or her chapter and at the end of the book. You may contact these experts for advice or clarification, or even choose to engage their services.

The goal of *Secrets of Successful Inventing* is to provide you with the most current and comprehensive information on the world of inventions available. I have attempted to create an all-in-one guide that addresses the many issues novice inventors might not initially consider, and that gives advice on how to improve the methods of slightly more seasoned individuals. You will learn all the inventors' jargon— which is to say, all the terminology and expressions that are commonly used in the industry. What is a non-disclosure agreement? A logo? A "country of origin" tag? Social media? A packaging mock-up or a virtual prototype? By the end of this book, you'll be speaking the language of inventors like a pro.

Throughout your journey, please be prepared to expect the unexpected. If you do your homework and listen to these guides, however, I am certain you will become a wiser, better educated consumer, and, more importantly, a successful inventor. Who knows how far you will go? Happy Inventing!

1. Inventors' Groups

Leo Mazur

This is a conversation I have several times every week:

"Hello. It's Leo."

"Hmmm, ah, is this the, ah, invent . . ."

"Yes it is! How can I help you?"

I have been told that some people have been taken aback by my very cheerful opening. People expect a very businesslike greeting, such as a simple, "Inventors Society of South Florida." But I use my cell phone for personal calls as well as business calls, and I feel that a brief awkward moment is a small price for callers to pay to have me available almost any time of day. I also get numerous emails from inventors, both local and international. These inventors range from rank beginners to people with products in the market. The one common thread among all of them is their enthusiasm. God, I love it! Once we get past the cautious, "are you going to rip me off?" stage, and they start to talk about their projects, every one of them displays a powerfully optimistic attitude. Even the ones who are very shy seem to "just know" that their products are going to be "huge." It is my unpleasant task to bring these

Leo Mazur is a former president of the Inventors Society of South Florida and continues to field questions of all types from inventors located all over the world. If he doesn't know the answer to an inventor's question, he will work to find the answer, or show the inventor how to find it.

mazurelectric@earthlink.net • www.inventorssociety.net

folks back to reality a bit because no one truly knows if a product is going to make it in the marketplace. Even the biggest companies in the world with all their research can never be sure of how a product will fair until that product has been launched.

No, I'm not some horrible ogre out to crush other people's dreams. Being an inventor is a very complicated business—one with lots of rules and lots of ways to lose lots of money. I want to educate others as much as I can, especially if they are completely new to inventing, but it can be a real challenge. I need to make new inventors aware of elements of the business, including public disclosures, non-disclosure agreements, assignment clauses, and so on. By the time they get off the phone with me, their heads are often spinning, and they are probably wondering whether it is all going to be worth it.

At the end of our conversations, I always make sure to include the names of books and helpful websites to get them started. This gives them resources they can refer to as they take the next steps. Hopefully, these steps will include coming to meetings of the Inventors Society of South Florida, where they may learn firsthand from experts, who are frequently asked to be guest speakers. If the people I speak to are not local, I let them know of the clubs closest to them. I truly feel the more they know, the more likely they will be to find success, and I want everyone to be successful.

My story is not unlike most of the stories I hear. From the time I was a kid, I always thought it would be great to become an inventor. I was always tinkering and making things that I needed myself. At one point, I had come up with some tools that I thought would have real appeal. I had used them on the job and had found that my coworkers and those in other trades were interested in them. What I didn't know at the time was, by showing other people the tools, I was starting my one-year grace period to file a utility patent application. To make a long story short, the patent on those tools is now out of my hands due to my ignorance. That's all right, though, because I have since cured my ignorance with knowledge.

Around the same time, I shared another idea of mine with a coworker. He loved it and started to make suggestions. I told him I had already considered those options and had discarded them for various reasons. A week or two later, when the matter of this invention came up again, he asked me, "When are you going to build OUR invention?" Years later, I shared this same idea with another individual, and a few weeks later he asked me, "When are you going to build MY invention?" These experiences made me realize that sharing ideas for inventions was unwise. I realized how dangerously close I had come to having unexpected, and unwanted, partners. Had either of these products become successful, I would have done all the work for only a portion of the rewards.

Finally, I went from dreamer to doer with a phone call to one of those invention companies that advertises on late night television. It seemed a logical decision to me. I came up with something for that particular market, and my wife and I met with a representative of the company. After the meeting I said to my wife, "So, what do you think?" She said, "I think if you don't spend the $800 for the market research blue book I don't ever want to hear about being an inventor again." I replied, "You are the queen of catalogs and online shopping. He showed us a book full of great products. Have you ever seen any of them in stores? This is not the way to make money in this business." Thus began my journey. I read everything I could on being a successful inventor. I went to seminars and took courses. I had realized that this was a business, and that I had much to learn.

It seemed like everywhere I turned, a new idea would pop into my head. I'd go to make some eggs in the morning and end up reinventing the frying pan or the spatula. I'd go to hang a picture and come up with an invention to make the job easier. I couldn't go anywhere or do anything without coming up with "a better way." I started to think of myself as an "idea guy."

Through my research, I found a local inventors' group and nervously gave it a call. The woman on the other end of the line asked me to tell her a little of my background and why I thought I was an inventor. When I told her I get all these great ideas every day, she burst with excitement saying, "You must be an idea guy! Oh my God, do you know how long we have been looking for someone like you?" I couldn't contain my excitement as I answered, "I am! I am an idea guy!" She replied, "So is every other person you will meet at our meetings, and only a few of them have made any money." At this remark my heart sunk, but I knew it was going to have a huge impact on my new career.

The meetings with the group were great. Every month there would be new stories and new subjects brought up. The best part was networking with all the other people. We helped each other and shared our resources. These days I run into "idea guys" all the time, beginners who think like I did. They see themselves as special, and believe that someone would be willing to pay a lot of money for their talents and do all the work to bring their products to market. But as I discovered, this is not the case. It is not a bad thing to come up with so many ideas, of course, but the true inventor needs to sort through these ideas quickly to find the one or two that may have serious potential. Once this is accomplished, the true inventor will start building a case for the product and implement a plan to make the idea a reality. Sadly, this is where I find most inventors fall short.

In general, a new inventor will come up with an idea that he thinks has potential and believes that everyone else can see this potential. If he is handy, he will probably make a prototype. If he goes to a patent attorney, he will file a patent application. Somewhere along the way he will realize that this process costs a lot of money, and that to get this money he is going to need to prove that his idea truly has the potential he believes it to have. In other words, he will realize that his idea requires a business plan. Many times, as a new inventor does the research for a business plan, certain inconsistencies crop up. Maybe the market isn't as big as he had thought. Maybe it is going to cost more to manufacture the product than he had expected. Maybe there is something out there already that is better than his product. By this point, the inventor has all his hopes, dreams, and money invested in his creation, so does he want to hear that it may not fly? I don't think so. That's why I encourage people to start with a business plan. It is easier to be objective and drop a project that has no clear path to success at the beginning rather than to give up on something you have put your heart and soul into for years.

BEFORE PROOF OF CONCEPT

While the subject of doing a proof of concept (POC) prototype will be discussed later on in this book, I would like to shed light on a few important points that should be addressed before taking this step in the process. First, do patent, product, and industry searches to find your competition, and possibly add some features to your concept to make it better. Next, determine how much of your product you can own and whether this amount will be enough to achieve your ultimate goal.

Learn the standards of the industry you are working in, including price points, manufacturing methods, methods of distribution, and the way in which a new product penetrates the market. Define all the gate-keepers and how you will overcome them. Finally, and perhaps most importantly, hear the voice of your customer.

With less than a 1-percent success rate for new products on the market, the first and second points seem fairly obvious. Similar products could inform an inventor about the probable success of his own idea. While there are thousands of products out there that will likely never be seen, should one succeed, an unknown patent holder could become an unexpected partner if you are not careful. And if an inventor's ultimate goal is to license his product to a large company, his patent needs to be strong enough to warrant making the deal.

Every industry has standards that it must follow. You can learn about these standards by researching the companies you want to do business with. Read trade magazines and join trade associations. You may need to research associate trade groups. For example, if your product is a new carpentry tool, you would, of course, want to learn about carpenters and companies making carpentry tools, but you should also learn about the companies that sell those tools. It is vital to understand their buying methods and their rules for submitting new products.

Think of the road to success as blocked by gatekeepers. Sure, the typical gatekeeper is the executive assistant who always tells you the boss is out of the office, but there are many other obstacles to overcome, including such issues as third-party testing requirements and government regulations. You should determine what these obstacles are and figure out ways to surmount them before you start spending any money. The toughest gatekeeper may end up being the buyer for the retailer. Although the end user may love your product, if it doesn't meet with the buyer's specifications there will be no sale.

The thing inventors seem to neglect most is the need to understand the customer. This is one of the biggest issues separating inventors and the big corporations, which, by the way, have an 80-percent chance of success with any given product they choose to launch. They spend a fortune having focus groups, doing surveys, and testing marketing strategies. It could be said that the consumer actually develops their products for them. It makes sense. Let the customer tell you what they want and then give it to them. Unfortunately, most inventors go with their guts. As I've said before; new inventors "just know" their products are going to sell. But the truth is that, in most cases, this "knowledge" alone is not good enough. As an inventor, you will need to convince an investor or licensee—and ultimately, retailers—that your product is going to outsell what they already have on the shelf. The more proof you can put together, the better chance you have of success. You are going to have to do the work at some point. Why not start at the beginning and first prove to yourself that you are on the right track?

In the beginning, you don't have to reveal what your product is. An invention is meant to solve a problem, and you can simply talk to your target market about the problem your invention seeks to solve. Find out what these people use to solve the problem. In fact, find out if they feel it is a valid problem, for that matter. For example, I have seen a number of nail-holding devices at trade shows. If you have ever hit your finger instead of the nail you were holding, you know a problem exists. Those who hang the occasional picture might find a nail-holding product quite clever. But those who are handy or swing a hammer for a living realize that the same function can be achieved with the pliers they already have in their tool pouches. They would never buy such a device, which is why you will probably never see one in a store.

Many inventors feel they question their customers adequately, but just talking to people is completely different from interviewing them. Before an interview, you must set up the key questions you want answered. During an interview, you must document your results. Documentation is a key factor because without it you will likely remember only the positive comments afterwards. Interviews can be done in casual conversation, through focus groups and surveys, or in meetings at trade shows or similar events. You can use combinations of these methods, of course. You can use a confidentiality agreement (CA) or a non-disclosure agreement (NDA) if your product is not patent-pending and you wish to reveal proprietary information about it. Once you have a patent application in place, you can make a public disclosure, and it is a very common practice to do so, but you are not really protected by your patent until it has been issued, though large companies launch products all the time that are patent-pending.

In the beginning, any data you can collect is wonderful. The more data you have, the more confident you can be. I have been advised, however, that at least 385 respondents are required for data to have the statistical significance to make a business decision with a 95-percent confidence level, with a margin of error of plus or minus 5 percent. You need approximately five times this number, or 1,884, to raise your confidence level to 99 percent, with a margin of error of plus or minus 3 percent. Some inventors' groups allow their members to present to the group under a collective non-disclosure agreement. Although you will get excellent feedback from other inventors, you will not get the same information that comes from talking to ordinary consumers. Inventors will often give you opinions with a focused or business-minded view of the market, which, while helpful, will ultimately prove insufficient for your needs.

My group allows its members to introduce their products at meetings, but it does not use a collective non-disclosure agreement, so presenters must have their products protected or suffer the consequences. One of our members came in with a product for which he had already envisioned a fairly large market. The group started brainstorming and the next thing he knew his market had grown tenfold. This led him down a completely different path. He changed the name of the product and is now making some serious headway.

Inventors are often inspired by the news. I don't care if it is an oil spill, a mass shooting, or a cheating scandal, inventors see a problem and they try to come up with a solution. That's what they do. When inventors contact me for help, they don't tell me how their ideas are going to solve certain problems, and I don't want to know. I usually try to find a way for them to submit the idea to the appropriate party. Frequently, an inventor will tell me that his invention will save lives, and that the government is sure to mandate the product. While this article does not aim to determine whether a government mandate is a good thing, it must be said that it is next to impossible to get the government to mandate anything. It takes tons of money and a huge public outcry to get merely a debate started in Congress. Consider the effort Mothers

Against Drunk Driving (MADD) has already expended trying to persuade the federal government to mandate a breathalyzer in the vehicles of repeat drunk drivers. This breathalyzer would disable the car's engine if the driver's blood alcohol level tested over the legal limit. Although bills with such provisions have been passed by a number of states, requiring breathalyzers in the cars of repeat offenders is a great idea that has yet to be embraced federally.

A long time ago, one of our members gave a presentation on why nobody wanted his product, and it was a real eye-opener for me. What he had invented was a simple device that would help users place eye drops on their eyes. Older patients especially have problems doing this and end up wasting a lot of expensive medication. Of course, this inventor first went to the pharmaceutical companies with his idea. After all, the company with this product would surely have an unfair advantage over its competitors, and customers would certainly choose the company with the device that would prevent them from wasting their medication. But the pharmaceutical companies did not agree. They didn't care where the medicine went as long as the customer bought more. He went to the insurance companies, thinking his product would save them money. They also did not agree. As far as they were concerned, they covered a certain dollar amount of the cost of a prescription per month, and once that amount was reached the rest was not their problem. This inventor went to the government and to pharmacies. He even went to AARP. Nobody was interested in helping older people save their eye drops. As far as I know, he finally gave up on the project. Since then, I have seen other products that were very similar trying to climb that hill unsuccessfully.

What inventors need to realize is that even a product that can help millions of people will not do well unless there is a real profit to be made. We need to identify how our project will be received by the industry. What new advantage would it bring to the table? I often see or hear of "me too" products. This is when a product is really selling well and an inventor decides to make an incremental improvement to it, thinking he'll land on a gold mine. In a way, there are a lot of products that make it into the marketplace on the coattails of other inventions, but these generally do not do as well as the originals, and if they somehow start doing better than the originals, lawsuits may appear.

Combination devices are a different story. If you can eliminate a tool in a tradesperson's pouch, that person will take a serious look at what you have. I knew of an ingenious tool that was given a second function simply through the addition of a set of jaws to its handles, which eliminated the need for pliers. A major company was very interested in licensing the product, but lost interest when it found out its inventor had only a design patent on the device.

INTELLECTUAL PROPERTY PROTECTION

I speak to a lot of inventors who ask me if I know of an inexpensive patent agent, as attorneys are too expensive. This one really makes me shake my head because intellectual property (IP) protection is not a "one size fits all" matter. People will comparison shop for the best value when buying potato chips, but think only of price when getting a patent. Writing a patent is an art. The wording is very critical. The product and how it relates to its industry should decide how much to budget for its protection. To understand my point better, think of your product's industry as a neighborhood and your product as a house in this neighborhood. If every one of your neighbors has bars on his windows, you may want to think about putting bars on yours as well. In addition, if your house is the nicest one in the neighborhood, you are probably going to want to add some extra security to it. If it is one of the least attractive homes, maybe you can get away with the bare minimum. As you necessarily plan on selling or renting this house, how desirable it is and how well you have protected it will determine the price you can expect to get for it.

The electronics industry is probably the most volatile industry there is. Low-level products come and go so quickly that it probably isn't worth the effort to patent them. If a product is a radical improvement, however, it will start to look like the best house on the block, and will then need some serious protection, as the electronics industry is filled with litigation. On the other hand, there are all sorts of industries that are not as complicated—pets and novelties come to mind. We have all seen dozens of variations regarding a leash and a flashlight. I did a quick search online using those two terms and got dozens of hits. I am sure there are more products that are not patented, but I could not find an infringement suit regarding any of these devices. This could be because the projected rewards that might come from a successful lawsuit are outweighed by the cost of the lawsuit itself.

The word "rewards" is the key. It sums up what type of action you must take as an inventor to achieve your goal. What rewards are you looking for? Many of the older members of my group tell me that they simply want to supplement their incomes and maybe leave something of value behind for their kids and grandchildren. Most inventors, however, are looking either for the "big score," or for numerous smaller returns from numerous smaller yet profitable products. Many inventors do want to do all the work involved with launching an invention, but they soon understand that this business is a "no pain, no gain" situation. What all inventors must do is define the rewards they are looking for, and then determine the best methods to achieve them. It sounds simple, and it is. It just requires a lot of hard work.

More often than not, the ultimate goal is to license a product to a large company. To many this might seem like trying to climb Mount Everest with one hand tied behind your back. But, believe it or not, big companies are always on the lookout for that next big product to license. So what's the problem? Maybe I should have put more emphasis on the word "big." Companies are inundated with tons of incremental improvements to and new uses for their existing lines of devices. A business faces a huge liability issue when it looks at the ideas that people submit, as these ideas may already be in development within the company. Large companies are a huge target for people trying to make a quick buck through litigation, so it is no wonder they can be a bit guarded. But a licensing deal with a big company can be done.

The phrase "open innovation" was coined by Henry Chesbrough in 2002 and has developed into a portal through which companies may bring in new products from the outside. Each company may handle the concept a bit differently, but the ways in which businesses now accept external ideas are still quite similar. I don't know of any company that will sign a non-disclosure agreement. A business will usually make inventors sign a disclosure agreement, which states that it can use any submissions without any required payment, and that it is up to the inventor to protect his intellectual property. In addition, a company will typically provide a form to be filled out that includes questions covering topics that would be in a business plan. Sometimes you can access this form from a company's website by searching the words "outside submissions," "open innovation," "new product submission," or other combinations of these terms. You can also do an online search using the same key phases and the name of the company you wish to reach. Sometimes you really have to work hard to find the entryway to a company.

If you go for it, be prepared with a well-documented, complete business plan. The people who go over submissions are very busy. They will not fill in the blanks for you. Any inconsistency will result in quick rejection. Remember, each time a gatekeeper gives the go-ahead to a new idea, his job is likely on the line, so put your best foot forward.

CONCLUSION

"Do I really have to do all this stuff just to get a simple product in the market?" The quick answer is no. The more you know about your industry and the stronger the case you can make for your product, the better your chances of success will be. But there are many other ways to participate in the process, although the rewards may not be as great. My group provides free information via email about contests, product hunts, and educational and media opportunities. All you have to do is sign up on our website, www.inventorssociety.net. Websites such as www.edisonnation.com constantly run product hunts in which you can submit ideas without doing all the legwork. If your project is accepted, it may be developed at no cost to you.

The best piece of advice I give everyone who contacts me is to get involved. Get involved with your industry's trade organizations. Get involved with various inventors' online groups. Most importantly, get involved with your local inventors' group. You will learn so much in such a short time about the business of inventing that you will surely be able to take on the challenge of being an inventor. Use your monthly meeting as a benchmark to see what you have accomplished and let it inspire you to move forward in the month ahead. Little by little, month by month, the knowledge you gain along with your accomplishments will build your confidence to the point at which success will not be a matter of "if" but of "when."

ONE BIG IDEA

Slinky was invented in 1943 by naval mechanical engineer Richard James. Soon after, he and his wife, Betty, started a business by taking a loan for $500 to produce a few hundred Slinky units to sell to toy stores. After a demonstration of James' compressed steel coil at Gimbel's department store in Philadelphia, Pennsylvania, in 1945, the simple toy became a big hit, delighting children ever since with its amazing ability to propel itself down stairs.

2. Prototyping

Jack Lander

When it comes to inventing, you should know which manufacturing processes and materials you will use to produce your invention in its final form. You should then begin your design around these processes and materials. Finally, you must work backwards from these chosen processes to find the appropriate methods of prototyping and the materials that you will use in prototyping, which will be different from those used in production. You may not be entirely certain of the manufacturing processes and materials, but an intuitive guess is better than complete uncertainty. An educated guess is better still.

For example, assume your invention is a novel kitchen tool. From your knowledge of similar and complementary kitchen tools, you acknowledge it will have to be made of metal or plastic. You suspect that plastic will be more practical and less expensive than metal, so it becomes your first choice. You've heard about plastic injection molding, but discover that injection molds typically cost between $10,000 and $100,000. Obviously, you aren't going to spend that amount of money to create a prototype or even a pilot run (although, I know of one inventor who did exactly that). What you need to know is how to make one

Jack Lander is a seasoned inventor and mentor to inventors. With thirteen patents, Jack is also a small-business veteran, having founded eleven businesses. He is a past president of the United Inventors Association, and served as Vice President of the Yankee Invention Exposition for fourteen years. He is the founder of DIG, the Danbury (Connecticut) Inventor's Group.

JackL359@aol.com • www.inventor-mentor.com

piece, or even a few pieces, without a production mold. I will explain how to accomplish this task, and how to do so at minimum cost.

The main difference between a production process and a prototyping process is the tooling that is used. In general, the higher the production quantity, the more money is invested in machinery and tooling. Prototyping tooling ranges from almost none (in the hands of a highly creative person) to sophisticated machines used by the major industries to get their prototypes out quickly, when cost is a secondary consideration.

THE ORIGINS OF PROTOTYPING

The origins of modern prototyping date back to when the United States Patent and Trademark Office required a physical prototype as proof that an invention had been "reduced to practice." Since then, most inventors have followed this tradition, creating working prototypes of their inventions. Of course, in many cases, ergonomic needs and the uncertainties involved in making mechanical devices are compelling enough reasons to make physical prototypes. Moreover, a prototype can serve as proof that your concept actually works. This kind of prototype is known as a "proof of concept prototype."

In the past few years, the "virtual prototype" has become a major option for many inventors. In other words, even the inventor of a complex mechanical product does not have to prove that it will work provided she is absolutely certain that it will. The United States Patent and Trademark Office considers the act of drawing an invention in detail and describing its operation sufficient to satisfy its rule of "reduction to practice." So, today we have two basic categories of prototype: physical and virtual. I should add that a virtual prototype is never a fiction, nor is it even speculative. It consists of a computer-generated image or video representation of an invention that can be realized in functional, physical form if and when it is practical to do so. A physical prototype may be subdivided into the following categories:

- **Proof of concept prototype.** A crude version of a product, ranging from a basic "balsa wood and rubber band" construction to a fully functional and durable device that lacks only cosmetic refinement.

- **Presentation prototype.** The "looks like, works like" version. Essentially, the off-the-shelf product. May be presented to potential licensees, partners, financiers, individuals for testing, etc.

- **Pilot run prototype.** The production of a small quantity of the invention, perhaps ten to fifty pieces, to be tested by people who will give you their opinions, or to be used to gauge sales response on a small scale.

A virtual prototype may be subdivided into the following categories:

- **Lifelike image.** An image created by CAD (computer-aided design) using a 3D program and sometimes called a virtual photo. Along with the sell sheet, it is one of the two main components of a virtual prototype.

- **Sell sheet.** A single-page brochure that illustrates the lifelike virtual image of a product and stresses in writing the product's features and benefits to the end user.

- **Animated program.** An animated image created by CAD using a 3D program and manipulated to show motions that help explain the nature and benefits of an invention.

- **Video.** Typically, a video that displays a real person demonstrating the physical prototype. (I classify this as virtual because its recipient does not see and handle the actual physical prototype.)

These subcategories are, of course, a generalization, but they are sufficient for this discussion. I must, however, clarify the minor distinction between the first two categories. Practically speaking, a lifelike image and a sell sheet form one and the same item. Use the term "sell sheet" when your purpose is marketing-directed, and use the term "virtual prototype," or "lifelike image," for all other purposes. When in doubt, use the term "sell sheet." After all, your overriding purpose is to convince someone to sell your product.

VIRTUAL PROTOYPING

Although my purpose is not to bias you towards virtual prototyping, there are many advantages to this method. The cost of a virtual prototype is often much lower than that of a physical prototype. It is also much quicker to make a virtual prototype. Because a sell sheet must be prepared in almost all cases to explain the benefits of an invention effectively, the cost of a sell sheet must be added to the cost of a physical prototype. This extra cost, however, may be eliminated through the use of a virtual prototype, which often doubles as a sell sheet, as previously mentioned. A virtual prototype may be used to determine interest in an invention, helping the inventor to make an informed decision before investing in a physical prototype and a full utility patent. The computer-generated virtual prototype becomes the master document with which to explain an invention and boast about its benefits to individuals, beta-site testers, prospective partners, prospective financial investors, potential licensees, retailers, and catalog managers.

Another advantage to virtual prototyping is that countless reproductions can be printed quickly and relatively inexpensively once the master computer model has been created. Similarly, if a physical prototype is lost or its return is delayed by a potential licensee, money and time must be spent in its retrieval. If a virtual prototype is lost, the consequences are of little concern. In addition, if an invention is large or heavy, a physical prototype poses a problem, especially when the product needs to be demonstrated at a distant location.

In terms of demonstrating a product, if an invention has internal working parts that must remain hidden or cannot be easily viewed, a virtual prototype can show any number of cutaway perspectives. If an invention has internal working parts that operate too quickly for the eye to follow, such as those of a combustion engine, a virtual prototype video in slow motion may clarify its operation.

A virtual prototype consists of two main parts: a virtual photograph and the writing that describes the invention's features and benefits and sometimes its technical details. A virtual photograph alone has been referred to as a virtual prototype, but a photo on its own may fail to describe what the product is and how it may benefit users. Just as a picture of a person is not a résumé, so a lone photograph of an invention is not a virtual prototype. A virtual prototype begins as a sketch, which usually evolves through several iterations until a rough design is deemed satisfactory. Although these sketches need not be artistically refined, the final version should be dimensioned, and include notes on materials and colors. It will serve as the basis for a three-dimensional computer-aided design, or 3D CAD. The CAD draftsperson will create what is known as a wireframe, which is a skeleton of the design. The wireframe is then filled in to become a virtual solid object. The object, of course, consists of a digital file within the computer, so remember to ask for a copy of the digital file on an external storage device.

The writing component of the virtual prototype must follow the rules of writing advertising copy. Unfortunately, many small advertising agencies and other service providers often lack this ability, having made names for themselves through the use of computer graphics, which emphasize artwork at the expense of effective writing. In addition, even those who appreciate the art of writing advertising copy are not always trained in the subject. Large studios, however, may dread working with amateurs, who are unfamiliar with the process and simply don't know what they want. To cover the increased time they may have to spend on such accounts, they may hike up their prices. I advise any new inventor to resolve what she will furnish and what she wants at the end of the day before she contacts a sell sheet service.

A sell sheet essentially is an advertisement, a proposal that attempts to convince someone to buy something. The time-honored and most effective format for an ad or proposal is represented by the acronym "AIDA," which stands for attention, interest, desire, and action.

If you have ever been approached by a person trying to sell you something, you know that your first reaction is resistance, or at least skepticism. The AIDA approach effectively breaks down this resistance by presenting a sales pitch gradually, in steps, each of which is non-threatening.

If you doubt this method, test AIDA against the next few written sales pitches that elicit a positive response from you. The headline and photo likely attracted your attention. The bulleted list of benefits probably aroused your interest. The testimonials created your desire for the product. Finally, the information on how to acquire the product facilitated the act of purchasing it. Note the word "facilitated." This means more than merely telling a potential customer how to make a purchase.

It means the process has been made easy and painless, usually by the inclusion of a phone number and a website or email address.

Graphic artists are clever at creating eye appeal, which is paramount to attracting attention, but when graphic artists are not guided by AIDA they can produce some of the greatest wastes of paper imaginable. I've seen sell sheets that couldn't convince me to do any more than crumple them in a ball and toss them into my waste basket. Insist that whoever prepares your sell sheet follows the four AIDA steps in sequence.

The ideal sell sheet will feature a tagline in bold print at the top of the page. A tagline is a single brief sentence that expresses what the product is and directs its major benefit to the ultimate user and not to the intermediate customer, which may be the catalog or retail store buyer receiving the pitch. A tagline must attract attention and arouse interest within a few seconds. Statements like "we are proud to announce" or "presenting" are turn-offs, distractions from the vital content, and a waste of precious space. No one except you and your loved ones cares how proud you are of a product. Think only from the viewpoint of the end user, which is usually the consumer. A brief tagline may have a sub-tagline below it. In general, avoid questions, such as, "Do you spend too much time washing your car?" Questions are weak statements and do not always elicit the desired answer. Instead, make a declarative statement, such as, "The new XYZ sponge washes your car in seven minutes flat!" In the previous case, you could probably add a sub-tagline, such as, ". . . and saves an average of four gallons of hot water."

Once the tagline has been chosen, place a color photo—either a virtual photo or an actual photo—of about 3 by 4 inches below it and towards the left side of the page. If appropriate, show the product being used by a person. Get in close. Show hands only unless otherwise necessary.

To the right of the photo, just below the tag line, include a brief statement that defines the product, if the tagline hasn't already done so, but don't get carried away. Remember to avoid placing too emphasis on features. Features don't sell a product; benefits sell a product. Inventors think in terms of features and must be especially disciplined to change this perspective when working on any kind of advertising.

Also to the right of the photo, mention any subordinate benefits in a bulleted list.

Below the photo and the list of benefits, include the most positive testimonials you have of the product. You may have to lend your prototype to a few friends or acquaintances in order to get honest testimonials, but be sure they don't all come from the same region, or even from the same state. This may be a troublesome step, but testimonials convince people to purchase products more than any other words ever could. Below the testimonials, you may cautiously discuss features, but only those that yield benefits. Use the following sequence: feature and resulting benefit. For example, state, "Built with stainless steel ball bearings that will never rust or corrode, thus guaranteeing product XYZ's long life." This is also the area in which to write the product's UPC code and the company's liability insurance, if applicable. Lastly, below the features, divide the remaining area approximately in half. In the left section, enter your company's address and contact information. Place a rectangular box around the right hand area and leave it blank. This space is for rubber stamping information such as a distributor's contact information.

Follow this format and don't get too fancy. The objective is to sell, not to dazzle with glitzy artwork. Remember that the best formula to use is "AIDA." It's what I call the "gradual induction principle." Treat the sales process as you would the act of courtship. First comes the date, which is followed by infatuation, which is followed by true love, which is followed by lifelong commitment.

PHYSICAL PROTOTYPING

The following methods are used to make prototypes and small production runs. They imitate the appearance and qualities of production parts that will eventually be made by an injection molding machine, which typically uses one of two processes: plastic injection molding or metal die casting. The same digital information used for 3D CAD drawings, with a few program amendments, can now be used by a variety of machines to create a physical model that looks exactly like the virtual model on the computer screen. These processes have been informally labeled "rapid prototyping" and include stereolithography (SLA), 3D printing, selective laser sintering (SLS), the Z process, investment casting, plaster mold casting, and material removal machinery such as milling machines, lathes, abrasive water jet, laser cutting, and chemical milling.

Material Additive Processes

Stereolithography, 3D printing, selective laser sintering, the Z process, investment casting, and plaster mold casting are known as "material additive" processes because they start with a "clean slate," that is, a bare platen on which material is added and built up. Think of the process as similar to a child building a clay model on a wire frame, or making a clay mold of his hand and then pouring plaster in it to create a replica of his hand. These methods typically employ a plastic material, although metals may also be sintered using the jetting process or cast in a mold. Since material additive processes build an object layer by layer, the result of an angled edge of an object built is known as "stairstepping." If you are familiar with the stone layers of the Egyptian pyramids, you'll be able to visualize stairstepping. Stairstepping is acceptable for most early purposes of the prototype, but for final "show and tell" issues it may be reduced to a smooth surface by sanding.

Stereolithography (SLA)

This process begins with the three-dimensional digital image of an object. The image is then cut into slices of about .005 of an inch thick, although layers as thin as .002 of an inch may be used for particular applications. The thinner the slice, the longer the process takes, and the more expensive it is. The slices are, of course, imaginary, and only take place within the digital data.

The production aspect consists of a vat of liquid plastic that can be hardened by an ultraviolet light. It begins with a platform at the top of the vat of liquid polymer, or liquid plastic. This platform drops down about .005 of an inch—about the thickness of two human hairs—and a layer of liquid plastic is swept across it by a blade. This thin layer of liquid plastic is then scanned by an ultraviolet laser beam according to information from the bottommost slice of the 3D image, which hardens the plastic. The platform continues to drop down in equal increments, adding and hardening subsequent layers of plastic, bonding each new level to the previous one. Layer by layer, the physical model is created. Once the last layer has been completed, the complete piece rises from the remaining liquid plastic and is allowed to drain for a time. It then gets washed to remove any remaining liquid and is placed in an ultra-violet "oven," where it is flooded with ultraviolet light that further cures the plastic.

SLA is the oldest computer-driven material additive process, and the one that inspired the creation of many other material additive meth-ods. One disadvantage of stereolithography, however, is the high cost of the photopolymers used to make the hardened plastic.

3D Printing

A recent addition to material additive processes, 3D printing is very similar to ink jet printing, except the material ejected is a molten plas-tic, not ink. The 3D model is constructed layer by layer. The printer is driven by the slices of digital data, much in the way stereolithography works. 3D printing is presently the least expensive rapid prototyping method. Desktop machines are available at prices approaching those of ink jet printers. The only downside to owning a desktop 3D printer is the need to learn how to use computer-aided design to draw objects in 3D, though drawings may be obtained from outside services, if necessary.

Selective Laser Sintering (SLS)

Metal sintering is the heating of very small metal particles, which are eventually fused together through the use of CO_2 pulsed lasers. Selec-tive laser sintering starts with a thin layer of powdered plastic, or for metal parts, a powdered metal mix. A blade swipes across a deposit of the powder, leveling it precisely to the proper thickness, which, again, is approximately .005 of an inch. A laser beam heats and melts the plas-tic powder layer by layer. Although metals can also be sintered, the process is much more demanding.

In many cases, depending on the design of the part, it is less expen-sive to machine the part rather than to sinter it. But certain parts, such as boat propellers or those with many undercuts, are difficult or even impossible to machine by metal removal. Metal sintering requires exacting control of temperature and is significantly more demanding for metal than for plastic. Consequently, it is much more expensive.

The Z process

This process is similar to selective laser sintering, except that the powder is not plastic but a kind of starchy material that is hardened by a liquid binder rather than by heat. This is the original ink jet process that led to the ejection of molten plastic. The Z process is able to create parts in several colors, and can make an assembly of parts in one setup, each with its own color, if need be.

Casting

If you wish to make several identical copies of your master prototype, you may do so by making a silicone rubber mold and casting a two-part liquid material, usually polyurethane, that will harden into a durable plastic or rubber-like part. Casting refers to introducing a liquid into a mold without the use of pressure. The casting process begins by making the mold, such as a block mold, using a two-part liquid elastomer, or rubber-like material, such as silicone rubber, that cures when the two parts are mixed together and allowed to stand for a time. Making the silicone rubber mold is itself a casting process, in fact.

A single-stage mold may be used as cast, or may be separated into two parts by careful cutting after the material has cured. A two-stage mold is made by casting the first part, allowing it to cure, applying mold release to its common surface with the second part, and then casting the second part. A single-stage mold may be used as a one-piece mold for a part that does not have undercuts, which refer to any hollows in or protuberances on a molded piece.

While a two-piece mold will generally permit easier removal of the hardened part, one exception would be a one-piece mold known as the blanket mold. It is made by brushing a very thin layer of the mold-making compound onto the master. This layer would then be peeled off the cast part in the same way you would remove a rubber glove from your hand. Such a mold, however, is very flexible and easily distorted without some form of external support. Thus, before removing the master and after the brushed-on mold material has cured, a very thick shell of plaster is cast over it, making it, in effect, rigid. To remove the casting from the mold, the blanket and the casting inside are pulled from the shell, and then, of course, the rubber-like blanket is peeled off.

Casting the elastomer must be done in a leak-proof container. A loaf pan, a paper or plastic cup, or even a specially constructed box should work. Molds made from silicone elastomer usually don't need a mold release in order to remove the mold from the container. Other elastomers, however, may stick to their containers, but this may be avoided by spraying the containers with a mold release, or even coating them with Vaseline or a similar grease. Once the mold is complete, you may cast a two-part polymer or elastomer, thereby producing your prototype.

When casting metals, the choice is typically between investment casting and foundry casting. Investment casting dates back thousands of years, having been used to make icons and jewelry in Egypt and Africa. It is the process by which much of today's jewelry, dental crowns, and complex parts that cannot be machined by metal removal are made. Originally, a beeswax model, or master pattern, of the desired item was carved by hand. The wax was then invested, or coated, with a form of plaster and left with a protruding stem. The plaster mold was then placed in an oven with the stem pointed downwards and the wax was melted out of the mold. This left a hollow shell into which molten metal could be poured.

This method is still used today, except that a special wax and a low-ash plastic are now available to create the master pattern, which allows rapid prototyping methods such as investment casting to use 3D CAD digital data to produce the master pattern as well as the metal casting. Silicon compounds, rather than ordinary plaster, are now used for a first coating, providing a very fine finish. A rough mix of sand and plaster are then employed to strengthen this first coating.

In contrast to investment casting, which typically makes small parts, foundry casting is usually chosen for larger parts made of zinc alloys or aluminum. The master pattern is made using one of the rapid prototyping processes, or is machined by a material removal method, and a sacrificial plaster mold is made from the master. Unlike investment casting, foundry casting is seldom used for volume production. It is generally considered for small runs or prototyping before the creation of molds for die casting.

Other Material Additive Processes

Vacuum forming, or thermoforming, is a process that consists of heating a sheet of plastic, placing it over a mold, and drawing a vacuum on the sheet in order to suck it down into the mold. Sometimes pressure is added to ensure conformity to detailed features. Molds for short runs are made of wood or wood-like material. While many plastics are not suitable for this process, the plastics that are used include PET, acrylic, polycarbonate/ABS, high density polyethylene, and PVC/acrylic. The most common product that is vacuum formed is the blister package.

Rotational molding is a process for molding large, hollow items, such as shipping drums and tanks, from plastic. Tooling for rotational molding is far less expensive than tooling for injection molding. Prototypes of rotationally molded parts are sometimes made by vacuum forming sheets and welding them together. And yes, many plastics can be welded in much the same way metals are, but with much less heat.

Blow molding is the method used to make the millions of clear plastic bottles in which products such as condiments and cleaning chemicals are sold. It's a fantastic production process, but difficult to prototype. The best process is to vacuum form the desired part in halves, and then weld or glue the parts together, finishing the seam as best you can.

Material Subtractive Processes

In contrast to material additive methods, material removal machinery may be considered analogous to a sculptor, who starts with a block of marble and chisels away until the statue appears. This method is sometimes referred to as a "material subtractive" process, though it was simply called "machining" before the advent of material additive processes.

It starts with a bar or block of material from which pieces are cut away until only the part remains. Automatic material removal developments occurred more or less in parallel with rapid prototyping, the most notable of which was computer numerical control, or CNC. The most recent form of CNC uses digital data from 3D CAD drawings to drive material removal machines directly, rather than having a human being write a program to produce the part based on a drawing. The main amendments to the 3D CAD program are determining the sequence of the cutting operations and its appropriate cutting tool, and specifying allowances for the tool shape and size. For example, the digital data is unaware of the tool diameter, and, unless changed, would define the axis of the tool path. Thus, an end mill of half an inch in diameter would require that the axis of the tool path be moved outwards a quarter of an inch to allow for the tool's radius. In addition, end mills with curved tips, known as ball end mills, are often used to soften the effect of stairstepping when curved surfaces are cut.

Although other means of removing material are available, including grinding, drilling, burning, and electrical discharge, the workhorses of material removal remain turning and milling. The essential difference between these two machines is whether the cutting tool or the part being made is in constant motion.

Turning

This process consists of gripping the metal—usually in a rotating chuck—and turning it and moving it against a non-rotating cutting tool, which cuts away the material. The machine that does this is called a lathe.

Milling

This method consists of clamping the material on a movable bed that slides left to right or right to left (the X axis), and front to back or back to front (the Y axis). The bed can also be raised or lowered (the Z axis). The milling machine's cutting tool constantly rotates, and the work is moved against the rotating tool. Most milling machines are vertical mills, which somewhat resemble a drill press, but horizontal milling machines are also used for certain operations, mainly those that require the removal of a lot of material, sometimes with less precision than is typical of the vertical mill.

Chemical Milling

Chemical milling, or chemical etching, is a precision photographic process that produces sheets of parts, and often several parts per sheet. It deals with thin metals relative to abrasive water jet and laser cutting.

The master is a photographic negative. The master is made by photographing a drawing of the part, and the exposure is stepped and repeated to fit as many parts on the negative as possible. The drawing does not consist of the usual lines that outline the part, but depicts the part as a two-dimensional solid white and solid black, wherever the sheet is to be etched. The metal to be etched is coated with an emulsion that resists the etching chemical. It is then exposed through the negative, which is in direct contact with it, developed similarly to a regular photograph, and the areas to be etched are washed away in the developing process. The sheet of metal is then sprayed with an etchant, and the metal is etched away, leaving a sheet of parts connected by thin sacrificial "runners." The remaining protective emulsion is washed away and the parts are separated from the runners using scissors or sheet metal shears.

Chemical etching is sometimes used to produce delicate, lacy-looking jewelry such as earrings, or similar Christmas tree ornaments. It is the capacity to produce extremely fine and precise detail that distinguishes chemical etching from abrasive water jet cutting. For less demanding detail, either process is acceptable. The mix of tooling and unit costs is such that only obtaining and comparing the prices for a specific quantity made by each process can determine which is the more economical. Although chemical milling is not a rapid prototyping process, it is an affordable process for producing a small quantity of precise, thin, flat metal parts.

Machining Centers

These machines combine the features of a vertical milling machine with the ability to change tools automatically to make different cuts, and to lubricate and cool the cutting process with a spray. Because they are production machines that are computer-program driven, they are typically enclosed to prevent chips from falling to the floor, and lubricant from spraying onto the floor and the operator. Machining centers operate without constant operator attention, and are programmed to shut off when the part is completed.

Abrasive Water Jet Cutting and Laser Cutting

Abrasive water jets or lasers may be used to cut shapes from plastics, rubbery materials, and even metals. This process is considered rapid prototyping, although it is not available to desktop machinery and, therefore, must be obtained from vendors. It uses 3D CAD digital data from drawings and produces precise prototypes that simulate parts that would be stamped in volume production. The abrasive water method uses a jet of water, typically loaded with garnet abrasive particles and ejected at greater than 50 thousand pounds per square inch of pressure. It has the advantage over laser cutting for thick parts. Some vendors have facilities for bending the cut parts, but precision sheet metal shops can be used for secondary operations if bending is not available from the cutting vendor.

Laser cutting uses a powerful laser to cut materials that are predominantly less than one quarter of an inch thick. The thicker the material is, the slower the process will be, and the less accurate the cut will end up. Thin sheets can be cut very precisely. Copper cannot be cut by this process because of its reflection, and because it conducts the heat so rapidly that melting is not practical. Aluminum, too, offers problems in cutting for the same reasons, and many shops will not process aluminum. Both steel and stainless steel are easier to cut, and ordinary cold-rolled steel parts are the most common. Like abrasive water jet cutting, laser cutting is driven by digital data from 3D CAD drawings.

Spinning

Spinning is a process that creates axially symmetrical bowl-like parts, such as light reflectors, vases, etc. The process starts with a disk of metal placed in a lathe. The metal is usually formed against a mandrel that has the inside shape of the desired part. Small diameter parts can be formed from tubing in many cases. Spinning is a practical way to produce parts in relatively small quantities, while avoiding the expense of a die for drawing the part. Spinning is used for limited production runs and prototyping. Cost per part is substantially higher than that of deep drawing, but tooling is far less expensive.

Stamping

This method produces parts from sheet metal by either a short-run process that uses standard, individual punches and dies, or a volume process that uses a custom die set. The short-run process is available at precision sheet metal vendors, and is practical for prototypes. The punches and dies are used in a turret machine that is programmed to change from one tool to the other, and to position them on the sheet metal blank. Holes are positioned and stamped one at a time through the programmed series. Because the machines and tools are universal, a die set is not needed. If the part involves bending or shaping, this is done as a separate operation on a press brake, or bending machine, after the part is punched. Volume production is achieved using a die set designed to punch either all of the holes at once, or in a series of stages that may include bending or shaping. Die sets are very expensive, and the parts produced are relatively inexpensive.

The Four-Slide Process

This method involves a machine that processes a coil of wire or a relatively thin and narrow strip of metal. The metal is advanced to a first position, and one of the slides moves its forming or punching tool against a stationary opposing tool. The material is then advanced, and a second tool slides against or through the material until all features of the part have been formed. The part is then cut off at the last slide station.

Flat springs, brackets, wire forms, paperclips, and electrical socket parts are some of the typical items made on a four-slide machine. The main advantage of the four-slide is that expensive permanent tooling, such as a progressive die set, is not needed. Four-slide machines take time to set up, and therefore small quantities are significantly more expensive than a run of perhaps 10 thousand parts. But if your prototype requires a number of similar small stamped or formed small parts, the four-slide process may be a good choice.

PROTOTYPING COSTS

Prototyping—and production processes in general—almost always consists of a mix of five basic costs: tooling and other nonrecurring requirements, setup time, running time, direct material, and surplus material. To explain the subtleties of the prototyping process, consider yourself a baker. If you were in the business of baking cakes, you would intuitively, if not formally, base your costs on the aforementioned elements. Suppose that your customer wants a shamrock-shaped cake for

St. Patrick's Day, but you don't own a shamrock-shaped baking pan, and you're fairly sure that you'll never have the need for one again after making this customer's cake. You inform the customer that she'll have to pay for the pan, for the time you spend ordering it, and for the UPS charge to deliver it. These elements make up tooling and its related costs. You don't have the Irish recipe that your customer is asking for, so this means you'll have to research it and copy it, which are nonrecurring needs because if you receive succeeding orders for this same cake, you won't incur theses expenses again.

Now you've got everything you need to begin baking. You assemble the pans and mixing bowls, get all the ingredients together, set the temperature and time on the oven, and begin mixing. These steps are your setup time. You pop the cake in the oven and watch over it, testing it with a toothpick near the end to be sure you haven't under-baked or over-baked it. These steps are your running time.

You know the amount of each ingredient you've used, so you know their costs. The cake flour is something you use for most of the cakes you bake, so you are going to charge only for the two cups of flour you used. That's direct material. However, you had to buy a special spice for the batter, and you used only a fraction of it. The rest is surplus, but it's likely that you'll never use it before it loses its strength, so you've got to charge the full cost to your customer, again, including the time and costs associated. Finally, after the cake is finished, you must wash the mixing bowls and pans, put away the ingredients, clean up the counter top and floor, and deliver it. These elements are also considered part of the setup, as they are tasks that occur each time you get an order.

Thus, you may see that even the seemingly simple task of baking a special cake can involve costs that you must include in the sales price, and that are independent of the number of cakes produced per setup.

Now translate this example to your prototype. Tooling includes drills, end mills, and holding fixtures that are special for the job. A prototyper can be expected to furnish standard-size drills and common-size end mills without an extra charge. These are a part of his "tool chest," and are included in his hourly rate. A drill size in millimeters, for example, or an end mill that cuts an outside corner radius, is typically not part of the tools a prototyper is expected to have on hand. He must look them up in a catalog or online, order them, charge you for his time, pay for them to be delivered, and, of course, pay for the tools.

Nonrecurring charges, sometimes called nonrecurring engineering, or NRE, do not include setup costs, and consist of anything that must be done to produce the prototype, including tooling if it is not quoted as a separate item. Examples include amending the 3D CAD digital data, preparing production sketches and sequence instructions, finding outside sources to handle unusual operations that the prototyper must delegate, and designing features that were not detailed in the drawings. In short, these costs are incurred once, the items preserved, and their expenses avoided in the future. Always insist that nonrecurring charges be itemized in your quote so that you won't pay for them again on reorder.

Setup costs, which are mainly time, consist of getting out the tools, installing them in the machines, installing the program in the computer or the machine, loading the material, and "pressing the start button." Setup includes any task that must be done each time the job is run. And when the parts are completed, all of this must be reversed, of course, and the machine cleaned to remove the chips. Setup costs also cover materials used in setting up the machine until the operator arrives at the first acceptable part. Setup is typically spread across the quantity ordered, being added to the cost per unit. For example, an order of one thousand pieces, having a setup cost of one hundred dollars, and a running cost of fifty cents each, would be quoted as sixty cents per unit. This merging of the setup costs with the running costs accounts for the decrease in unit cost as the quoted quantity increases.

Running time is simply the time the machine runs to produce parts, or the operator's time spent working on the parts. Some parts must be manually deburred, and this is also running time if it cannot be done during the time the part is being machined. Running time is basically the same for the tenth unit as it is for the hundredth unit, although when manual work is involved, operators generally reduce the time per unit, up to a point, as the quantity increases. Prototyping quantities are generally too small to reflect any increased operator efficiency in the pricing.

Direct material is the amount used to create the part, including an allowance for scrap. Cost is the simple calculation of amount per unit multiplied by the quantity. Surplus material is that which is left over due to a minimum practical purchase quantity. For example, if a prototype requires a material that is not inventoried by the prototyper—let's say a length of brass bar stock—and the prototyper must buy a twelve-foot-long bar, despite the fact that the prototype will only require one foot of the bar, guess who pays for the other eleven feet? The inventor pays for it, of course. Most of the time this cost will be included in the unit price that the vendor quotes, and it is understood that the leftover material is the property of the prototyper.

Standard, or inventoried, materials are more common for the material additive processes due to the limited number of materials that lend themselves to these processes. But materials for the subtractive processes come in a near-infinite variety of sizes and shapes, and chances are the prototyper will purchase the material.

Reducing Costs

There are a few things you can do to reduce your costs. Work with an industrial designer to determine the best materials for your design. And explain your design, always asking if there is a better way to accomplish your objective. Industrial designers specialize, so don't hire a package designer to create a kitchen gadget. Call around until you find a designer who has experience in the category that your invention falls in. Do as much of your own designing and sketching as you can before consulting with an industrial designer. Even crude sketches are far better than verbal descriptions. Be sure that your 3D CAD designer's program is compatible with your prototyper's preference. Most vendors have a program that they prefer to work with. Ask your CAD designer if she can use this program for your drawings.

Your designer should specify the most appropriate raw material for your product, and possibly even for your prototype. Many industrial designers have a prototyping shop on their premises, and will recommend the right materials without being asked. If your prototype is made from material not in your prototyper's inventory, ask what quantity she will have to procure. State in your purchase agreement that you will pay for this material as a separate item, and that you want what is left over. This way you won't have to pay for the material a second time if you need to purchase it again.

Ask about any nonrecurring charges. You don't want these added to the unit price. Remember, nonrecurring charges should be one-time charges that you pay for in the first order. If you must order a second time, you don't want them loading the unit price unfairly. Ask that any and all nonrecurring charges be spelled out in the quote.

Get price quotes from at least three vendors. Pricing depends on a vendor's cost to produce, of course, but it also depends on the kind of machines a vendor uses, her skills in creating imaginative ways to make prototypes, and her workload. All vendors are not created equal. A vendor with up-to-date machines, and who needs the job, may quote half the price of a vendor with older machines and a heavy workload.

FINDING PROTOTYPERS

Inventor-friendly prototypers often place advertisements in *Inventors Digest*. If you don't subscribe to this magazine, you should. If you know the process you'd like to use, consult websites such as www.thomas-net.com, www.macraesbluebook.com, and www.jobshop.com to find a prototyper that meets your specific needs.

CHOOSING A PROTOTYPING PROCESS

Most prototypers who use material removal processes have a lathe and a vertical mill, although their machines are generally smaller and simpler than production models. Small vertical mills are often bench-top size, and today, small computer-driven vertical mills are affordable and frequently found in shops operated by lone prototypers. Prototypers usually specialize in either material removal or material additive methods, although you may see these processes combined in the future due to the commonality of the 3D CAD digital data that drives both.

The main difference between the appropriate prototyping process and the volume production process for a given part is found in the custom tooling investment. The higher the volume required, the greater the cost of custom tooling, and consequently, the lower the cost per part. Prototyping processes, in a sense, are the opposite of volume production processes. The custom tooling either does not exist or it is minimal, often in the form of a digital data rather than hardware, and therefore its cost is low. Conversely, the cost per prototyped part is high compared with the production part.

Many options often exist to prototype the same part, and the reasons for using one process over the other is generally not clear until investigated with a degree of patience.

CONCLUSION

You can learn a lot from visiting production vendors and prototypers and asking questions. But vendors and prototypers tend to specialize, and production vendors frequently do not know or care about appropriate prototyping processes. If you choose a certain prototyping process that works for your prototype but can be done better and for less money using another process, don't expect prototypers to send you to their competitors. It's up to you to investigate and learn. The Internet is a great place to start.

Best wishes in your venture.

ONE BIG IDEA

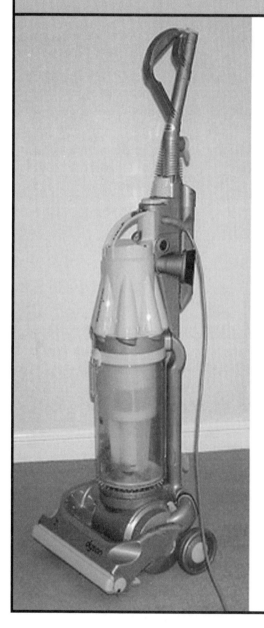

Created by James Dyson, the Dyson cyclonic separation vacuum cleaner was originally licensed by the Japanese company APEX in 1983. Named the G-force vacuum cleaner, it went on to win the International Design Fair prize in Japan less than a decade later. Its success provided Dyson with the funds to launch Dyson Ltd in England and produce his own version of the design.

In 1993, he set up a factory in Wiltshire, England, as well as a research wing of his company. Dyson's second production version of the dual cyclone vacuum, the DC01, soon became the United Kingdom's best-selling vacuum cleaner.

A serial inventor, Dyson has brought many of his subsequent ideas to fruition, including the Dyson Airblade hand dryer and a washing machine called the Contrarotator. He now sponsors the James Dyson Foundation, a charitable trust that seeks to inspire young people around the world to become engineers.

3. Patenting

Andy Gibbs

Patents have been described as the most complicated type of document in the world, intertwining technology, business, and the law. While most new inventors think of a patent as a means to protect their inventions, they should make an effort to understand the business and financial reasoning behind investing in a patent, so they can make an informed decision on whether to file a patent application on a new invention. They should also recognize the importance of meeting all the legal requirements under US patent law. Most inventors spend thousands of hours becoming the leading technical experts within their fields. They do not spend their time reading do-it-yourself patent books or hoping to become authorities on patent law. If you really want to become a patent expert, then go to law school and become a patent lawyer. If you want to become a successful inventor, then become an expert within your industry, and work with trustworthy people who can help you attain your patent. A solid plan, an effective strategy, and strong teammates go a long way towards your becoming a successful inventor.

If you were to ask 100 successful inventors their recipes for success, you would likely get 100 different answers. But every recipe would

Andy Gibbs has more than thirty years of technological, corporate, and market development experience. He has founded eight manufacturing and professional service companies, and is an inventor with twenty-five issued and pending patents in the automotive, medical device, electronics, sporting goods, methods of business, and software industry segments.

andy@andygibbs.com • www.andygibbs.com

share some common ingredients: planning, strategy, and trusted team-mates. A patent just might play a key role in helping you create your own American dream. Then again, you may consider alternatives to spending big money on patent drafting and filing fees. Contrary to the popularized metaphor, the world will not beat a path to your door just because you have a newly patented invention. In fact, statistics show that 97 percent of all patents cost their owners more money than their inventions make, which is what I'd describe as a business failure.

If you had only a 3-percent chance of successfully completing your daily commute to work each day, would you even leave the house? If you knew that your marriage would have only a 3-percent chance of lasting, would you ever consider walking down the aisle in the first place? I don't like the prospect of investing thousands of hours and dollars in an invention only to have a 3-percent shot at success, but those are the United States Patent and Trademark Office's published facts. I've made money from more than 90 percent of my inventions because I understood that to succeed, I would need to become an expert in my field. I've invested literally decades of time learning from experts, assessing existing technologies by reading thousands of patents, finding the right people to join my team, and studying markets and competitors. Each time I embark on a new invention, I roll all my legwork into a financial plan and patent strategy before ever filing a patent application.

In this chapter, I will tell you my hard-earned secrets of successful inventing. You will learn why and when you should file a patent application, as well as when not to file one. This chapter will also teach you the United States Patent Office's requirements for patentability, when filing more than one patent application is a good idea, the advantages of a provisional patent, and much more. Do not pass up the opportunity to learn a few important tenets of the business of inventing that could make the difference between success and failure.

If you're inventing with the idea of making money, then you should understand that making money with patents is a tough and serious business. Inventing is not a dream, a wish, or a prayer—it's 100-percent pure capitalism. Successful inventors are entrepreneurs, marketers, and small business financial managers. As an inventor with about two dozen US and international applications and granted patents, I rely on patents to help my businesses make a profit. My products have sold more than $500 million internationally. But I've designed and sold just about as many unpatented products as patented products—perhaps even more. I've been a consulting patent strategist for some of the world's largest patent owners, including Microsoft, IBM, AT&T, and others. They've paid hundreds of thousands of dollars to learn some of my most valuable secrets, which I will now share with you. Make no mistake, though; I am my own toughest critic, and I work hard to uncover every possible flaw in my business, technological, and financial assumptions, looking for reasons not to patent an invention. Success is forged not by finding every reason an idea will succeed. A successful inventor searches for every flaw in his design, his thinking, and his planned execution, and then he creates solutions to those problems before starting any patent process.

Most new inventors I've encountered are so emotionally attached to their ideas that they find any way to justify filing patent applications on their inventions. They never want to hear someone say anything negative about their ideas. The fastest way to waste a lot of time and money is to let ego drive your decisions, never considering the possibility that your invention may never make one business dollar.

WHY PATENT?

As an inventor, why would you even want a patent? Is it because you want a pretty engraving to hang on your wall and you're willing to pay ten thousand dollars for it? Is it because you want to make believe that you're the Scarecrow in *The Wonderful Wizard of Oz,* and that being granted a patent is like getting a brain? Is it because you want to prove your critics wrong? The sad fact is that these are just a few of the wrong reasons that have actually driven many of the thousands of inventors I've coached over the past few decades. I really don't know whether inventors have higher Intelligence Quotients, but such brilliance certainly isn't always reflected in their actions. I've watched thousands of inventors waste their savings and throw away years of time just to get a patent.

Right now, I'd say that you are probably thinking about getting a patent for your idea, but you haven't yet written a business plan, you haven't plotted every step concerning how you're going to get your product to market, and you haven't recognized the real costs of developing and filing a patent, or of litigation against patent infringers. If I'm wrong, I'm happy to be. You may become one of the few success stories in the world of inventing.

Over the years, I've gathered some interesting metrics from hundreds of successful inventors. On average, inventors spend over $35,000 getting their inventions to the point of making money (and these inventors are part of the 3 percent who succeed). Before you say, "I'll never spend that kind of money," let me say that most inventors have said the same thing. Inventing is like an addiction. Inventors start out on the cheap by spending just a few dollars to get their projects going, and then they discover that they need to spend just a few dollars more, and somehow find the extra money. After years of money trickling away, they wake up and realize the total cost has ballooned to over $30,000.

You should also know that successful inventors typically invest about seven years of work in their ideas, between when they first conceive their inventions and when they finally begin making money from their efforts. My personal experience is very much along these lines as well, with some inventions getting to market for about $15,000, and some requiring much more than $50,000. Of course, there are a lucky few one-hit wonders that blast out of the idea box and hit $1 million in sales in the first year, but they are extremely rare. Perhaps you're better than the average successful inventor, or at least you think you are. But if you want to take a more realistic look at what it takes to succeed, at least in budgeting terms, know that the rough total of government fees to file a patent presently amount to $3,720. If your yearly household income qualifies, you may be eligible for the lower, micro entity fee levels established by the America Invents Act. This assumes a do-it-yourself approach for inventors who are expert in writing a beautifully detailed invention specification, and who can draft strong, enforceable claims. Everyone else should find a capable patent attorney or agent, and rely on those legal experts to draft and file an enforceable legal document. For attorney fees, budget another $10,000 for a basic utility patent. Make that $15,000 or more if the invention is a method of business, electronic device, or composition of matter patent. Of course, patent application costs will vary considerably depending on level of complexity, how many drawings you include, the number of independent and dependent claims, and whether you meet the statutory definition of micro entity, small entity, or large entity patent filer.

So far, with attorney fees, you're nearly half way to the $35,000 I mentioned, and you haven't even started to add the costs of prototyping, traveling, or miscellaneous expenses, or the opportunity cost of the thousands of hours you'll invest over seven years. Common sense would dictate that if you are one of the 3 percent who succeeds, there's a good market demand for your invention. Where there's a market opportunity, there will be knock-offs. There's no shortage of people or companies that would attempt to grab a piece of your market, even if it means infringing your patent. Therefore, "owning a patent" is nearly worthless unless you are willing and able to enforce your patent against an infringer. Launching a lawsuit against a large company that you believe infringed your patent will cost more than $500,000. By the way, I should mention that you should never (without solid legal advice and support) threaten suit against suspected infringers. This is a mistake too often made, and always regretted. In any case, lawsuits certainly are not inexpensive for either party. Legal fees can be crushing, even if your business is generating $10 million in profitable sales. If you never expect to sue an infringer, then why do you want (or need) a patent?

By now, you may be thinking I am against patenting. You may be thinking, "I have no chance of success, so I shouldn't even bother." Of course, both thoughts are untrue. As an independent inventor and small business owner, I have a great many patents issued and pending on more than two dozen different inventions across varied industries. My experience tells me not all business opportunities related to my inventions will pan out. Naturally, I'll abandon the inventions that won't make money before I waste too much time and money. Your approach should be one that is conservative, like mine. It should be well planned, fully informed, and carefully executed.

Pursue your invention ideas, but if you discover that there is simply no way to make a profit from your idea, walk away from you invention and proceed down another invention path. Inventing is a business, and it's important that inventors not become emotionally attached to an idea. Instead, they should take a logical business approach to patents.

But back to the question: Why do you want a patent? Here's one correct answer: "I want a patent because I understand the time and costs involved, I understand that inventing is a business and not a get-rich-quick scheme, I know what experts I will need to help with the areas I really don't know, I've completed my budget and business plan, I have a smart business opportunity that could be profitable, and I want the market advantages a solid patent will afford."

Now you know you have used sound business judgment to determine your need for a patent, but should you actually file a patent application? Here's a concept that too many inventors never really grasp: Patents are merely business tools that allow the patent owner to protect a market, not an idea. Most inventors think that patents protect their ideas. They are wrong. Besides, you might ask, what is protection anyway? Physically, a patent is no more than a multipage document with a ribbon and seal. It can't necessarily keep predators from copying your invention and competing against you in the marketplace, but its weight as a powerful legal document eventually can make invention thieves sorry they copied. Your patent, distinctly defines your invention and the extent of your patent coverage. A court of law determines the existence or non-existence of infringement. All this sounds quite academic, but the point is that the patent is only as strong as its enforceability in court.

Infringement, however, is relatively rare, with perhaps less than 2 to 3 percent of US patents ever ending up in court. Most conflicts result in licensing agreements between conflicting parties. Again, a patent does not give the patent owner exclusive rights to a product or market, but simply gives the owner the right to enforce the patent against an infringer. This is a critically important concept to wrap your head around. Patents are used to secure and enforce market share. Market share means sales and profits. If you can't clearly see where profits can be made (develop your financial projection spreadsheets), then you have no business thinking about a patent.

If your business plan is good and you have charted all your costs and sales (and hopefully show a profit), then it may be time to file for a patent on your invention. Oh, you don't have a business plan? Remember, I said successful inventors require a plan and a strategy. Get to your local small business development center (SBDC), service corps of retired executives (SCORE), or other government or nonprofit agency for entrepreneurs and develop your business plan. Oftentimes you can get help for free, or for a small fee.

Manufacturing and selling a product isn't the only way an inventor can profit from his invention. The business plan may outline how to earn royalties by developing an invention and licensing the patent to a manufacturer. As a new inventor, you might want to patent your invention because you have clearly identified a revenue opportunity through invention licensing and can present to the licensee incredible cost savings, increased sales, improved systems, or more profits. You might want to patent your invention because you wish to introduce a product to the market and need to protect your tooling, startup, and manufacturing investment. You may need to raise capital from investors who expect you to protect your superior product or technology with a patent. Maybe you have discovered a fast-moving product trend in a very large market and want to beat the competition by patenting the next generation product three to five years out. My own business plans lay out three-year to five-year strategies for selling my products, patents, trademarks, and other intellectual properties to one of the competitors for a big cash-out when the market demands my next generation products. Then I'll turn to other inventions, and start another business.

There are many other reasons that inventors and companies choose to file patents, but the clear point is that every valid reason is based on an understanding of commercial potential and follows a plan to profit from this potential. If you have convinced yourself that you are going to file a patent application, timing will be a critical element to your patent strategy. You'll need to determine when you should file.

WHEN TO FILE

Through decades of casual observation of and discussions with would-be inventors, I have discovered that 97 percent of them never analyzed the commercial and business potential of their ideas before running off to spend money on filing their patents. Is it merely a coincidence that these 97 percent never made money from their inventions? I think not. The answer to when to file is simply driven by the inventor's own timeline, the sequence of information collection and business planning, and, of course, the available money to support the patenting efforts. I developed a "when to file" process years ago and continue to use it to evaluate every invention before making filing decisions. There are three major components to the sequence. The first is exhaustive product, market, technological, and competitive research. If you are not an expert in your field, you're not ready to file a patent. The second is budget planning. If you simply don't have enough money to take your invention to its successful conclusion, take another part-time job, or find an investor. Think of the minimum budget using this analogy: If you need four tires to drive your car, buying only three tires is a waste of money. Success dictates that you wait until you have the money to buy all four tires. The third is drafting a comprehensive patent specification and then filing the patent application. This phase cannot be started until you have completed the first two steps in this sequence.

Keep in mind that under "first inventor to file" rules, inventors should always file their patent applications before making public disclosures of their inventions. Although US inventors still have a one-year grace period to file their patent applications after publicly disclosing their inventions, public disclosure before patent filing may eliminate the chance of ever receiving patents in foreign countries. In certain instances, an inventor's early disclosure may pose problems if the content of the patent application filed later deviates from the disclosure. So, your best bet is to keep a lid on your invention and then file at the earliest opportunity. It's best for inventors to adopt a series of thoughtful steps in navigating the patent application process. This process extends beyond simply writing and filing the formal application documents and paying the associated fees.

Before an inventor can begin writing a great invention disclosure and specification, he must understand what competitive products do or don't do. Inventors who say, "I have no competition," will fall into the 97-percent failure group every time. Every successful product has a competitive alternative, so if you don't know all the competitive products and which companies make them, it's time to find out. As you analyze the companies supplying the competitive products, find answers to a few basic questions. Is your targeted market served by just a few huge multinational corporations? Are their products sold through a distribution channel that you will find impossible to enter? Do they have a history of filing suits against companies that threaten their market shares? All these questions should guide you through whether or not you want to step in the ring with these heavyweights to battle for market share and sales. On the other hand, you may find that they move much slower than you, and that they have a history of simply buying out smaller, innovative companies. Selling my innovative new company to a competitor is actually my personal strategy to profit from my patents.

After becoming an expert in the market you are about to enter, develop a business plan, including a patent and financial strategy. How will you address the market? What's your budget? How long will it take? What experts do you need on your team? With answers to these questions, you can begin writing your business plan and creating your financial projections. If you don't have a solid plan, you're not ready to file your patent.

After you have your plan and your invention concept, develop as many alternatives to your invention as possible. There is always more than one way to create your product or invention—different materials, different manufacturing processes, more features and functions, lower cost, higher quality, and so forth. There is no end to the options, and at each turn you will discover different nuances to your idea, many of which might be patentable. After this analysis, determine the best approach to your invention based on market opportunity, revenue, and profit potential.

Armed with your invention ideas, go online to a patent database such as the United States Patent and Trademark Office (www.uspto .gov), or access other patent search engines with the search terms "free patent search," and familiarize yourself with all the pre-existing technologies related to your invention. When researching, you may uncover many ideas very close to yours. You may find that your invention already exists, or you may learn how to make your invention even better and more advanced compared to patented technologies that already exist. After completing your research and becoming acquainted with the document content and format, you will be able to define your invention clearly and precisely. Finally, you'll be ready to get down to the patent drafting phase.

Draft your patent specification. I do not mean write your own patent application, but only draft your specification. The specification is the written portion of your patent that fully discloses the background of your industry, technology, or product, and describes what your invention is and why it delivers significant commercially valuable advantages over the prior art. The specification not only lays the groundwork for the claims, it establishes the broad functionality of your invention, while at the same time details how your invention works. This could be reviewed by a trusted engineer under a confidentiality agreement or by your patent attorney or agent prior to putting it into its final form.

At this point, you may prepare and file your patent application. This could be a provisional or non-provisional application, depending on your business and patent strategy.

Cost

If an inventor were to hire out all the necessary research, product development, patent drafting, business and financial planning, and patent filing, the hard costs would be between $15,000 and $25,000. I know there are many books out there that say you can write your own patent—in fact, I've written one. But books that suggest that you can do everything yourself for very little money even if you are not skilled in patent law, engineering, or financial planning are simply not being honest about the complexities and costs associated with inventing. Their prime motivation may be to sell more books, not to create successful inventors. You'll rarely see these high costs presented in do-it-yourself books, but at the end of the day, they remain a reality. If you are a skilled marketer, expert financial planner, credentialed engineer, or accomplished business person, then you will be able to handle a portion of the work yourself, but your costs will likely still be in the $10,000 to $15,000 range. Therefore, when to file will be determined as much by available cash as by anything else. The bottom line is this: Don't expect to build a $1 million invention enterprise by investing $50 in a patent book and spending $130 to file a self-drafted provisional patent application. Work three jobs if you need to make more money, but without the financial resources, you will not be able to feed your golden goose.

WHEN NOT TO FILE

There are times when an inventor should not file a patent application. If for no other reason, an inventor who has not completed the research and planning as earlier described has no business filing a patent application. Understanding when not to file a patent application will prevent you from wasting time and money. Do not file a patent if:

- You have not completed your market, product, and competition research, or if you are not skilled in these areas, have avoided this step, or haven't hired a business research professional.

- You have not completed a plan that clearly illustrates your strategy on how to commercialize your invention.

- You do not have the financial resources to fund complete patent and business development. Wait until you can afford it.

- Your invention does not meet United States Patent and Trademark Office requirements for patentability. (See pages 48 to 52.)

- You did not invent your product. You cannot file a patent application on someone else's invention.

- Your research or financial plan shows inadequate commercial profit potential.

- The technology will evolve faster than you can acquire patents. By the time you receive your patent, your technology may already be obsolete.

There are two more notions that you might consider. First, if no one says, "Wow, what a stupid idea," then you're only asking unqualified people who don't want to hurt your feelings. Open up and get some qualified criticism, and then find ways to overcome the problems before you continue. Finally, if your spouse says, "Spend another minute or dollar on that stupid invention and I'm getting a divorce," you should probably take heed. If you're spending family money on your invention, I always recommend including your family in your patent investment decisions.

PATENT OFFICE REQUIREMENTS

As previously discussed, one of the reasons not to file a patent application is when your invention fails to meet the United States Patent and Trademark Office's requirements for patentability.

As this subject is complicated, I strongly recommend that you rely on a patent attorney or patent agent as your ultimate qualifier of patentability. It's important for you to understand that this section is not meant to be the ultimate do-it-yourself guide to teach inventors what is or is not patentable. If you expect to become a patent expert, study the United States Patent and Trademark Office's *Manual of Patent Examining Procedure*. It is the definitive information source.

I've already made clear my opinion that no inventor should draft and file his own patent application unless he is well versed in patent law and has the appropriate experience and credentials to be writing and prosecuting patents. The purpose of this section is to educate inventors on the general guidelines of patentability of their inventions, so they can speak intelligently with their patent attorneys or agents.

I've written a great many patent specifications, both for myself and for my clients. Your expertise should be focused on the invention, not on patent law. Great patent specifications are invention disclosures that have been written to highlight the important commercial advantages of a present invention over the prior art. Most importantly, a specification should establish a foundation for claiming the broadest commercial value of a patent once it has been granted. Most patent attorneys and agents simply don't have the time or the front-line industry experience to understand your business, your markets, industry product trends, competitive products, or key selling points of your product like you do. That's your job! When it's time to draft a patent claim, file the application, and prosecute the patent, I have always recommended using competent attorneys or agents to convert specifications into a defensible application and an enforceable patent.

If you sue an alleged patent infringer, his attorney will pull out all the stops to destroy the validity of your patent. It's my firm belief that few inventors, if any, have the legal skills to write and prosecute patent claims that would survive such litigation challenges. So, the real objective is to make inventors conversant enough to discuss the patentability of their inventions with a patent legal professional. I would expect inventors to first spend their time completing invention prototypes and improvements, industry research, and their business and financial plans.

What Is Patentable?

Simply put, the United States Supreme Court has set clear the three subject matter categories for which inventors may not obtain a patent: abstract ideas, laws of nature, and natural phenomena. Therefore, what you can patent must fit the strict definition of patentable subject matter. Here is how the United States Patent and Trademark Office determines the patentability of any invention filed. The patent examiners review each application to determine whether the invention meets the statutory requirements.

Utility Requirement

Under this requirement, an inventor must show that his invention is credible, specific, and useful. Considered another way, an invention must be operable and produce some kind of intended result, and not lack credibility, for instance, by claiming to change the laws of nature.

As one example, a round steel ball merely sitting on a table would have no utility, is not operable, and therefore would not satisfy the utility requirement. However, if this same steel ball were one of many steel balls, all of which were captured between two cylinders, the resulting assembly would be a roller bearing, useful in moving heavy materials, and thereby producing a functional outcome of its operation.

Furthermore, an invention must be founded on credible fundamentals. The laws of nature, physical phenomena, and abstract ideas have been held not patentable. For example, Newton would not be allowed a patent on his law of universal gravitation, and Einstein would not have been granted a patent on his "E=MC2" formula.

The United States Patent and Trademark Office will favorably consider patentability if utility falls into one of these five primary types of patent classes:

- **Processes and methods.** Defined as one or more steps for doing or making something, such as a manufacturing sequence to make rolls of paper more inexpensively, or an improved process for spray painting cars.

- **Articles of manufacture.** Defined as objects that produce a result with few or no moveable parts, such as a new slotted spaghetti spoon with no moving parts, or a shovel manufactured from many parts, but these parts are generally static relative to the other parts.

- **Machines.** Defined as devices with more than two interacting parts that produce a certain outcome as a result of the interaction of these parts, such as the rotating head and cutting string of a weed eater.

- **Compositions of matter.** Defined as the intermixing of two or more ingredients or materials that produces a desired result, such as the synthesis of a new organic compound that produces stronger plastics.

- **Improvements.** Defined as advancements or novel uses of existing inventions, such as the creation of a method to turn on windshield wipers intermittently for light rain.

Novelty Requirement

I've had would-be inventors ask me to help them patent a product they saw in Europe because they've never seen the product sold in the United States. Let me be clear, if a product has ever been used, or the description of the product or invention has ever been published in a patent or printed publication anywhere in the world more than twelve months prior to a new application, then the United States Patent and Trademark Office will not issue the inventor's new patent. Besides, in this example, note that the would-be inventors saw the product, but did not invent the product. With rare exceptions, patents are granted to the named inventors. If you think that you can outsmart the United States Patent and Trademark Office by not disclosing the existence of the invention somewhere else in the world (and some inventors do), understand that even if you are granted the patent, the United States Patent and Trademark Office could later invalidate your patent if it learns that the invention existed before you filed your application. All your time and money will be lost. Furthermore, if you assert your patent in litigation, the rigorous background investigation that ensues may expose your secret. Since you signed an inventor's declaration and oath, your willful misrepresentation or deceit could be considered a fraud against the United States Patent and Trademark Office.

A new invention must also differ physically, functionally, or operationally in some way from existing inventions found anywhere in the world in order to meet the novelty requirement. In other words, your invention must be substantially different from or functionally improve upon that which the United States Patent and Trademark Office refers to as "prior art." There are nuances to the novelty requirement that require a deeper look into what this body considers new and novel, and what it would disallow based on whether a claim of the new invention was anticipated by an earlier invention. For example, if an earlier invention disclosed a bicycle gear ratio that would allow a rider to pedal the bike at a speed of 30 mph, a new gear ratio claimed as a new invention that would allow a rider to attain a speed of 33 mph would have been anticipated by one skilled in the art. Although not claimed in the earlier invention, one could anticipate that a higher gear ratio would allow a higher speed, and that a lower gear ratio would limit maximum speed. The claim on the new gear ratio, anticipated by the earlier inventions, would therefore be denied as a failing to meet the novelty requirement.

Non-Obviousness Requirement

To figure out whether your invention meets this requirement, you have to consider whether experts in the field of your invention would consider your new invention obvious. As described earlier, the first three steps necessary to determine whether you should patent a new invention all require extensive research. While observing and coaching hundreds of inventors, I've found that most of them do a little research on their idea, but they do not take the position that they must become experts in their fields of invention. Unless you become fully skilled in your field, you cannot know what those who are would consider novel or obvious.

You must demonstrate to the United States Patent and Trademark Office that even those skilled in your field would consider your invention new, novel, and useful, and prior to seeing your invention would not have considered your idea a casual evolution within their industry. In other words, your invention as a whole must have a "wow" factor, even to those who are experts in the field. After you make the determination that your invention would be considered patentable, you can proceed, knowing that your time and money will not be wasted. Of course, this assumes you have first completed research, and have determined that your invention would be marketable, able to be manufactured, and profitable.

WHEN TO FILE MORE THAN ONE PATENT

It would not make sense for a hunter to pursue big game armed with only one arrow. Why then would it make sense for an inventor to take on the 900-pound gorillas of his industry with only one patent? Most of the time, it could be a losing proposition. For every invention, there are most likely another two or three alternative inventions or alternative embodiments that could be patented. As I've already noted, if there is market demand for your invention, then someone else will try to take a piece of your business. Sometimes, this person will improve upon your invention and receive his own patent—beating you to the punch on your next generation product. There goes your business! When it makes sense to file a patent on one invention, it makes sense to file more than one.

As an example, a new invention may be a new crop picker for the farming industry. In addition to the novel function of separating the fruit from the stem (a device patent), a new process may be required to manufacture the picker in the first place. This could be a process or method patent. After the picker picks the fruit, it may begin processing the fruit for packing. This could be yet another process patent. When the inventor was creating the prototype of the invention, one prototype yielded to a better system, and then to an even better device—the "best" invention possible. The wrong approach is to file the patent only on the newest, "best" device. There is no shortage of companies that succeed in selling inferior products, and unless an inventor also discloses (and perhaps claims) an earlier "inferior" version of his invention in his patent, he will be leaving the door open for a competitor to enter his market. Professional boxers know that if they miss with a left hook, they can come back with a right uppercut. Inventors should also be armed with multiple weapons before entering a competitive market.

Always look for every angle to increase your number of patents. Be sure to include variations that would result in lower production costs, higher quality, easier operation, or any other element of your invention that could be improved upon by a competitor. I can hear you asking already, "If it's going to cost me $15,000 to get one invention patented, then how am I going to afford filing patents on three or four inventions?" Here's where patent strategy comes in. The reality is that you may not want to file patents on all these inventions. But if you're going to file a provisional patent application (PPA) at the start of the filing process, then you can certainly disclose the different inventions and embodiments in one PPA. You then have up to twelve months to refine the business approach to commercializing your inventions, and during this time you could perhaps polish your business plan to attract some investment. As you continue to develop your business, track the competition, and plan your market entry, you may decide that only two of the four inventions are commercially valuable. By filing non-provisional applications on the final two patents, you've accomplished two important goals. You've protected what you believe are the two most valuable money-making inventions, and by disclosing all four inventions in your non-provisional patent application, you've created "prior art" that will prevent your competitors from ever patenting the other two.

HIGH-VALUE PATENTS

What makes a patent valuable, and how can you be sure that you are filing a high-value patent rather than a patent that will fall into the "97 percent that never make money" category?

Three elements are required to create a high-value patent. It must be commercially valuable, technologically advanced, and legally enforceable. Understanding what creates a valuable patent reinforces the arguments I made earlier in this chapter regarding the necessity of doing your homework on business and financial planning, market research and patent strategy, and competition.

Commercially Valuable

The patent must protect large commercial market opportunities. Most venture capitalists will not invest money into a business unless it enters a market with at least $2 billion to $3 billion in annual sales—and growing, not shrinking. If they won't invest in small, niche, or shrinking markets, neither should inventors. For instance, the pet products industry in 2012 was $55 billion, up from $53 billion in 2011—definitely a large and growing market to address with an innovative product. However, the mere fact that the pet market is large doesn't mean any invention will become a million-dollar winner. An inventor's business plan must lay out a very specific and credible plan to enter this market, demonstrating a keen understanding of how major pet retailers qualify and buy new products. Did I mention inventors have to do a lot of research to become experts in their fields?

Technologically Advanced

Patents protect the most advanced technology. Does this mean that an invention is hopeless if it's simply a new dog collar rather than the next generation microprocessor technology? Not at all.

However, it does mean that the simple dog collar must deliver some real value that's tied to technology. Let me explain.

If the dog collar is manufactured on a machine that can produce three times as many for the same cost as traditional dog collars, then the product will have a competitive advantage. Referencing back to my earlier discussion of filing for multiple patents, perhaps one patent would cover the manufacturing method (so other companies could not use the same manufacturing method to make a competitive product), and another patent would cover the material elements of the collar's construction that result in the product never pinching the neck of the dog wearing it. There must be a core process, system, method, or technology directly tied to the commercial opportunity.

Legally Enforceable

Since most inventors are not legal experts, they wrongly assume that just because they have been granted a patent, the patent is legally strong. Don't forget that the patent attorneys representing the company you are trying to sue for patent infringement will go to the ends of the earth to destroy your patent claims. Since most patent attorneys and patent agents are patent legal experts, most will agree that they can successfully circumvent or invalidate most inventor-drafted patent claims without an awful lot of effort. Well-written claims define the legal metes and bounds of an inventor's patent rights. Some claims are very broad in the hope of claiming more commercial territory, while others are narrow, focused, and bulletproof. All claims must be adequately and unmistakably supported by the specification, which the inventor should write.

The patent attorney or patent agent should, in my opinion, also draft claims with the express purpose of suing an infringer, or at the very least defending against attempts by other attorneys to invalidate your claims. Since an infringement suit is the only effective way an inventor can enforce his patent, claims that cannot be argued and defended in court are quite literally worthless. The bottom line is clear. If an inventor is going to invest thousands of hours and dollars in an invention, attempting to become his own patent lawyer is the recipe for writing a worthless patent.

As a final point regarding legal strength, under the new America Invents Act (AIA), a company that has an interest in your patent, for instance, a competitor, may challenge the validity of your newly granted patent within the first eighteen months after issuance by declaring "post-grant opposition," providing relevant documents to the United States Patent and Trademark Office, and asking it to invalidate your patent. This is a much less expensive way to eliminate the potential for an infringement suit. The company's patent attorneys will challenge your patent, so you'll need your attorney to represent your interests.

ADVANTAGES OF A PROVISIONAL PATENT APPLICATION

Under the AIA, the United States joined the rest of the world in adopting a "first inventor to file" patent system. Previously, the United States patent system was based on the "first to invent" rule. This is a significant change in the law that, in my opinion, gives inventors a huge advantage over big corporations in many ways, and which should be incorporated into your fundamental patent and business strategies. Generally speaking, here's how simple this type of patent system is: The first inventor to file a patent on an invention gets it. The second inventor to file a patent on the same invention does not.

A provisional patent application enables an inventor to establish the earliest possible filing date by immediately filing an application through the United States Patent and Trademark Office website for a fee of $130 (although filing fees occasionally change). It also enables an inventor to market his product for one year with a "patent pending" notice. It allows the inventor to keep the details of his invention secret for more than two years. (Regular patent applications are routinely published publicly after eighteen months, but PPAs are never published.) It allows an inventor to make incremental improvements or add related inventions during the twelve-month term of his PPA, and to incorporate all improvements and related inventions into one patent application at the end of the twelve months. It enables an inventor to split one provisional patent application (with the earliest filing date) into one or more non-provisional patent applications, each benefiting from the earlier PPA filing date. It buys time to test the marketability of a new product, or to determine whether companies might license an invention. It does not require an inventor to write the legal claim.

Note that some patent attorneys strongly suggest writing at least one claim in order to be considered a valid patent application under international patent law, although there are no instances of a provisional patent application without claims being denied consideration as a valid patent application if the non-provisional patent application was filed within the twelve-month window.

There is one major disadvantage to the PPA. If an inventor fails to file a non-provisional patent application (with claims) prior to the expiration of the twelve-month term of the PPA, he loses the ability to protect his invention forever. Another issue worth mentioning, and perhaps a disadvantage in certain instances, is that any foreign patent application (based on the same invention) to be filed downstream of the PPA must also be filed within the PPA twelve-month period. Attention to such issues should evolve from your plan. A smart inventor should know he shouldn't file his PPA until he has completed his market research, budget analysis, and business plan, and has developed a clear patent strategy.

Protecting a large market opportunity is vital, especially if you are planning to license your patent to a multinational corporation. In the example of a new pet product, perhaps you're looking at licensing to a manufacturer that sells pet products throughout Europe. The value of your invention increases significantly if you preserve the possibility of filing patents in Europe as well as in the United States. There are two approaches to maintaining international patent rights after you file your PPA. It's critical that you remember that the PPA term is only one year, and if you do not continue with one of these approaches prior to the expiration of this one-year term you will lose the entirety of your patent rights.

Filing a PPA does, in fact, preserve your opportunity to file patents in Germany, the UK, and most everywhere else in the world as long as you file a non-provisional patent application prior to the expiration of your twelve-month PPA term. Rather than filing a non-provisional patent in the United States, you may opt to file an international application, known as a patent cooperation treaty (PCT) application. Without getting into the mechanics of international patent law, suffice it to say that you can preserve your patent filing options in any of the 117 country members of the PCT for nearly three years, giving you time to test the marketability of your product, or to leverage your patent licensing opportunities with potential licensees.

There are many nuances to filing a PCT, not the least of which are budgeting and timing concerns. If you believe that your invention really has commercial potential internationally, you should discuss your options in detail with your patent attorney or patent agent.

BEYOND PATENTS

You should now understand that the entire concept of patents makes sense only if they are used directly or indirectly to protect profit opportunities or generate revenue. But patents are just one piece of the intellectual property puzzle. Even if you do not end up filing patents on your inventions, you may still leverage a trademark, trade dress, or copyright for these same purposes.

Trademark

Even if a product is not patentable, it can still leverage the power of a registered trademark. For instance, a plastic water pistol may not be patentable, but if the new company makes the most powerful, most accurate, highest quality water pistol, it can create customer demand and market share with a strong trademark. Just as there are United States Patent and Trademark Office rules for patentability, there are United States Patent and Trademark Office rules for trademarkability. It is not my intention, however, to go into detail regarding the legal requirements for trademark registration, but rather to inform inventors of the possible use of trademarks with or without patents.

As with patents, there are many laws guiding the creation, maintenance, and enforcement of trademarks, so it pays to engage a patent or trademark attorney for assistance in clearing your use of a new trademark through a registered and common law trademark search, as well as for registration filing and prosecution. Smart entrepreneurs will also check out domain names for the same trademark, registering desired domain names so they can later build their websites with the same domain names as their trademarks.

Trade Dress

Somewhat related to trademarks, trade dress is the legal term that refers to the appearance of a product or its packaging that signifies the source of the goods of service. However, the packaging cannot be functional; otherwise, the function would be covered under patent laws.

Examples of trade dress would be the blue boxes used by Tiffany, or Kodak's yellow and red color combination on its consumer packaging. In the case of Kodak, a consumer could walk into a camera store and spot the Kodak products from across the room, even before they could read the word "Kodak" on the boxes.

Copyright

Finally, a copyright can be used to protect original creative works, including photographs, paintings, illustrations or cartoons, theatrical performances, musical scores, records, computer software, poems, movies, books, and other authored works. A copyright may also be used to protect unique designs, such as a specific design of a boat hull. In business, a copyright might be used to protect the unique graphics used on a product's packaging (perhaps along with the trade dress mentioned above), even though the design cannot be protected with a patent. Copyright registrations are inexpensive to obtain, and should be used wherever they might add commercial value to an enterprise.

CONCLUSION

It's clear there are many forms of intellectual property rights available to inventors and entrepreneurs. In all cases, it's important for an inventor to become generally informed on these options, how and when they might add commercial value to an enterprise, and which legal professionals should be relied upon to provide the knowledge and skill to maximize the legal strength, defensibility, and enforcement capacity of these intellectual property rights.

Perhaps the best place to find resources on intellectual property rights is the website of the United States Patent and Trademark Office, which I encourage you to visit.

ONE BIG IDEA

Initially created by John Pemberton as an alcoholic nerve tonic in 1885, the former Civil War colonel developed a nonalcoholic version of the drink in 1886, selling it at the soda fountain of Jacob's Pharmacy in Atlanta, Georgia, as a patent medicine. To this day, the headquarters of the Coca-Cola Company remain in Georgia.

4. Crowdfunding

Steve Greenberg
and Gary Greenberg

As any inventor can attest, once you develop an idea you think is unique, you live in fear that someone may also have a similar idea that could get to market faster and cheaper. Coming up with a product is just the beginning. Without enough quick funding, your idea may never see the light of day. Today, the potential to promote an idea has never been easier, given the pervasiveness of the web and social media. But raising funds for your product is not as simple as posting your idea online and waiting for the money to roll in.

When it comes to the process of inventing a new product, the biggest "game changer" in the world is crowdfunding. In the past, the typical "garage inventor" would borrow from family and friends, max

Steve Greenberg is a product scout, author, and TV personality. When Steve is not hunting down new products, he routinely appears on *The Dr Oz. Show* and *The Today Show*. He was also the host of the Food Network's *Invention Hunters*. Each month, Steve can be seen demonstrating innovative products in America's top TV markets, including WGN Chicago, ABC Dallas, NBC Seattle, CBS Houston, and others.

innovationinsider@gmail.com • www.stevegreenberg.tv

Gary Greenberg has designed, negotiated and implemented hundreds of transactions involving M&A, real estate, outsourcing, and partnership agreements. He also has extensive experience managing professional services operations for large companies. As a consultant, Gary assists companies to improve their client relationships, turn around problem situations, and enhance their strategic positions. Gary is on the Dean's Advisory Board of Rider University, where he also teaches a graduate course. He has also served on the Dean's Advisory Council of the University of Maryland Smith Business School.

garyagreenberg@gmail.com • www.garygreenberg.net

out her credit cards, or take a second mortgage on the family house to fund her project. Today, inventors are turning to crowdfunding to fill their capital needs. Simply put, crowdfunding refers to raising a small amount of money via a large number of people. Crowdfunding has garnered buzz in the marketplace for funding new ideas and projects that have very specific goals. The biggest names in the crowdfunding business include Kickstarter (www.kickstarter.com), which has generated over $1 billion for inventors, as well as Indiegogo (www.indiegogo.com), CircleUp (www.circleup.com), Launcht (www.launcht.com), and others.

Although the term "crowdfunding" is new, the concept has existed for ages. It originally encouraged individuals to make donations if they simply believed in an idea. Today, donators seek a return for contributing, especially when the project reaches its specified goal or targeted funding level. These rewards have come in many forms, from physical gifts like t-shirts, to recognition of the donator's name on the product's website, to promises of early adopter products from the first manufacturing run. The latter acts as a preorder of the product and enables the inventor to begin production. Some campaigns offer different rewards based on the size of the donation. No matter how hefty the donation, however, donors cannot get equity or rights to the company or product as a form of reward unless they follow today's investment rules established by the U.S. Securities and Exchange Commission, or SEC.

GUIDELINES

Currently, the general public cannot invest in any product or company at will. There are limitations that require investors to be qualified (based on SEC guidelines regarding investors' income levels and net worths) and validated before they are allowed to make investments. These rules may change, of course, with the goal of opening the door for everyone to invest in companies, products, and new ideas, supporting creativity by easing access to money. By expanding the pool of investors, the hope is that more ideas and companies will develop and become successful, creating more jobs. Assuming the SEC develops workable guidelines for non-qualified investors, there could be an explosion of funds available for investment purposes.

So, what does this mean for inventors? It could mean a simpler way to find funding without the task of searching for and presenting to multiple traditional funding sources such as venture funds, angel investors, family, and friends. Crowdfunding offers a level of transparency and confidence. You should know if you're going to meet your funding target within weeks of a post, or a few months at the latest. Still, there are potential roadblocks about which inventors need to be aware.

The SEC's guidelines could slow down non-qualified investors, or even curtail investment for those not qualified completely. Ryan Caldbeck, CEO of CircleUp, feels the rules could potentially make it difficult for non-qualified investors to own equity in companies because the registrations and audited financials required of companies and inventors could be too egregious. But he does say there is still a large untapped market of qualified investors that, if enticed with an equity position, could directly fund many new companies via crowdfunding websites.

The quality of your posting can be a major differentiator. The level of sophistication of crowdfunding websites is increasing not only in terms of content, but also in regard to the quality of videos, interchanges with social media websites, and rewards offered. Sally Outlaw, CEO of Peerbackers, noted that the professionalism of its video may be the single most important aspect of a campaign achieving success. There are studies that monitor a website's levels of success in meeting its campaign targets. The length of a campaign—whether thirty, sixty, or ninety days—can directly influence its success, as can the rewards that stimulate donator participation. The success rates achieved at each website differ greatly, and what works and what doesn't continue to change.

Social media plays a powerful role in the success of a campaign. Crowdfunding campaigns that achieve their targeted goals are almost always linked to well-designed social media campaigns. Social media takes many forms, and a good public relations plan takes time and preparation. The groundwork for media success requires months of work, including a concerted effort to pinpoint the intended audience and develop a plan that targets the right people and addresses their needs. Getting referenced by others, blogging, and finding email lists will help distinguish the better inventors' campaigns.

Once an inventor decides to crowdfund, she needs to have a proper funding plan. The fee to use a crowdfunding website could range from 2 to 7 percent of the funds received. For example, a crowdfunding website could charge an inventor 4 percent of collected funds if the campaign successfully achieves its targeted funding amount, and a 9-percent fee for the funds received if the campaign is unsuccessful in reaching its goal. Each site's fees and approaches are different. For example, Kickstarter only charges a fee when a project's target is met. If a campaign is unsuccessful, it requires all funds to be returned back to the donators.

According to Freeman White, CEO of Launcht, "the inventor must understand his or her capital needs by developing a cash flow plan that accounts for manufacturing costs, inventory build out, marketing expenses, distributions approach as well as many of the unforeseen obstacles most inventors face when going forward." Without a model that captures a realistic assessment of the cash needed, the inventor will be required to return to the well again and again, seeking more funds from angel investors, family, and friends.

Once a product is posted, and even after funding targets have been met, the inventor needs to be aware of the potential for copyright and trademark infringement. The possibility of lawsuits always exists, but doing the homework upfront could avoid a costly situation. On the other hand, inventors need to protect their intellectual properties (IP), which may be easily copied or stolen. Offshore counterfeiters have been known to steal inventors' information directly from crowdfunding websites. Most inventors are aware of this concern, but proper protection of their IPs should provide a level of safety. There are multiple ways to get this protection, but provisional patents and design patents are lowest in cost, and should allow the inventor enough protected time to assess the marketability of her product before seeking a full patent. International registration of copyrights and trademarks is required as well. Still, an inventor's best protection is to keep her "secret sauce" a secret and only divulge what is critical to the project. When sharing information with investors, secure a signed non-disclosure agreement, and keep an eye on social media, as friends and family may share too much information in their endorsements.

Each crowdfunding website has its own guidelines that restrict how creative projects may be displayed and how rewards may be structured. Kickstarter, for example, offers two main guidelines. According to the website, "[e]verything on Kickstarter must be a project. A project is something with a clear end, like making an album, a film, or a new game. A project will eventually be completed, and something will be produced as a result." In addition, Kickstarter projects must fit into one of the following categories: "Art, Comics, Dance, Design, Fashion, Film, Food, Games, Music, Photography, Publishing, Technology, and Theater." Other guidelines include showing your work. "Projects must be clear about their state of development, and cannot be presented as preorders of finished products. Projects must show details (photos, videos, sketches) of their progress so far, along with a prototype demonstrating the product's current functionality. Projects must explain how the final design is likely to differ from the prototype, and include a production plan (i.e., how you're going to make it) and an estimated timeline." Furthermore, "[p]hotorealistic renderings and simulations that could be mistaken for finished products . . . are not allowed," but "[t]echnical drawings, CAD designs, sketches, and other parts of the design process are awesome and encouraged."

Finally, "[p]roduct design and hardware projects can only offer one reward per pledge. Offering multiple quantities can imply that rewards are shrink-wrapped and ready to ship when they're not. With some projects, [Kickstarter will] make exceptions for . . . things like salt and pepper shakers, notebooks, building blocks, etc."

Based on these guidelines, it is clear that inventors need to have products ready for delivery or in beta form with approved manufacturing designs. Funding by the masses becomes much easier when a product can be visualized. Even with a finalized product, however, the inventor must realize there will be many unexpected costs that will need to be absorbed, especially in areas such as manufacturing, legal, distribution, and marketing.

Lastly, inventors need to find a way to get their products to market for distribution. Getting funding is critical, but achieving sustainable distribution is a must. The number of crowdfunding websites is growing fast and could soon find its saturation point. In the end, a limited number of sites will remain, and for those sites social media will be a major feeder. Large companies and institutions will want to establish their own websites, and Indiegogo and Launcht are creating crowdfunding platform products to do just that. When large retailers such as

Amazon and Target enter the crowdfunding market in a big way, the rules will change, and inventors could be the beneficiaries.

WHEN CROWDFUNDING WORKS

Many of those who have planned and executed their projects well have found success through crowdfunding. Actually, 44 percent of all campaigns on Kickstarter achieve their goals, with Indiegogo having slightly lower levels of success, but still many good results. An example of crowdfunding success would be Charles Michael Yim of San Francisco, who ran a very successful campaign on Indiegogo. His product, the Breathometer, is a small gadget that plugs into a smartphone. When paired with an app, it turns the phone into a device that can analyze breath. Initially it started off as a smartphone breathalyzer, and then evolved into a breath diagnostic platform through which users could measure a broad range of health conditions based on their breath. Just as everyone has a unique fingerprint, everyone has a unique breathprint. Breathometer currently detects alcohol levels, but will soon be moving towards the detection of halitosis and diabetes. Charles's Indiegogo campaign had a modest goal of $25,000, but ended up attracting four thousand backers and raising more than $138,000. That's a huge success in the world of crowdfunding.

When we asked Charles why he needed a crowdfunding campaign, his answer was simple—he needed the money to manufacture the first four thousand units, and he believed a successful crowdfunding campaign would "validate the product, while gaining exposure to the brand." Why did Charles succeed where others have failed? He says, "We were tactical about the entire Indiegogo campaign, from setting the fundraising goal, pricing the perks, working with key PR outlets, generating compelling content, having a genuine story, and timing everything around developing momentum. The product, of course, has to be compelling." His best advice to other inventors is to keep it simple."Focus on making a killer product and clearly message the key value points around that."

Charles says the crowdfunding experience taught him so much about his own product. He learned who his customers were by including a survey in his crowdfunding campaign, which revealed that his typical customers were males between the ages of twenty-five and forty-five with high incomes. Charles had actually created a new product category. In his survey, he found that 84 percent of his customers had never owned a breath analyzer even though the technology had been around since the 1950s. By putting the technology into a small device that could work with a smartphone, Charles brought new customers to the marketplace. Crowdfunding also helped Charles fine tune his product's price. Exploring different price points, he was able to recognize $49.99 as the perfect price.

As Charles understands, "the product won't sell or market itself. You need to make investments and put in a strong effort to spread the word and gain as much exposure as possible."

WHEN CROWFUNDING DOESN'T WORK

An example of when crowdfunding doesn't work is Derek Hoy's Cooler Cannon. We first met Derek while shooting a television program on the Food Network called *Invention Hunters.* Derek's invention, then called Shoot-A-Brew, was showcased on one of the episodes. The Cooler Cannon is the world's only remote-controlled beverage-tossing cooler. Perfect for a tailgating party, this ice chest shoots cans of soda (or any beverage) to a thirsty crowd. Derek's invention was great for the television show, being very visual. In fact, it was so eye-catching that the commercial for *Invention Hunters* featured the Cooler Cannon.

Soon after *Invention Hunters,* Derek landed a manufacturing deal that seemed like the perfect fit. Unfortunately, the deal fell through and Derek decided to manufacture the Cooler Cannon himself. To do that, he needed $275,000. After knocking on lots of doors, he came to the conclusion that crowdfunding was his only option. Derek decided to use Kickstarter to launch his crowdfunding campaign. Most successful Kickstarter campaigns offer multiple tiers of rewards to attract different types of supporters. To capitalize on as many interested supporters as possible, Derek created the following tiered reward system for his campaign:

- **$1.** Updates on the latest happenings with Cooler Cannon. Geared toward people who simply liked the cause and wanted to contribute something.

- **$10.** Cooler Cannon Koozie. For those who had a little more interest in the business's success.

- **$15.** VIP club membership, which was listed on the website, and which allowed members to post their tailgating pictures on the website. For those who wanted to make a declaration of support.

- **$20.** Cooler Cannon Soft Cooler. This allowed people to pitch in at a lower cost and get something in return.

- **$200.** Early Bird Cooler Cannon. Meant to reach the supporters who wanted to get their hands on the product right away. The first 100 supporters at this level got free shipping.

- **$240.** Cooler Cannon. Same as "Early Bird" option, but shipping was included.

- **$270.** Cooler Cannon and Extra Remote. Offered a bonus feature for a few dollars more.

- **$300.** Designated beta tester. For a select 20 people who wanted to be part of the development and get their hands on the first prototypes.

The campaign also included extra rewards that would be added if things went well. T-shirts, personalized or logoed coolers, or even a Cooler Cannon tailgate party were all ideas for these prizes.

Derek produced a video to meet Kickstarter-required content and created a comprehensive marketing campaign. His marketing strategy was to generate traffic on the Kickstarter page, with the end goal being the funding of his project. His target audience was primarily tailgaters, but Derek also catered his message on Kickstarter towards other possible supporters as well, such as friends and family. The first wave of the campaign launch targeted obvious supporters, intending to get pledges going and push the first surge of social media coverage. Derek also leveraged prior website subscribers by utilizing over one thousand sign-ups from his initial website, and by contacting people via email and Facebook in a push for prospective supporters. Derek planned to send periodic updates and even phone calls to keep supporters' attention and provoke action.

Kickstarter campaigns live and die by exposure, so leveraging all aspects of social media in order to maximize exposure is important. Because the ultimate exposure targets the end customer, Derek even made plans to demo his Cooler Cannon on site at numerous tailgating events.

In today's world, no marketing strategy would be complete without a social media plan, and Derek's plan hit social media in a big way. A typical social media campaign will direct traffic towards a website. Derek's efforts differed in that he pushed everything, including the product's website, toward his Kickstarter page. Derek used Facebook, LinkedIn, Twitter, blogs, and email blasts as part of his social media campaign. As noted, friends and family received personal calls to action, as did the leads from the Shoot-A-Brew website. Derek was able to get placement in many media outlets including radio, tailgating blogs, *Tailgater Monthly, Million Cups, Inventors Club,* and more. After all his effort, however, Derek's results were eighty-four backers, $17,358 pledged (very short of his $275,000 goal), an average pledge of $206, approximately eleven thousand video views, and few conversions of visitors to backers.

Derek's poor conversion rate might have been due to the Cooler Cannon not appealing to the masses. His conversion rate of 0.76 percent was low. The campaign's lack of success might have been due to scarcity of fresh PR. Unfortunately, Derek's product had gotten so much coverage before the Kickstarter campaign that the novelty of the invention had faded. Conversion of Derek's email list was also low. This was likely due to the long period of time (3 years) between when many of them had expressed an interest in his invention and when they finally saw results. At the end of the day, Derek's product may have been inappropriate for crowdfunding. Its high cost and long lead time may have caused it to lose its mass appeal.

We asked Derek what he should have done differently. His response was that he should have worked harder to establish more PR connections earlier. He should have been more aggressive with social media frequency. He should have added some of the bigger rewards at the outset, and taken advantage of friends and family that were willing to pledge large amounts. Derek had reserved a $3,000 tailgate party reward to drop in mid-campaign, but his campaign never got there. If he had included it at the beginning, it would have given him a bigger boost up front. Finally, he should have launched before football season. Doing so would have limited the time in which to film the video promo, but it may have generated more PR during that first wave of football season coverage.

CONSIDERATIONS

Although crowdfunding may help you achieve success with your invention, there are crucial factors to consider when crowdfunding your product. Unless your product goes viral (and that in and of itself will show results), the online crowdfunding community may not even see your idea. Generating traffic is crucial, but having a product that truly appeals to the masses is also critically important. Derek's cooler did not connect with the masses, but another cooler on Kickstarter, which had a built-in stereo and blender, and which targeted a different audience, did make a connection. Once your conversion rate is known, you will have a realistic view of how many people need to be reached, how many outlets and what coverage you will need, and how much effort you will need to expend.

A powerful video is a must-have, so budget for a good one. You should expect to pay between $1,000 and $3,000, depending on the complexity and professionalism of the video. Remember, PR is critical. At some point you will realize only so many people can organically be reached through networks. Unless there is a viral launch, your reach will plateau. A powerful public relations campaign may reach many more thousands of people—people to which you as an inventor do not have access. So, if the funds are available, budget for a PR firm. Derek had a friend help him for free. This resulted in approximately four mainstream blogs and a radio spot, which reached thousands beyond his network of contacts—but it was still not enough. Create a press release with a good back story that news outlets will want to cover. Keep the Kickstarter angle subtle, as there are thousands of other campaigns looking for coverage, and journalists will not want to write at length about it.

Once the campaign is off and running there will be little time for anything else besides execution. Inventors need to hit their Kickstarter launch dates with full momentum. Get all your tools (email service provider, website, Facebook page, QR codes, and so on) in place ahead of time. Research and understand how to leverage all the available tools. Build email lists and relationship lists in advance. You don't want to start blasting the email list the first day, get flagged as spam, and then have to shut down. It would cripple your campaign. You must build your social media connections, including your Facebook fans, blog, and Twitter followers. Get your PR outlets lined up a month or more in advance. It will take them time to schedule coverage and record the events.

Use your contacts. If you have a friend of a friend who works at a television station, magazine, or other media outlet, this is the time to ask for a favor. Success on a crowdfunding website is all about traffic; you need to get eyeballs to your page. Set a schedule for your email and social media. There may be optimal times for emailing, social media, and other forms of communication with your prospects. You should know them and set a schedule, so you're not scrambling or winging it by randomly posting and emailing. Timing and frequency do affect response. It's also important to write your email messages and social media content ahead of time, otherwise you'll be up all night trying to stay on schedule.

Consider the crowdfunding sweet spot. A successful product on Kickstarter, Indiegogo, or another crowdfunding website usually has mass market appeal, low cost, and short lead time. Derek's Cooler Cannon did not hit that sweet spot, since it cost too much, had a long lead time, and didn't have mass market appeal.

Running a crowdfunding campaign is a ton of work. This work includes scheduling, planning, shooting video, script writing, applying to a crowdfunding website, maintaining your website, updating your blog and social media content, and so on. It isn't just posting a video and watching the money roll in.

CONCLUSION

Inventors know that getting an idea to market is a cutthroat business. So, you need to ensure that you have the right stuff, both literally and figuratively. The bottom line is if you really want to succeed in getting your product to market, crowdfunding can be a critical element in finding the necessary money, but only if you have a complete business plan, understand the limitations, and find ways to team up with people that can help you put a successful campaign together.

On the road to invention, crowdfunding is a new path to explore, but inventors need to know there are still lots of bumps and potholes along the way. Ultimately, it's all about putting more money and more power in the hands of individual inventors, which is always a good thing.

5. Packaging

Josh Wallace

As an inventor, you know how important it is for your product to stand out. When a prospective customer browses the retail aisles, your product has fractions of a second to catch his eye, which is why packaging is so important. Research package design and you'll see this phrase repeatedly: "Packaging is just as important as the product." It's almost common sense, really. Some people may even go as far as to say, "The package is the product," which may be bold a statement, but nevertheless, packaging plays a tremendous role in sales. It's the final opportunity to advertise your product before the consumer makes a choice. Moreover, studies have shown that most people make brand choices at the point of purchase.

Spend time researching packaging, thinking carefully about your audience, and considering in which stores your product will be featured. Bring in a designer, who will help you find the answers you require. There is a lot to consider. What type of packaging should be used? Of which material should it be made? How will the packaging sit on the shelf or hang from a rack? What information will need to be included on or inside the packaging? What kind of graphics or photos

Josh Wallace earned his degree in graphic design at the Art Institutes International, Minnesota. He remains in the Twin Cities, where he works on a variety of projects in the fields of graphics, advertising, and illustration. His main clients have always been small businesses and proprietorships, including inventors.

joshw@joshwallace.com • www.joshwallace.com

should be added to the packaging? Does your product need a logo? Where should you manufacture your packaging? Will it be outsourced overseas? Are there any specific regulations that you'll need to follow?

If you think carefully about all these considerations and find the right professionals to consult, designing your product's packaging won't be much of a problem. It can actually be a fun process, and the result can add so much more personality to your product.

BASICS

What is the general purpose of packaging? A product's packaging adds protection from shipping damage, consumer handling, dust, moisture, and so on. It is usually needed for containment, especially if the product isn't solid material or if it's composed of many pieces. Portability is another perk, as it allows shippers to easily stack and transport crates or pallets of product. Finally, and just as importantly, packaging communicates a certain need to the consumer.

First off, you'll need to figure out where you're going to produce your packaging. Will you be working with a local manufacturer or an overseas factory? Choosing someone local provides a more hands-on experience, with experts assisting you face to face, or at least by phone, if they're not directly in your vicinity. These companies have teams of professionals to work with you from the beginning through the finished, packaged product. The alternative to staying local is to cut production costs, which also lowers the cost to consumers, by outsourcing. The package design options may be a little more limited, but foreign companies have most of the same capabilities as any American company. In this case, it would be worth your investment to hire a sourcing expert to communicate with the factory, and a graphic designer to handle the creative end. No matter who produces your package, you will have to begin an in-depth exploration of what your product is and how you want it represented through your packaging. It's necessary to personify your product, thinking of its personality, which leads us to branding.

Companies brand themselves to configure their ideals, benefits, and identities, and then develop ad strategies from these characterizations. Branding helps keep their images consistent, ensuring that their messages won't stray. Products need to do the same. What are your product's advantages? How is your product different from the competition? What sort of feelings could your product produce? You have to do more than inform customers. You must provoke emotions by branding your product through the use of logos, advertising, press releases, and, of course, packaging. Your product's brand encapsulates its name, slogan, graphics, shapes, colors, copy writing, website, and practically everything to which the consumer has access. If you've established anything with your brand yet, then share this information with your designer. Have you started a website? Do you have any sell sheets, business cards, or flyers developed? These items could begin telling the story about your product, helping your designer understand what you are trying to accomplish.

Regarding most advertising and design projects, a creative brief is written to set a foundation from which to work. It lays out the details needed to help begin the whole design process. If you were to hire my company for your project, I would send you a questionnaire to fill out and discuss with me, or we would meet in person or over the phone to go through the brief. This document consists of questions relating to ten topics. It's best to answer each question with as much information as possible. The more detail, the better—you need to teach me everything about your product because you never know what I could find useful. The topics are as follows:

- **Overview.** What's the background of your product? What's the big picture you're working towards? What's going on in your product's market—the history and current trends? What kind of opportunities or issues do you face? I might not know everything about your product, so explain what it does, why you developed it and why you believe in it.

- **Deliverables.** What are all of the packaging elements that you need designed? Do you have any thoughts on what kind of package you want or which kind of materials should be used? Some other items you may need include logos, product photography, illustrations, and help writing copy, instructions, or diagrams on the packaging itself or within a manual inside the packaging. You may also need a physical mock-up to submit to potential manufacturers.

- **Objective.** What should the objective of the packaging be aside from its basic functionality? What effect should the packaging have on consumers? What should it make the audience think, feel, and do?

- **Audience.** Who is the audience that will make up your prime customers? The more precisely detailed the answer, the better. Think demographics, but go beyond just age and sex. Does your main customer base consist of young urban professional mothers or out-doors-loving new-age hippies? It's a good idea to specify before broadening your focus. And don't go too broad, or you'll become too generic.

- **Tone.** Describe the overall tone you're looking for and consider how it would transfer to the packaging's ad copy, imagery, graphics, color scheme, and so on. What feelings are you trying to evoke? What kind of impression are you trying to make? Is your product formal? Sophisticated? Casual? Funny? Serious? Shocking? Keep your branding in mind.

- **Competitors.** List your competitors and explain how your product is different from theirs. What would a competitor's customers think and feel about your specific product and brand?

- **Value.** Why should consumers buy your product? What reason does the consumer have to believe that your product would be useful to their lives? What value does the consumer see in your product? Include all the copy that you would like to print on the packaging. Think of everything you could possibly say to help you explain and sell the product.

- **Main Reason.** What's the single most important thing for your packaging to say to the consumer? What could be stated that would be the most persuasive reason for your audience to purchase your product?

- **Other Considerations.** Is there anything else that you can think of in terms of your product's creative development?

- **Timeline.** What do you need and when do you need it?

Once the creative brief has been written, you, your product, and what you're trying to accomplish with your product's packaging should become clear. Additional questions may come up after reading the brief, of course. Open communication is very important. When it comes to my clients, I would like them to let me know whenever they think of something to share, and I always do the same for them.

RESEARCH

Research is the next step before any sketching of ideas. This step could be started before the creative brief, but should definitely become more aggressive afterwards. You will have researched plenty during the development of your product, and you'll continue to do so throughout the duration of its life. Assuming you've already studied the market and your potential audience, you should now begin learning about packaging. I, a designer, am also an avid researcher, but it never hurts to find out what a client finds attractive. Go to different stores and look at packaging. Focus within your product family and the stores you'd like to be featured in, but also look beyond. You never know where you may discover something useful. See what your competitors or others within your category are doing. What kind of packaging are they using? How does the packaging sit on the shelves? Study the personality of other products. How do they use design to attract a consumer's eyes and stand out?

The Internet has become an amazingly useful research tool. Use Google image searches to find other packaging samples that may spark ideas. Look for graphic design or packaging design websites to find the best work out there. There are tons of online publications, blogs, and portfolio sites to explore. Pretty much every industry has a trade publication. What might you find there? Check the library or book stores for more books and magazines offering packaging information and examples. Find a handful of inspiring ideas and trends to lead the way towards your own packaging designs. I also like to have the actual product in my hands so I can test it out and get a feel for how it actually works. It makes sense, right? How could I possibly create an effective package for something that I haven't even had the chance to play around with?

Figure out what will be written on the packaging before you dig too deeply into the design. Space is limited, so be brief and figure out a hierarchy. Leave room for the brand name, the company name, a slogan (if desired), some quick but important descriptions, and any supplementary copy (instructions, storage info, warnings, etc.) you may need to include. Copy is another branding tool where you can be creative. If you want to be as clever and brilliant as possible, you may consider hiring a copywriter. They know how to use the written word to get into people's heads. If you have a surfing product, for instance, it would be great to have the copy written as if it were being said by a hip, young surfer dude.

Connect with your audience. The copy should advertise your product as a very useful part of people's lives. You want to be flashy, but you have to be honest. You can't use any false advertising or the FCC will be after you to pull the product off the shelves. A package's shape and material play a big role in communicating to the customer. While strolling down the grocery aisles, notice all the competing brands within the same product category in many different shapes and sizes of packaging, each creating a unique perception. Some products aim to be higher end, others to be affordable. Some are concerned with being taken seriously, while others would rather be a fun part of your day. A straight and narrow glass bottle will look classier than a plump plastic one. An uncoated cardboard box will look more environmentally savvy than a plastic wrapped container. How can the structure and material of your packaging expand your brand?

TYPES OF PACKAGING MATERIAL

There are many different types of packaging, and some are the obvious choices for certain products, like bottles for beverages. But what kind of bottle? Glass? Plastic? Aluminum? Do you want to be conventional or do you want something completely custom? Does the product need to be mounted in the package? Does it need to be tamperproof?

Cardboard boxes and cartons are among the most common packaging types. They come in countless shapes and sizes. If the entire box is closed with no windows, then product photography is typically used to show the consumer what is inside and how the product works. Some boxes have windows to show the product. The window might be made of plastic or it might be completely open. Some boxes are made to be re-sealable, or to be used as a spot to store your product when it's not in use. A simpler form of packaging is a bag with a cardboard label folded in half, closing the top of the bag (usually with a staple). This inexpensive solution is often used for cheaper products like certain toys and party favors. There are almost endless variations of cardboard that can be utilized for different functions.

Plastic is another common choice, especially in the form of clamshell packaging. Those are the one-piece plastic containers that consist of two halves coming together on a hinge, which is usually located at the bottom. There is typically a label inside each clamshell that the consumer can see through the plastic, or there's one adhered to the outside of the packaging. Some clamshells are easily opened because they're just taped shut by the label. Some clamshells, on the other hand, are very difficult to open because the halves of the plastic have been fused together. These are usually the culprits responsible for the phenomenon known as "wrap rage." Wrap rage occurs when a package is so difficult to open that people become overwhelmed by frustration trying to get to the product inside, sometimes cutting themselves or spraining their fingers accidentally in the process. There are ways to make these clamshells more accessible, so be sure to speak with your manufacturer if you choose this option. Blister packs, conversely, are easier to open. These are commonly used for over-the-counter medicines when each pill is in its own plastic bubble against foil. Blister packs are also used for other consumer goods when the product would be in a single plastic bubble against a cardboard backing. The product is easily visible and there should be space on the cardboard for information and graphics.

Obviously, there are many other options for packaging, including bottles, cans, buckets, and so on. Any material can be customized to fit your product perfectly. Cost, however, will play a major role in deciding the structure and material of your packaging. It's good to stand out, but you need to stick to a budget. Think at a practical level too. I like to keep mixed nuts around my house for snacking, and I've purchased both plastic jars and plastic zipper bags of them. At some point I stopped buying the bags because I like the jars better—I think they're more user-friendly. Do you notice any ways that you gravitate towards some forms of packaging rather than others?

One way for your product to stand out in stores is through a "point of purchase," or "P.O.P.," display. This refers to having your product featured in its very own setup. P.O.P. displays can be made out of cardboard and come in many shapes and sizes. They may be as tall as an average-size adult, with shelves displaying many products, or they may be small enough to sit on a checkout counter and display just a handful of items. This option will obviously cost more, but it would surely get your product noticed. You would also have to work with your retailers to ensure available space in their stores for any P.O.P. displays. These displays usually have a short lifespan of a few weeks, as retailers continuously switch out products and shift things around. It would be nice to have your own permanent display in each store, but such a thing is not likely.

Other questions to consider include: Will you be outsourcing your packaging? And what will the factory be capable of? Are there any government regulations or safety concerns with your packaging? You must be particularly diligent in finding the answer to this last question if your product is in the field of foods, toys, baby items, medical devices, or cosmetics.

GRAPHIC DESIGN

Graphic design compels the audience and quickly communicates significance. Graphics can either be printed on the packaging materials or may appear on a label or tag of some sort. The basic design essentials are: color, typography, composition, logo use or development, photo or illustration use, and the overall style. This is another area in which research is important to see how other companies and products use design effectively. Let's say you have an exercise product that's branded as a high-quality, high-energy, extremely efficient piece of equipment. Research those themes to inspire provocative imagery. What are some sources of energy that you could conceptualize around? How could you tweak it to connote quality and efficiency as well? With these rough concepts in mind, what kind of typefaces, colors, and graphic elements could work together to harmonize your brand identity? If you know your brand well, these answers should come relatively easily.

Color is one of the most fundamental tools for designers of all types. Color is used to create mood, contrast, and also harmony throughout a design. You should choose colors that make sense for your product and package—don't just make choices based on your personal preference. Think of the meaning of different colors. White is clean and pure. Blue is calm and relaxing. Red is exciting and sexy. Green is natural and lucky. It's good to play around with a few different color schemes to find the best possible choice to complement your brand. With the high-energy exercise machine, what are a couple colors that would be obvious choices to use? What are a couple colors that would not work with this theme at all?

Typography is another one of design's fundamentals. There are thousands of typeface choices to add to the mood you're setting with the packaging. Which one shares the same mood with your product? Do you want something classy and very elegant or are you looking for something more edgy and untraditional? There are plenty of unique typefaces to represent the writing on your package. Designers usually choose a couple—one for headlines (this can be a more flashy choice) and a different one for the body copy (this should be a simpler, more legible choice, as not to strain the eyes of your customers). There are conventional ways to use typography and also many experimental ways to use it. With the exercise equipment, you may consider a slanted typeface to connote motion, or maybe you want a more energetic, electrified choice.

Speaking of typography, do you want just a bare typeface used for your product's name, or do you want to push it further with the creation of a logo? The most basic piece of any brand is the logo. It sets the tone for everything else. Products also commonly have logos or at least some catchy typeface that fits its personality. If you decide to go with a logo, it should evoke feeling, just like every other element of design. It should visually sum up your product and tell a story that will relate to your customers. It can be something concrete or abstract, simple or complex, literal or metaphorical. Your logo should subconsciously say things about your product so that it gets into people's heads at a glance.

While this can be a challenge, with proper preparation, the ultimate solution will soon follow.

Will your package need any photography? If the product isn't visible within the package, then product photography is necessary so people can understand what's going on. If the product is new to the market, showing a photo of it in use would be a great idea. The alternative is an illustration of some sort, but you don't want to misrepresent the product in any way.

Composition is the part of design in which everything comes together—how every element is laid out, and how each aspect intermingles with the others. Graphics placed in relation to any photos, illustrations, sections of copy, color, and so on, is the art form of composition. Any famous artist will tell you that they carefully consider the placement of every element within their paintings to assure a proper flow of interest.

One additional option (although not necessary because of the added expense) is specialty printing, which consists of several eye-catching ways to extend the graphic design. Foil stamping uses a metallic foil that is applied with heat and pressure. This creates shiny graphics or lettering for a high-quality, more expensive look. Embossing uses pressure to create a raised, multi-dimensional graphic. Debossing creates an indented graphic. Die cutting creates unique shapes by cutting away some of the material (like a business card shaped like Minnesota or Arizona). Spot varnishing applies a glossy or matte (or a step in between) layer of finish to allow specific areas to stand out. There are more options available, and as technology evolves, more options will be introduced.

INSPIRATION

After I do my research, explore colors, and dig through typefaces, I create an "inspiration board" full of found photos, graphics, patterns, objects, other products' package designs, and anything that could help inspire some ideas for the project. Let's say I'm working on a label for a new barbecue sauce. I'd compile tons of imagery from restaurants, kitchen utensils, food items, cookbooks, appliances, and so on. I would also attach potential typeface and color choices. With my inspiration board at hand, I would then take out my mechanical pencil and some blank sheets of paper and begin sketching ideas. At this point it would be quantity over quality. I would sketch out all my ideas because doing so would get the clichéd ones out of my head, allowing me to narrow my choices down to the best ones. I'd combine images from the inspiration board—a drawing of a tomato with a pan, the name of the barbecue sauce in a pan, barbecue utensils crossed, etc. I'd also study the letterforms from the typeface choices to find relationships between those and the shapes of the objects and images being used.

I'd then sit in my computer chair and draw up a few polished digital pieces using the fundamentals of design explained earlier. I'd create some good mock-ups to present for discussion before setting off to touch up the final piece. I'd also tap into my network of design colleagues to get additional opinions. Closer to the finish line, I'd create a final mock-up of the packaging to make sure that everything is working properly before handing it off to the manufacturer.

At this point, I'd like some version of the product (the actual product is always best) to be sure that it fits in the packaging and will remain secure. Package size adjustments may need to be made at this step. Without the actual product to work with, I would need to work with an estimate for the packaging size and make adjustments later. Creating a mock-up is especially important for outsourcing. The factory needs to understand what it is you're looking for. Will the same factory produce both packaging and product? If so, send them both the product prototype and packaging prototype.

CONCLUSION

By getting to know you and your product, while researching the competition and finding inspiration, a designer should be able to find the right path to the finished piece. Design can sometimes be commoditized, but it's a lot more than just making pretty pictures. It's a process of problem solving. It's coming up with a strong concept to justify the details of the designed piece, which will be facilitated through a thorough creative brief. If you want your package design to make sense and have meaning, make sure your graphic designer is proficient in the fundamental areas of design: color, typography, and composition.

Remember to be practical. Of course you want to stand out, but your package can't be too outlandish or exceed your budget. Research pricing and be honest with manufacturers about your possible need for short runs where custom packaging would be too expensive. There are plenty of stock choices that can be tailored to your needs, so spend more time thinking intelligently about branding with graphics.

Do you think packaging is the product? When it's on the shelf introducing itself to shoppers, the answer should definitely be yes.

6. Manufacturing, Importing, and Product Safety

Edith G. Tolchin

Inventors who choose to manufacture their own products have either attempted licensing or decided from the beginning to control the destiny of their own businesses. If you have decided to deal with manufacturing, please do the necessary research involved and follow the guidelines I have provided below. Since I manufacture my clients' inventions in Asia, I will specifically address guidelines for manufacturing overseas. Please note, however, that many of these principles will apply whether your product is made in the United States or overseas.

PROTOTYPING

The best way to begin the manufacturing process is with a prototype that is as close to perfect as possible. Factories in Asia work best with a physical prototype, because the "what you send is what you get" rule applies. If you send a rough prototype, for example, or a drawing, you will receive a very rough counter sample, which in all likelihood will not

Edith G. Tolchin, "The Sourcing Lady," started EGT Global Trading in 1997, with a goal to link US inventors with Asian manufacturers, and to provide an exclusive import service for sourcing, quality control, production testing and safety issues, manufacturing, international financing, air and ocean shipping, customs clearance arrangements, and dock-to-door delivery. Edith is also a contributing editor and freelance writer for *Inventors Digest Magazine*.

EGT@egtglobaltrading.com • www.egtglobaltrading.com • www.edietolchin.com

be what you are looking for in your finished product. Drawings are also subject to the factory's design department, which may interpret it very differently from your intention. Translations for tweaking may help, but based on my work with Asian factories since 1990, I have found that perfect physical prototypes are best and will save you money in the long run. For example, you'll spend a lot in courier charges sending samples back and forth without a good working prototype, not to mention fees to your consultant to correct prototype issues.

PACKAGING

Your packaging brands your invention, and if done properly it makes it very visible in stores. Carefully consider your brand or product name and logo. Your product name and logo should blend well together and define your product. Done poorly, no one will pay attention, and your product will sit on shelves collecting dust. Unless you plan on manufacturing your product in just a plain poly bag for sale on your website and shipping from your basement, please have a packaging mock-up ready to send to the factory, along with your best prototype, and information on how your product works (sell sheet) translated into the language of the country where your factory is located. Pay close attention to government regulations pertaining to product and packaging labeling.

PRODUCT DESIGN EVALUATION

The category of "consumer products" generally includes household items, items that come in contact with food or the human body (such as beauty products, cosmetics, and kitchen items), electrical items, apparel and shoes, all products for babies and children up to the age of twelve, and items that may have had previous regulations, restrictions, or bans according to the Consumer Product Safety Commission (CPSC). If your invention belongs to this category, then for the safety of your customers, as well as to protect your new business, you must submit your prototype to a CPSC-accredited laboratory for what is known as a product design evaluation (PDE). Go to the CPSC's list of accredited laboratories (www.cpsc.gov/cgi-bin/labsearch) and choose one that is qualified to evaluate your type of product. Send a few inquiries to a few labs and ask if they do product design evaluations for product safety issues, government import regulations, and proper product marking. Get a few price estimates, and ask what type of report they will furnish you with. Make an educated comparison. When you have decided on the proper lab, you will complete its application for the PDE and send them your best prototype, along with packaging mock-ups, product instructions (if applicable), and your sell sheet or product brochure.

Aside from providing you with the lab's special design concerns, safety issues, any "red flags" regarding your product, a list of import regulations, and mandatory and optional production tests (of which your appointed factory must be made aware), your PDE report will also help you obtain product liability insurance, which every business involved in selling consumer products must have. Make sure you thoroughly read and understand your PDE, and do not be afraid to ask questions of the engineers who performed your evaluation. You will usually have up to thirty days after receipt of report to resolve any issues. Be certain to heed the advice of the lab's engineers if they provide recommendations for revisions to address design concerns or red flags. Remember, even though you know your invention inside and out, the engineers are specifically trained to spot problems, so please respect their knowledge. Depending on the outcome of your report, you may need to go back to tweak your prototype a few more times before you submit it to your prospective factory.

GOVERNMENT REGULATIONS

In addition to the need for a PDE report, there are many other government regulations to consider when manufacturing a new invention. For example, labeling your product (and its packaging) "permanently, indelibly, legibly and conspicuously" with country of origin (e.g., "Made in Italy") is a requirement issued by U.S. Customs and Border Protection (www.cbp.gov) in order to import a new product legally into the United States. For a textile invention, you may require a registered identification number (RN), which is basically an importer's registration number. Information on this can be found on the Federal Trade

Commission website (www.ftc.gov). And as mentioned above, the Consumer Product Safety Improvement Act governs the manufacture of all children's products up to the age of twelve, requiring that various testing be done for issues such as toxic chemicals, flammability, choking hazards, and so on. Children's products also have very detailed labeling and marking requirements, which include tracking labels, and you must also have a children's product certificate prepared and readily available to U.S. Customs and Border Protection. If your invention is, for example, medical- or health-related, or comes in contact with food or the human body (as in a cosmetic product), you may want to check the Food and Drug Administration (FDA) website (www.fda.gov) for requirements. Better to investigate government guidelines for manufactured products to avoid expensive mistakes—or even jeopardize your ability to import your product legally into the United States—before you place a purchase order with your chosen factory.

FINDING A FACTORY

For first-time sourcing ventures, I always recommend hiring a consultant who is well versed in working with overseas factories. Your consultant can screen a prospective factory for communication problems (how fluent will your factory contact be in English?), production capacity for reorders (once your invention takes off—and of course we wish you success!), shipping terms (such as who will make the arrangements with the steamship company or freight forwarder), and many other issues that you may not know to ask about. Here are some questions I always recommend asking a factory before you place a purchase order:

- Can the factory furnish references of United States-based companies for which it has manufactured products?

- What are the holiday closings for the factory for the coming year? Note that, for example, Asian factories can be closed for a full month during Lunar New Year celebrations and have many and frequent holiday closings throughout the year. You do not want to encounter delays even before launching your new product.

- Is the factory willing to work with an appointed independent safety testing laboratory for production testing?

- Will the factory suggest possible alternative materials that might enhance the design of the product? This is not absolutely necessary, but it will certainly show creativity on the part of the prospective supplier.

- What policies does the factory have in place for replacement of defective merchandise? I normally write a stipulation in all my purchase orders that clearly spells out how the supplier will replace any defective items, beyond the typical industry standard, indicating that the supplier will be responsible for not only replacing defective merchandise, but also for arranging for the collection and return shipment of these items.

- Does the factory work with a Chinese freight forwarder who could arrange shipment? Regarding small initial orders, it can be easier and more economical for the supplier to arrange for the ocean freight and marine insurance to be prepaid and coordinated by its appointed freight forwarder at the port in China. Also, sometimes the factories get cheaper freight rates than if arranged in the United States. The unit cost will increase by a few cents, but it will be worth not having to deal with steamship companies for quotes, making the arrangements with unreliable trucking firms in China, inferior roads and transportation systems within China, and so on.

- What is the factory's minimum order quantity (MOQ)? If you are only in the position to purchase a small number of pieces to begin with, as most startups are, you must state this fact directly. Many Asian firms—especially the larger ones—will assume you are interested in purchasing their typical MOQs from the start. These MOQs can be upwards of fifty thousand to one hundred thousand pieces. So, if you only want to buy one thousand pieces to "test the waters," that should be the very first subject you discuss. You don't want to get too far along with prototypes, counter samples, and so on, only to lead the supplier on, who will assume you are interested in buying huge quantities. You can certainly volunteer that you will be buying only a small quantity to begin with, but that if your product sells well, you will return to them in the future for a quote for larger quantities.

PRICE QUOTES AND COUNTER SAMPLES

Let's say you've found a reputable factory and have done your home-work. Now you are ready to send the factory your prototype so that it can review it, comment on it, create a counter sample, study the materials and components involved, and then provide you with a price quote.

For each sourcing inquiry, prepare one prototype of each desired product style, a product brochure with photos thoroughly explaining the use of the product, and a list of specifications and components, including possible alternative components, packaging samples, logo and labeling information, and desired purchase quantities—and make sure all this information has been written in as simple English as possible, without any jargon or colloquialisms. Include a list of required production tests and any optional tests you may want done. If it is at all possible, try to have your information translated into Chinese, if applicable. You should give the factory all your contact information, including your email address. Use FedEx, UPS, or a similar courier to send your parcel. Most suppliers will begin to email questions about your product within two to three weeks. Their promptness and ease of communication in English will be an asset to your business relationship. Counter samples and price quotes usually begin to arrive within three to four weeks.

Learn about shipping terms in price negotiations. You will see terms such as "US $4.50/pc. FOB Shanghai" or "US $10.00/pc. CIF Miami" in the quotes. These indicate who is paying for the air or ocean freight and marine insurance. FOB pricing usually indicates that you will arrange and pay the freight and insurance, and CIF indicates that the freight and insurance will be prepaid by the seller. For more information about shipping terms, do an online search for "Incoterms" and you will find many websites with information on international shipping terms. Also make sure your price quote from the factory includes packaging, printed inserts, hangtags, your logo (if applicable), and any other labels or markings as required by government regulations (such as the "Made in China" label). Most imported products require a country of origin label. It is normally much less expensive and more efficient to have all the packaging done by your overseas supplier, making your product shelf-ready when it arrives in the United States.

Carefully review the counter samples. They may need revisions before you place a purchase order. Look for the supplier's willingness to cooperate by making necessary revisions. If the supplier says, "We can fix that after your purchase order is placed," don't count on it. Typically, packaging samples are not sent with the initial set of counter samples. They are normally sent with production samples, after the purchase order has been placed. If your packaging is particularly complicated, ask the supplier to send a sample of similar packaging they have done in the past, so you can assess their abilities in advance.

PURCHASE ORDERS

For your protection (and that of your new startup business venture), make sure a properly written purchase order (PO) is drawn up. This is a contract between you and the overseas manufacturer. Include buyer and seller names and addresses, phone and fax numbers, email addresses, quantities, unit pricing (determine in advance if you will be paying "FOB China" pricing, which will not include ocean freight and marine insurance, or "CIF USA" port pricing, which will include freight and insurance), and mold and tooling charges. In addition, include wire transfer details such as percentage for down payments (usually 30 percent down), percentage for balance due (which is paid only after presentation of a completed Import Security Filing document, which must be confirmed by U.S. Customs and Border Protection before you pay the balance due on your order), and other shipping documents as required by law, such as ocean bills of lading, commercial invoices, packing lists, non-wooden packing certificates, and so on. You do not want to pay in advance and then never see your shipment. Also include your list of production testing (as determined in your design evaluation), where testing will be done, and who is paying for the tests. Indicate your desired number of pre-production samples, as well as the number of mass-production samples you'll require (obviously after your pre-production samples have been approved), in order to assess quality and consistency throughout manufacturing.

The most important item to incorporate into your PO is a stipulation for defective merchandise. Under a "comments" or "remarks" section in the purchase orders I issue on behalf of my clients, I write,

"Seller (name) is responsible for defective merchandise. Seller will be responsible for the entire cost of merchandise, freight charges for return of defective items, to be returned to the seller, in addition to replacement of the defective merchandise or refund of buyer's payment (in US dollars, at the option of the buyer, via wire transfer)." Also provide all specifications, product descriptions, components, customs information, labeling and production testing (both in accordance with your design evaluation report), packaging information, and carton marks. For purchase orders, the more info you provide, the more protection you hold, and your supplier will not be able to say, "Oops, you never mentioned that!"

BINDING RULINGS

While your order is in production—and most initial orders take at least forty-five to sixty days—you'll have plenty of time to consider a very important issue: import duties. Say you visit a foreign country and purchase a good amount of souvenirs. When you arrive back in the States, you'll have to pass through U.S. Customs and Border Protection. Depending on the value of your purchases from this foreign country, you may have to pay duty on them. Similarly, you will have to pay import duties on your new invention once the shipment arrives at your chosen port in the United States. Now that you know what your unit cost will be, based on the price quote from the factory, how much extra money should you set aside for import duties? This is where a U.S. Customs and Border Protection binding ruling request is very important. Customs uses a gargantuan guide called the *Harmonized Tariff Schedule of the United States* (http://hts.usitc.gov), which consists of thousands of pages of import classifications and import duty percentages (percentage of unit cost, not including freight or insurance or the "FOB country of origin" amount) for products of all kinds—from apples to zippers. The problem is there are so many places to look for just one item that even a seasoned licensed customs broker can get confused. And, since your product is a new invention, odds are that U.S. Customs and Border Protection has not yet classified your product. So, a binding ruling request is another valuable tool in the development of your product.

You can go to the U.S. Customs and Border Protection website (www.cbp.gov) and look for information on how to apply for a binding ruling request, or you can have an international trade consultant or customs broker apply for the binding ruling request on your behalf. You may consult the National Customs Brokers and Forwarders Association of America, Inc. (www.ncbfaa.org) to find a broker. Once a sample of your product has been sent—along with descriptive literature, specifications, a list of components, etc.—U.S. Customs and Border Protection will review the product and classify it within thirty days after receipt. You may consult the Customs Rulings Online Search System (http://rulings.cbp.gov), also known as CROSS, for information about classifying your products. But again, since your invention may be a new product for the CROSS system, it may be to your advantage to work with a sourcing consultant, international trade consultant, or customs broker rather than risk incorrectly guessing the classification.

Customs will return your prototype, if you wish. Customs will also provide information on the duty rate and international labeling and marking issues, should you request it. Accurate labeling of your product will help you avoid the possibility of your shipment being detained for improper marking or labeling upon its arrival in the United States. Penalties can be steep. Later on, when your shipment arrives, a copy of this binding ruling is presented by your customs broker during clearance. Customs likes it when you make it easy for them.

QUALITY CONTROL

For quality control purposes, your PO should also include the number of pre-production samples your factory will provide. These samples should be thoroughly reviewed and evaluated by you to make sure the quality meets with your satisfaction. At this stage, typically, a pre-production sample is sent to a CPSC-accredited safety lab for production testing, according to the product design evaluation report's recommended tests. You, the buyer, are usually responsible for the costs associated with initial production testing. If the pre-production sample passes the tests, then the factory can proceed with mass-production, and will later provide you with mass-production samples to review for consistency in quality throughout the process. If the pre-production sample does not pass the production tests, then usually the factory will be responsible for making revisions to make sure future samples pass a retest, the costs of which should normally be paid by the factory.

Once your order has passed all production testing, mass-production samples have been approved, and mass production is complete, the factory will advise you that they are ready to ship. It should send you photos of shipping marks for your cartons (proper carton marking is a must for import compliance). Rather than rely on the factory's final shipment inspection, you should hire an independent agency to do this for you. Costing usually under $300, it's worth every penny. I normally work with a company called KRT Audit Corp (www.krtinspect.com), which has offices throughout Asia and many other parts of the world. You would prepare what's called final shipment inspection criteria, which would let the inspector know what she should look for when inspecting your order. Basically, you should include packaging, functionality, and appearance issues, and send photos of proper samples versus quality control issues along with a copy of your original purchase order, so the technician has a good idea of what to look for. Within a few days, you will have a thorough inspection report, which should include photos of the final shipment and packaging, and which should address all requested items. At this point, you should be able to determine if you are ready to accept shipment of your order.

SHIPPING AND IMPORTING YOUR PRODUCT

Depending on the shipping terms of your PO (FOB or CIF) and who is paying for the ocean or air freight, either the supplier or you and your consultant will make arrangements to get your order on a boat, plane, or air courier such as FedEx or UPS. Remember that your import security filing document, or ISF, must be filed with U.S. Customs and Border Protection with info furnished by the factory and its freight forwarder within twenty-four hours of vessel loading date. Customs issues costly penalties for non-compliance. Your consultant or customs broker should inspect the international shipping documentation provided by the supplier, such as the commercial invoice, packing list, bill of lading, certificate of inspection, marine insurance certificate, and so on, to make sure all proper customs information has been included, that the product has been properly described, and that quantities and costs are correct. If it is a children's product, do not forget to include your children's product certificate. It is always better to have more information than less when it comes to international shipping documents. Once your order reaches a port in the United States, your customs broker will clear your shipment through U.S. Customs and Border Protection on your behalf, prepay any import duties, and deliver it to your home, garage, warehouse, or other final delivery destination. Make sure to give your customs broker a copy of the binding ruling so your product can be properly classified for import duties.

CONCLUSION

Now, are you still certain you want to manufacture on your own? It can be done, but you must be an educated consumer, and you must not be afraid to seek help. If you have questions or need assistance completing a product design evaluation, finding a factory, or legally importing your product into the United States, feel free to contact me. Best of luck!

ONE BIG IDEA

You could say this invention was initially a bomb, as CorningWare cookware's heat-resistant materials were initially developed for a US ballistic missile program. Invented by Stanley Donald Stookey, PhD, this pyroceramic glass cookware was brought to market by Corning Glass Works in 1958 and soon became a staple in the kitchen for decades to come.

7. Marketing

Jack Lander

An entrepreneurial startup is dominated by a 500-pound gorilla named Marketing, and its keeper is a small-business heretic, namely you. Information about accounting, finance, forming a limited liability company, or LLC, is important, of course. But information on each of these subjects is abundant and readily available. Good marketing information for the small startup, however, is rare, which is why this chapter will concentrate on marketing. How well you perform the four essential marketing functions will determine your success. You can outsource or delegate almost everything else, but marketing ultimately comes down to you.

What does entrepreneurship mean? Let me put it this way: If you invented the incandescent lamp and made a working prototype, then you're an inventor. If you developed the incandescent lamp into a practical source of illumination and then brought it to market, then you're an entrepreneur. According to historians Robert Friedel and Paul Israel, twenty-three inventors had already invented the incandescent lamp prior to Edison's product coming to fruition, but it was Edison who made the first practical light bulb and took it to market. We tend to

Jack Lander is a seasoned inventor and mentor to inventors. With thirteen patents, Jack is also a small-business veteran, having founded eleven businesses. He is a past president of the United Inventors Association, and served as Vice President of the Yankee Invention Exposition for fourteen years. He is the founder of DIG, the Danbury (Connecticut) Inventor's Group.

JackL359@aol.com • www.inventor-mentor.com

think of Edison as an inventor, but my take is that primarily he was an entrepreneur who invented or modified products in order to satisfy his entrepreneurial drive. Entrepreneurship may be distinguished from ordinary business by its essential innovative ingredient. It must demonstrate innovation in the product or service, innovation in the marketing of the product or service, or innovation in both.

Marketing consists of four basic tasks: Finding or creating your product, positioning it, selecting the best distribution channels for it, and exposing it to people so they may discover it and buy it. Notice that the words sell and sales are not included in these four points. A small entrepreneurial startup should be organized in such a way as to encourage people to come to it and buy. Amazon and ebay are models of such organizations. Your time as an early-phase entrepreneur is too precious to devote to seeking potential customers and pitching them your product. It is in this sense that the entrepreneur is a heretic, which is a title that should not necessarily be concealed. The definition of a heretic is a person holding an opinion that is at odds with what is generally accepted.

FINDING OR CREATING YOUR PRODUCT

Entrepreneurship implies a certain novelty about the product in question, or a novelty in your approach to marketing—sometimes both. At the outset of your venture, you need every advantage you can get. Thus, you need to find or create a niche product that has a competitive edge relative to mainstream examples. There are three main ways to achieve a niche product: Find it among existing products, modify an existing product, or invent a product.

Finding an Existing Niche Product

There are five main places to discover niche products: printed catalogs or the Internet, angel or entrepreneur fairs, trade shows, retail stores, and local manufactures.

Printed Catalogs or the Internet

If your product selection cannot be sold through printed catalogs or online, it likely cannot be sold through retail stores. Catalogs and the

Internet allow you to determine if a product category exists (for example, books, tools, or sporting goods). Thus, your immediate search step is not to find a product, but to ensure that a marketing channel and category may be found for the product you eventually create or select. The point here is that a lack of category means that your product is an orphan, and reaching your buyers will be costly and difficult relative to a product that has an identifiable category. Once you've been assured that a category exists, proceed to search for a niche product.

Grey House's *The Directory of Mail Order Catalogs* is the only substantial printed directory at this time. But the fate of directories of all kinds is precarious. Many great directories, such as the famous *Thomas Register of American Manufacturers,* have bit the dust in their printed forms. *Thomas Register of American Manufacturers* may now be found online at www.thomasnet.com. If you can find a copy of *The Directory of Mail Order Catalogs,* whether used or new, consider it a treasure. It lists about twelve thousand catalogs, separated into forty-four categories. If you don't find an appropriate category for your tentative product in this resource, you will probably find difficulty in marketing it. Other sources for finding catalogs are www.flipseek.com, www. catalogs.com, www.cybercatalogs.com, and www.cataloglink.com. You may also visit www.amazon.com and see if it offers a category for your product.

The Internet provides hundreds of websites of inventors who are offering their inventions for licensing, or who are producing them on a small scale and may be receptive to a buyout or a marketing partnership. In the sixteen years that I've been mentoring inventors and start-up entrepreneurs, I've never heard of even one inventor licensing his invention merely by setting up a website and displaying the product without some collateral means of driving potential licensees to its website. Businesses that are receptive to new product proposals simply don't search for them on the Internet. The odds of a company finding a product that matches its product lines are slim. For the startup entrepreneur who has no preconceived definition of his product, however, there may be some value in such a search. In a sense, inventor websites are catalogs for inventions. A few are well managed and take an active role in finding potential licensees. Others are passive and ineffective. One of the best active sites is Paul Niemann's Market Launchers (www.marketlaunchers.com/licensingdeals.html). On his website, Paul Niemann displays products that he has helped inventors launch. He may also be contacted by those seeking licensees for their products.

Angel or Entrepreneur Fairs

These fairs are usually sponsored by angels, and attract entrepreneurs who are seeking finance for their ventures. They are found on the Internet by keying in "angel entrepreneur fairs" on your search engine. At these fairs you'll meet entrepreneurs and inventors who have products and inventions that they are trying to launch. Since most don't connect with an angel, the opportunity to find an available product, or even a business partner, is quite possible.

Trade Shows

Some trade shows have a section for inventors who are trying to license or sell their inventions outright. Inquire before attending. Seek out those trade shows that offer the kinds of products that interest you. You may have to join the sponsoring organization in order to attend. The attendance fee is sometimes expensive, but you'll learn more about the field by attending and walking the aisles than by almost any other way, and you'll meet people who will be valuable connections in the future. Be sure to collect business cards, and write notes on them so that you will remember your first impressions and recall why each person is significant with respect to the future of your venture.

Retail Stores

Products found in retail stores typically are well past the novelty stage. Thus, the intent of such a search is not to find a product directly, but to get ideas about what's hot in order to discover product gaps that may be waiting to be exploited. However, retail stores restrict their offerings to those products that move relatively quickly. So, the absence of a product may not be an indication of the absence of opportunity. As the cosmologist Carl Sagan once said, "Absence of evidence is not evidence of absence."

Local Manufacturers

Most products have a life cycle. As they age and approach obsolescence, they tend to become unprofitable due to competition and high overhead. A well-managed company will devote its resources to products that are profitable, and to the development of future products. However, many companies feel an obligation to their customers to continue to supply older products. But such companies may be receptive to consigning a product to you to sell in order to reduce their losses and still satisfy past customers. A small, lean manufacturer without an engineering staff will often be able to turn a respectable profit on such a product. Thus, obtaining such a product is a win-win deal for both parties. This may not be the most glamorous startup, but it can provide a base and cash flow from which you may generate other niche products. Many local chambers of commerce publish business listings that provide the names of local manufacturers.

Modifying an Existing Product

One of the easiest ways to enter the market is to modify an existing product. Such a product is already understood by customers and reaches them through an established market channel. Thus, two of the challenges that confront the startup entrepreneur—consumer understanding of the product and a market channel—are already in place. Modification typically consists of identifying special customer needs and adapting the product to meet these needs. Sales are a fraction of the sales of the main product line, but can be very profitable for the startup entrepreneur who exploits the product gap opportunity, and who is not yet ready for a product with mass demand.

Some modifications can be as simple as adding an accessory that works with the basic product. Others may require producing a new version of the product that incorporates the modification. In this case, a patent search should be made to assure that the new design won't infringe the original product's patent.

Inventing a Product

Inventing a truly novel product is higher risk than either selecting or modifying an existing item.

A sufficient number of potential customers may not buy it. It may not work as well as you expected. An appropriate market channel may not exist. Explaining its purpose and benefits in order to get sales may be too costly in the form of advertising and publicity. Its ratio of selling price to direct cost may not be sufficiently profitable. The cost of tooling up to produce your invention/product may exceed your resources. You may need to devote several thousand dollars of your capital to protect your invention with a patent.

Offsetting this higher risk are two advantages: If you are first in the market, you can "sew up" many of the best marketing channels. Catalogs, for example, typically will not accept a competitive product unless it has features that yours lacks, or a significant price advantage.

Because your product is novel, and demand for it didn't exist until you exposed your customers to it, you are able to sell it for a more profitable price than the price the market will settle on later, if and when it has completion.

Recognizing that the odds of success are lower, the payoff for an invention that takes hold in the market can be much greater than for an existing or modified product.

POSITIONING YOUR PRODUCT

Positioning is the process of deciding your product's features, benefits, deficits, quality, price, and channels of distribution, in light of knowing these same things about its competition. Positioning requires balancing your customer's ideal needs and wants, as well as his perception of the monetary value of your product, with your own need to make a profit, all the while knowing that you will have competition if your product achieves a significant sales volume.

You must consider all the features, benefits, deficits, and prices of products that compete directly with your own, and you must decide how to shape your product to fit advantageously into the market. Startups often fail because the inventor omits the painstaking positioning process and plunges in with only an intuitive approach. Intuition is valuable, but it should be challenged and disciplined. Positioning and finding or creating your product may occur simultaneously at the outset, but positioning will likely be an ongoing challenge. Markets change. The competition changes. In time, even your business objectives may change.

Deciding Your Marketing Channel

Early in your startup venture you will begin with low-volume channels in order to safely ramp up your volume as you gain experience, and as you shake out any problems with your product. If your product had to be recalled, for example, due to a certain unanticipated defect, you can easily be wiped out beyond recovery if you have shipped a large volume through the retail distribution channels. It may be difficult to accept, but a startup is very seldom ready for high-volume distribution. The section ahead on selecting appropriate channels to begin your marketing will provide the details.

Setting the Retail Price

There are two basic ways to price your product. You may multiply your cost by a certain factor, such as five; or you may arbitrarily decide the highest price that the majority of your customers will pay before it causes sales and total profit to decline. A longstanding rumor states that a product you produce on your own should sell for at least five times its direct cost. In a sense, this is true, but the process is upside down. You should set your selling price and then back down using the "five times" factor to arrive at your product's cost target. For example, if you feel that your retail price should be $19.95, and if you are producing the product yourself, its direct cost should be no more than one-fifth of $19.95, or $3.99. If you find that you can't achieve this direct cost, you must reposition your product so that you can.

The factor of five, however, is not sacred. You might use a factor of ten or more, as it is for greeting cards. It might be as low as four if you are selling only on your website. But in the absence of specific marketing discounts, you will probably find it perilous to use a factor of less than five. Retail price range affects the markup factor. Obviously, an automobile doesn't sell for five times its manufactured cost. The markup factor is reduced as the price range increases. In any event, you should always begin with the realistic approach of arbitrarily deciding the highest price that a majority of our customers will pay, and then work back to what you can afford as your manufactured direct cost.

Determining Total Direct Cost

Total direct cost is the ultimate dollar value of your product's materials and components delivered to you, including all freight charges, the time you or your employees spent getting your product ready to sell, and your product's retail box (which often costs as much or more than your product) and in-box packaging materials, including the instruction sheet. Even if you don't give yourself a paycheck, you must add in your imaginary pay, set at the level of an ordinary hired worker, so you don't fool yourself in regard to your venture's profitability. Eventually you will need to hire and pay an employee to do what you are now doing "free." No overhead is included in total direct cost, but be sure to identify and include all items that can be traced to shipment out the door. For example, if you ship free, your cost of shipping must be added to total direct cost.

Marking Up

There are times when you might like to compare marking up with working from the top (your arbitrary retail price) down. The markup is the factor or percentage by which you multiply your total direct cost in order to come up with a tentative "list price," or retail price. There is no sacred markup percentage. Use whatever works for you. But until you test various percentages, work with at least four or preferably five times your direct cost. At four times direct cost you'll probably lose money or barely break even on most products that you produce on your own. But if you are realistically counting on reducing costs as your volume builds, then four times may be a valid temporary markup. The advantage of thinking in terms of markup is that you become aware of the impact of added items. For example, if you add packaging material that costs only ten cents, you must think of this as adding fifty cents to your retail price, and you must ask yourself how this fifty cents will be recovered—how will it affect sales.

In the case of catalogers, the total of all discounts goes to one market channel. Some catalogers set an arbitrary price, taking something around 60 percent, and then compare what's left to your asking price. For example, if they decide $19.95 is the right retail price, then your 40 percent is approximately $8. If you offer your product for $8.50, they may or may not take it, as it does not meet their profit targets. But catalogs mainly think in terms of markup. An early test of whether the catalog will consider your product further is for it to mark up your price by two and a half and see if the resulting retail price would produce enough sales. For example, let's say that your product is $8 marked up by two and a half, making it $20. The catalog will want to know if a retail price of $19.95 would produce enough sales.

Including Features and Benefits

Start with 20 percent of your arbitrary retail price as your trial goal for maximum direct cost. Since you plan to produce your product on your own—which usually means buying most or all of its components and assembling it—the only limit to the features you may include is their costs. You must price each component and ask yourself how you can lower its cost without reducing its quality. Poor quality will ultimately hurt you by reducing customer satisfaction and increasing the number of returns. These choices require that you understand something about manufacturing options. Each manufacturing process generally has a spectrum of options that balances the increased cost of tooling against the reduced cost per unit produced. If you aren't well versed in manufacturing processes, work with your vendors and an industrial designer to become an expert. Your success depends upon you doing so.

Evaluating the Competition

As an entrepreneur, you are not interested in competing against the purest form of direct competition—a product that offers the same features as yours. You must modify an existing product and fill a niche, thereby avoiding direct competition, or you must create a product that is novel. But direct competition doesn't necessarily mean that your competitor's product looks or acts exactly like yours. A compass and a paper map compete with a GPS device. Havahart animal traps, which offer a non-lethal method of getting rid of unwanted critters, compete with traps that kill these critters, but the features and appearances of these products are entirely different. Still, the Havahart device is a direct competitor with the common rat trap, even though it is positioned quite differently.

Reviewing

You will never arrive at perfection, of course. Nor should you strive for it. Perfection is the enemy of progress. But you must periodically review your product's position based on the most recent customer feedback. You must also consider your competitors, who may reposition their products at any time. Entrepreneurs are often too certain that the market will be delighted with their products just the way they are. But the market is creative, too. Assuming that you are marketing through appropriate channels, the ongoing challenges in your creative endeavor are product refinement and possibly re-pricing—in other words, positioning.

SELECTING THE BEST DISTRIBUTION CHANNELS

Most small startups begin with an easy-to-enter, relatively low-volume marketing channel, and cautiously progress to mass distribution. Four main reasons work against attempting to market with the "big guys" early on. Retail chains don't like dealing with very small companies. They are skeptical of a small company's stability and don't trust its capacity to deliver reliably. Retail chains usually don't like to deal with a company that has only one product. They prefer dealing with companies that offer product lines. The startup entrepreneur typically does not have the financing for the essential high-volume tooling and methods that match high-volume demand and pricing. Therefore, the startup's wholesale price typically is too high. The startup entrepreneur can be easily overwhelmed by large orders from national distributors and wholesalers, causing delays. On-time delivery by the startup is essential if it wishes to remain accepted by traditional distribution channels. If brick and mortar retail store distribution is best reserved for future marketing, what remaining marketing channels are receptive to the startup entrepreneur?

Your website is where your startup marketing begins. Catalogs are an excellent early channel. Amazon and its affiliated marketers are also good. TV marketing (QVC and HSN) can be a great profit producer, but it has pitfalls and must be approached cautiously, and only after catalogs begin selling your product. Catalogs don't want products that have had the exposure of TV, or are already selling nationally in retail stores. Finally, local retail stores—generally the independent stores, not the chains—can provide insight into your product's eventual large-scale distribution.

Website

Your website will allow you to notice any defects in your product, or rough spots in your marketing process, which can then be corrected before you move on to other distribution channels, such as catalogs, Amazon, and QVC. Website designers focus mainly on graphics because graphic production is artistic work; they rarely focus on the words on the page. But words are not something you can scatter in any old order and hope to get results. The point is that website designers are naturally graphics people, so you cannot assume that they know how to design your website for effective word composition and placement. Sure, they know that you've got to have a home page, and buttons that take the viewer elsewhere, but exactly what those "elsewhere" pages must be is something only you can determine. These details are much too important to be chosen by a designer using a "one size fits all" approach.

For one thing, a website must have a landing page that has its own web address, or URL. This page is where browsers who see your classified ads or pay-per-click ads land. The landing page is designed as a full-page ad that draws your viewer in, and creates a desire to own what you are selling. You cannot allow your viewer to waste even one minute fumbling through your home page. You have mere seconds to get to the point and draw your viewer smoothly to the information that will arouse his interest. Your landing page must accomplish this, a fact that great graphic designers may not grasp as essential. Your landing page should be an almost exact copy of your sell-sheet. It should spark interest with a tagline that identifies your product and explains its main benefit. It should then create a desire for the product by listing its subordinate benefits and presenting testimonies from users, or "will be" users, if you are just introducing your product. Finally, it should provide simple, clear information about how to buy your product.

Your website designer is a technical expert, and may even be a good graphic designer. But you must take command and define which buttons you want, as well as the content of the pages to which those buttons will lead. Numerous good books exist on website design, but a good book on advertising theory and practice would be a better buy in your case.

Catalogs

Catalogs are friendly to small companies that have only one product to offer. You can grow slowly or rapidly depending on the number of catalogs that take on your product. Most catalogs also operate a website. After you are well established in catalogs, go to Amazon. The role of catalogs continues to change as more and more retail sales are handled by Internet companies like Amazon. Think of catalogs as an evolving market channel rather than solely as print sent through the mail. Catalogs traditionally buy from you, rather than ask you to consign your product. If sales are not up to expectations and they end up with inventory that they can't sell, the catalogs pass it on to dollar stores. Seldom will they ask you for their money back.

Television

Television marketing can make or break a small business if a product takes hold at a surprising level. If your product "bombs" on TV, you may suffer a major setback. Fortunately, the TV marketers have some idea of how much they'll sell even before your product is first broadcast. They may test it during the middle of the night to verify their forecasts. And they'll want you to have backup inventory available to insure against a greater demand than anticipated. But unlike mass retail distribution channels, if you are temporarily "paralyzed," they simply replace your product with another until you recover. They won't like the fact that you can't deliver, but they are set up to work around it, and probably won't dump you if you recover while your product is still hot.

TV selling will tie up a lot of your cash if your product doesn't sell as well as predicted, or if your quality suffers and you get a carload of your inventory back. (TV sellers are consignees, and will pay you after the fact, based on their sales, not based on how many you've shipped to them.)

Retail

Once you have mastered selling through these channels and are preparing for volume sales through brick and mortar retail stores, first work locally through a few independent retailers to get a feel for the differences. Once you've done this, approach the traditional distribution channels—distributor, wholesaler, and retailer—on a limited regional basis until your capacity is balanced with demand. Returns may increase. Shelving fees may be imposed. And any of the market channel entities may ask for advertising to introduce your product.

EXPOSING YOUR PRODUCT

There are two basic ways to expose your product so that people will buy it. There is free publicity, and then there is paid advertising.

Free Publicity

You do not get free publicity simply for being a nice person who is admirably struggling to start a business. There is no "free lunch." Free publicity is given when its supplier will receive something other than money in return. This generally refers to news that the publication's readers might welcome. Thus, you must be keenly aware of the need to provide news, not just the boastful statements of your product's benefits that you would include in your paid advertising. The publicity copy must be written as though you couldn't care less about whether or not the reader buys your product. All you are attempting to accomplish with your news release is to make the reader aware of "what's new." Of course, if you are clever, you can include subtext that might indirectly influence the reader to buy your product. In every case, you should state at the end of your release, "For more information, contact (name, phone number, and email)."

If you are still in the development phase of your invention, you aren't really entitled to free publicity. Editors know that many news releases for new inventions are merely "trial balloons" to test whether the eventual products will attract buyers. But since there is no easy way to determine the extent of a product's development, they may go along with publishing the news release. And in the overall sense, your release is still news whether your product physically exists yet or not. One way to satisfy your conscience, if it bothers you, is to advertise in the magazine or trade journal that published your news release later, when you are ready for cautious advertising. Sending news releases is a number game. Perhaps only one editor in four or five will publish your release, so be sure to send out several, all at the same time.

Press releases are great because they are free publicity, and because they are about five times as effective as advertising that uses the same amount of space. People believe this type of publicity because it looks like it was written by the editors of the magazines and trade journals in which it appears. These same people may pass over an ad because they don't trust advertising, often considering ads a distraction from real content. Another benefit to this publicity is that it can draw the attention of two different types of people: those who want to buy your product, and those who want to sell or distribute your product. Having these people reach out to you is much easier and less costly than you reaching out to them.

You'll find books at your library that cover writing publicity and news releases. Writing a news release for a new product is not an opportunity to be creative. Follow the format that is advised by the professionals. News releases must be in the standard format that editors expect. One rule is not to exceed two pages. Some editors prefer only one page, but for a new product, it's pretty hard to describe what it is, how it works, and what its benefits are in under a page. To send something other than a one- or two-page release in standard format, even though something unorthodox may seem better to you, will likely peg you as an amateur, and your release will be tossed in the wastebasket. You'll need a high-quality five-by-seven-inch photo to go along with your release. Send a color copy and a black and white copy, or simply a color copy. Most print media can convert a color photo to black and white. Internet freelancers and PR specialists will prepare your news release, photos and all.

Whatever you do, don't call yourself an inventor, but do create the image of a company. Newspapers and corporations are suspicious of inventors. Inventors have a bad image as nerdy people with half-baked ideas that were probably tried and discarded years ago. Not fair? Right, but that's how it is. So, make up a company name, and make yourself a letterhead and a matching envelope. And don't use the term "enterprises" in your company name; it is the sign of an amateur—someone who isn't sure of what he wants to do in business. Try to come up with a name other than your personal name. Personal names are fine for the neighborhood merchant, but not so effective for national producers. Always include your contact information as the last line of your release. For example: "For more information contact us by phone or email at . . ."

In addition to the publicity release, you'll need a sell sheet. This sheet is also called a brochure, bulletin, data sheet, or pitch sheet. The sell sheet is used to respond to inquiries that result from your news releases and publicity releases. Unlike the publicity release, the sell sheet follows the rules of advertising copy preparation. It must state clearly and boldly the benefits of your product.

Newspapers are usually a waste of time unless you can get into an invention feature column that some of the larger papers run, the reason being that their audiences are too generalized. If your business is based on a local service, however, it may pay to advertise in a local paper. Trade journals and magazines are just the opposite. They are specialized. You can reach the tight audience that will want your product. To find papers, trade journals, and magazines, go to your library—the reference section—and ask for any of the following: *Burrelle's Media Directory: Magazines and Newsletters, Gebbie Press All-In-One Directory, SRDS Business Publication Advertising Source,* or *Bacon's Publicity Checker. Bacon's Publicity Checker* also offers a press release mailing service, including photo duplication, which is very reasonable. It will also sell you a list of editors by category, and media personnel by category. If any of these directories is not in your branch library, ask if it is in your state's library system and might be borrowed from another branch. This service is free, of course. And remember, reference media is gradually phasing out of the printed volume, but not out of business.

Paid Advertising

One of the main reasons you may be tempted to think you understand advertising is because it is commonplace. Newspapers, magazines, and the Internet are full of display ads. What you probably don't understand is that many, perhaps most, of these ads fail, and those that succeed are but marginally successful. To understand these disappointments, you must be aware that there are essentially two different kinds of ads: institutional and action-demanded. The objective of an institutional ad—usually run by very big companies—is to create a favorable image of the product or company without expecting immediate or measurable results. The objective of an action-demanded ad is just that—to achieve an immediate and measureable reaction from the reader or viewer. "Act now! This offer ends at midnight on Sunday," or, "Buy before December 10th, and we'll ship it free." These are the kinds of actions demanded by the ad. The great thing about this kind of ad is that you can measure its effectiveness by the number of orders or inquiries you receive. Thus, you know quickly if your ad is successful or not. For most new products, early ads are failures, so feedback is essential. In my experience, there are ten main reasons that ads fail.

Medium Unfocused

Newspapers are delivered to a general audience. They are great for advertising products that are consumed by a general audience. Food, clothing, cars, and housing are the main items consumed by a general audience, and therefore newspaper ads for these items may pay off. But newspapers are almost always a waste of money for introducing a new product. Local newspapers, however, will often welcome a success story from a startup entrepreneur, especially if he offers a local service.

Ad Cost Too High

I learned about overpaying for ads the hard way early in my trials as a young entrepreneur. I had advertised in the *Los Angeles Times,* which used to have a page titled "Shopping at Home" in its Sunday edition. The ad featured a photograph and a couple sentences of copy. In today's money, my ads would cost about $550 each. I ran four of these ads, and the best resulting sales from one was for seven items at $13.95 each! The paper's readership was well over one million. What happened? The readership was too general. The only "Shopping at Home" ads that repeated, week after week, were for expensive items, some costing well over $100. The inverse is that ads that repeat consistently are clues to the kinds of products that are selling well—products that may be appropriate for a startup to modify or imitate.

Product Unclear

The best benefit statement that you can make will be lost if the reader doesn't grasp what your product is. Try to make this clear with your photograph. Your product photographed in action, showing the hands of the person using it, or even the whole person, usually works well. But consider the fact that placing a whole person in a photo will diminish the size of your product. If your product is so novel that it has to be explained because it won't be recognized, then your tagline will have to be longer to carry the explanation. Long taglines can work, but they must always emphasize the benefit. For example, "Your shoes will look like new in seconds with this new shoe polishing device," or, "Amazing device makes your shoes look like new in seconds." The second tagline is probably more effective because it's shorter, and, believe it or not, the word "amazing" still catches a reader's eye.

Benefit Unclear

If you expect to receive results from your ad, you must define your product and immediately tell your reader what benefit he will receive from using it. You have about five seconds to grab your reader and draw him into the ad, especially when the media is a magazine or Internet sidebar. Catalog and website readers are more relaxed, and more willing to tolerate longer taglines.

Graphics Overwhelming

This error occurs frequently when it comes to brochures and sell sheets. Graphic artists are not necessarily competent ad copy writers. Photographs and artistic graphics attract attention, but it's the words that sell a product. Splashy graphics may appear to make your sell sheet or ad look impressive, but they are not to be substituted for effective design.

Photo Unprofessional

Today, everyone with a cell phone is a digital photographer. But few product photos taken by amateurs are of sufficient quality to use in ads or sell sheets. If you don't have enough money for a professional photograph, then you probably don't have enough money for the rest of your enterprise.

Copy Poorly Written

Copy writing is half art and half science, and if you don't have at least a basic understanding of the science half, your ad and sell sheet will very likely fail.

Emphasis Misdirected

Entrepreneurs tend to think in terms of features, but those who buy their inventions or products think in terms of benefits, either to themselves or to their ultimate customers. Benefits arise from features, so it is fine to mention a feature in a benefit statement if it adds clarity. But your emphasis must always be on benefits.

Testimonials Lacking

Endorsements and testimonials are easy to get, even before your invention is a product on the market. You don't need to make them up. You can get honest endorsements from people to whom you've explained your invention. For example, "I've been waiting for someone to invent a device like your new X. Count on me to be your first customer." Testimonials and endorsements make even the best ad five times more effective.

Information Missing

There's nothing worse than an ad that's intended to sell a product but leaves the reader in doubt as to how to get it. A few years ago, I would place order blanks at the end of my ads. Today, I refer the reader to my website. Thus, the burden has now been placed on the website designer to call the reader to act, and to make acting easy. But few website designers are experienced ad copy writers. So, this burden is ultimately yours. Don't let the mystique of website design and execution scare you. The mechanics of website creation must always be subordinate to the rules of effective advertising.

Preparing Effective Ads

"Let's run it up a flagpole, and see who salutes." "We need more bang for the buck." These are a couple of expressions ad agencies of years ago tossed back and forth during their creative sessions. These expressions are trite, of course, but their messages and lessons are alive and well.

Entrepreneurs need exposure in order to produce and market their products or services. Some early exposure may come in the form of free publicity, but most will have to be paid for as ads, sell sheets, websites, and so on. Unless you have an understanding of advertising principles and techniques, most of your efforts will not produce your desired results.

Focus

If you have something you want to sell to inventors, advertise in *Inventors Digest*. Its readership is made up mainly of inventors. A prototyper who advertises in *Discover* or *Wired* probably isn't going to get enough response to make his ad pay, but prototypers who advertise in *Inventors Digest* tell me that their ads produce good results. If there were such a magazine as *Prototyping for Inventors,* its readership would be even more tightly defined, and the response possibly even better.

For Internet advertising, test pay-per-click ads. Properly worded pay-per-click ads attract only readers who are interested in your product or service, and you pay only for each person who clicks through to your website's landing page. See Google ad-words. This form of advertising, no doubt, is the most effective and economical available.

Cost

Startup entrepreneurs often make the mistake of paying for too much ad space. Start with the smallest space that enables you to get your message across. Several small ads are usually more profitable than one large ad costing the same total amount. The optimal way to use small ads is to use a tightly worded classified ad or small ad to drive prospects to your website landing page. Your website is the least expensive space of all. Large illustrations and photos, detailed testimonials, and lots of compelling copy are yours for pennies. And you can automatically monitor the number of hits you receive and test different taglines to determine which is pulling the best. This two-step process is even easier if it is pay-per-click, and a click of the button brings up your website. Classified ads and pay-per-click ads that lead your prospect to your website are relatively inexpensive. Your landing page is the equivalent of a magazine ad that costs several thousand dollars.

Clarity

Don't muck up your taglines with inappropriate words or outrageous claims in the hope of grabbing your customer's attention. Words other than those that identify your product and its main benefit are usually counterproductive. The identification of your product and its main benefit should use no more than ten to fifteen words. The photo of your product should clearly show what the item is and what it does, if possible. This will enable your tagline to be effective without excessive wording.

Because website designers are graphic experts, they are often given the responsibility for preparing the ad layout, including the written ad copy. These designers, however, may depend mainly on graphics to sell the product. Graphics attract attention and illustrate what a product does, but it's the words that make the sale. Learn to prepare your own ads, and to critique those prepared for you.

If you've ever growled while browsing a website, you know how important it is to have a smooth, step-by-step flow of information and instructions. Write your website copy in such a way that it may be understood by a twelve-year-old child. Have your friends and relatives actually place an order, pay for it, and then share their experiences with you. (Reimburse them, of course.)

Quality

Today, everyone is a photographer. The art of the excellent photograph has been largely displaced by point-and-shoot mediocrity. Professional photography isn't inexpensive, but if you are lucky enough to find the right photographer, the cost of quality photos will be paid back many times. Also consider virtual photography, which enables you to specify the exact composition of your picture and present your product even before it exists.

A certain standard of quality is also important in regard to ad copy. It's not easy to find a good ad copy writer. Big ad agencies have them, but small ad agencies may be hit or miss. If you farm out your ad copy writing, be sure to get a few samples of sell sheets and full-page ads that your candidate has prepared. Read a few books on the subject. Freelancers may be found online.

Emphasis

As you are the expert on your product, it is natural to think of it in terms of its features, but when you pitch your product to potential customers, you've got to stress its benefits. The main benefit belongs in the tagline in order to get the reader's attention. Subordinate benefits should follow quickly. A bulleted list is preferred. People find lists of short sentences more inviting than paragraphs. Browsers today want bites, not blabs. Once you have the reader drawn into your ad, and his interest has been aroused, you can relax a bit and allow a longer, more narrative style. But stick to explaining why your product benefits the ultimate customer. All of your writing—the benefits, narrative, and testimonials—should be directed to the ultimate user, not to the distributor, wholesaler, or retailer, even though these may be the entities that you are trying to impress. Distribution people understand how a new product will benefit their companies. What they want to be convinced of is that the customer will want to buy your product.

Testimonials

Nothing you can write is as effective or believable as a testimonial from a satisfied user. One ad professional claims that testimonials are about five times as effective as statements authored by the seller. And testimonials are not difficult to obtain. People love to see their names in print. Most people will give you permission to do so. Using only initials or just a first name needlessly arouses suspicion that the testimonial is a fake. In the many years that I've used only full names on my testimonial page I've never had even one client complain that he was bothered by someone checking to make sure he was a real person. If you don't yet have a finished product, ask "will-be" users to comment about how they can't wait to use your invention when it finally becomes a product.

CONCLUSION

The success of your business depends on how well you market your product. Marketing consists of four basic tasks: Finding or creating your product, positioning it, selecting the best distribution channels, and exposing it to the public so people will discover it and buy it. The easiest way to create your product is to modify a successful product to satisfy a niche market. The most difficult way to create your product is to invent it. One of the most important tasks entrepreneurs face is positioning their products. Set your retail sales price based on what your gut tells you the highest price your customers will pay before the sales volume drops off significantly. Then, divide this dollar amount by five. The result is your target direct cost for manufacturing. Five might actually be four, or it might be six or more. But use five as your divisor until you learn more. Early marketing starts with your website, and then moves on to catalogs. From there you may progress to Amazon and affiliate marketing sites, and from there to QVC, HSN, or other television resources. Be sure to approach national distribution gradually and cautiously.

Expose your product using free press releases early on, and then use inexpensive classified ads and pay-per-click ads that guide your potential customers to your website. Advertising can be very expensive when you don't get results, but classified ads and pay-per-click ads can be profitable. In a few relatively inexpensive words you may attract the attention of a select readership and arouse sufficient interest to lead many to visit your website's landing page. Your website may then finish the process and convince the reader to buy your product. Keep your costs low by using the two-step process whenever you can. Learn to write effective ad copy or have it written by an expert. Monitor your profit from each ad. Experiment with different taglines to maximize your ad's effectiveness. It's your buck, so get more bang for it. Some of advertising is intuitive, but not all of it. Study ads that repeat and repeat. These are profitable. Study advertising theory.

Don't be afraid to fail. Most inventors, including this writer, have failed often. It is the basis for learning how to succeed. As Louis Foreman, the publisher of *Inventors Digest* has said, "Fail often, and fail cheaply." As the writer Goethe said, "Whatever you can do or dream you can, begin it. Boldness has genius, power and magic in it." Go forth boldly and validate your dream.

8. Websites

Eddie Vélez

I remember when I first used the Internet. I was managing a computer company that offered sales and service, so when it was available to the public, I was one of the first to have access to it. I was so excited that I signed up for a personal account right away, ran home and had the Internet specialist set it up. I installed the Netscape browser, set up the modem, and heard all the beeps, whirs, and chirps. I was connected! I was ready to be blown away by a world of information, but what I saw was so disappointing—a simple website that was nothing but text, and very little of it at that. I thought to myself, "And I'm paying $19.99 a month for this?"

Fast forward one year, and my friend had created her own website. She was so excited by how easy it was to do. Now, being a graphic designer who majored in advertising and marketing, and who minored in cartooning, I was looking at the website from different perspectives (layout, balance, color, and so on), and I thought to myself, "That looks cheesy. Who'd want to look at that?" I was so shortsighted. I could not see the forest for the trees. I could not see that this innovation was going to grow into an economic powerhouse that would connect

Eddie Vélez is the founder and CEO of Success by Design, located in Tampa Bay, Florida, and has over twenty years of experience in formulating marketing strategies and implementing the tactics and support material necessary for a synergistic plan. Eddie is a graduate of The School of Art and Design in New York City, with a major in advertising, and has a bachelor's degree in Business Administration.

me@eddievelez.net • www.eddievelez.net

average citizens in multiple countries to mom-and-pop operations all over the world. Nor did I foresee online banking, education, music, movies, libraries, museums, advertising, or government administration—let alone smart phones and social media.

These days, a website is the first thing someone looks for, no matter how she found the business or product of interest. Moreover, the website has become the hub of a business's marketing wheel, connecting all the dots in an effort to deliver its message and penetrate the market. It's amazing how revolutions start with such humble beginnings. Let's take a look at how it all started, what innovations and industries it spawned, how it has leveled the media playing field, and why you need a website if you're in business or plan to promote anything.

INTERNET HISTORY

The Internet is an invention that has taken on a life of its own. It is so prevalent that it seems almost impossible to do anything without it. Think about it. How many things does the Internet touch that you depend on? How about banking, shopping, research, entertainment, business transactions, medical records, communication, defense and government administration, to name just a few? If it were to disappear, it would cripple the economy, hinder national security, and traumatize a generation that never knew life without it. Where would we go to "Google" things?

But how did it all begin? It began with someone like you, an inventor, who had a vision and the gumption to believe it could be accomplished. In 1962, J.C.R. Licklider of MIT envisioned a global network of computers, all interconnected and sharing the world's data—mind you, modems didn't exist yet, and no software had been developed that could facilitate two computers speaking to each other. However, he believed. So, he moved to the Defense Advanced Research Projects Agency, or DARPA, and started the work of developing this network.

While Licklider was at DARPA, Robert Lawrence, another MIT alum, managed to connect two computers, from Massachusetts to California, over a standard telephone line. He proved it could be done, but also suggested that phone lines were inadequate—a notion that would spawn a need for further inventions and innovations. Since Lawrence was able to prove it could be done, just one year later, he joined Licklider at DARPA. DARPA was renamed ARPA (dropping the "Defense" from its name), and in 1969, the very first Internet known as ARPANET (Advanced Research Projects Agency Network) was born. Fast forward a little over twenty years, and the Internet was coming together for public consumption. If you were born before 1980, then you probably remember the days of MS-DOS (Microsoft disk operating system). In those days, if you didn't know how to ask the computer what you wanted, you would simply receive a message that read, "Error: Improper command improper syntax." It was the Wild West era of computers, and many were trying to come up with their own solutions to this intimidating dilemma. After all, how was the average person with no computer skills, or any desire to learn them, going to be interested in a personal computer, much less in surfing a would-be Internet?

Many graphical user interfaces were created, including MS Windows, which allowed images and clickable commands to take the place of having to type it all out on a black or blue screen. There was also CompuServe, Prodigy, and America Online (AOL), to name a few. However, these were proprietary systems not universally available or compatible. This made it difficult to have a standard everyone could rally around, until one man came up with a universal solution. That man was Tim Berners Lee.

In 1990, at the CERN Laboratories in Switzerland, the World Wide Web was created. Tim Berners Lee devised what would become the standard for Internet websites: Hyper Text Markup Language, or HTML. By 1993, the first popular browser was Mosaic and only about twenty-six websites were available. In 1994, Marc Andreessen founded Netscape and the Internet was off to the races. Of course, early websites were very basic. The focus at the time was purely access to information for the purposes of research or news.

INTERNET FUTURE

Pandora's box has been opened. So, what happens now? Certainly the Internet will continue to evolve in ways no one imagined, but there are some trends you can look at that will give you an idea of the enormity of it all, and of what it all means to you, your invention, and the need to have a website. From the very first rudimentary website to today's sophisticated online community, a revolution in connectivity has taken place. It supports multibillion-dollar economies worldwide, and has truly made the world a global market place.

Social Media

There used to be a time when advertising was king and advertisers controlled what the public perceived. Complement this with traditional media (TV news, radio, and newspapers), and the average person was fed only what the seller wanted them to consume. Branding was controlled by major agencies, which were motivated to design campaigns and ads that would win awards, whether they boosted sales or not. Positioning could be manipulated, since backroom sessions could mold the message that would be delivered.

Branding is how the public remembers you. For example, your logo and slogan would become your brand, so when it was seen anywhere, the first thing that would come to mind would be your company. Positioning, however, is how people perceive you. For example, Amazon is perceived as the best deal in books online. When someone is driving down the road and thinks "book," Barnes and Noble may come to mind. However, when someone sits in front of her computer and thinks "book," despite the fact that Barnes and Noble has a wonderful website, she thinks of Amazon. Jeff Bezos, Amazon's founder and CEO, has done a wonderful job of positioning.

Today, there no longer exists a monopoly on getting one's message out to the public and controlling how it's delivered, and this is due to social media marketing and social networking (collectively known as "social media" even though they are two distinct mediums). There's power in being able to ask a question or share information with thousands to hundreds of thousands of people and not have it filtered by a business or a brand. What you get are raw, uncensored answers based on your own experience.

Billions of people worldwide congregate at online plazas and community centers, if you will, and converse. If they want to know about a company or product, they ask—and woe to the company that has done a poor job of taking care of the customer or of creating a quality product. On the flipside, those who care about quality and customer experience are rewarded handsomely. This freedom has become so popular that there are approximately one billion Facebook users, half a billion Twitter users, and half a billion Google+ users. When you consider that the average user in America spends over three hours daily on social media, you recognize what a captive audience is out there.

There are three main reasons people use social media: to be entertained, to be informed, and to be helped. If you do these three things, people will flock to you. So as you package your invention and start to promote it, ask yourself, "How can I make it fun, informative, and helpful?"

As you engage with your audience through social media, you will also be sharing your expertise through your blog articles, which will be posted in social media. This will drive traffic to your website, where people may read more of your blog and, if your website is designed well, discover what else you have to offer.

Smart Phones

Mobile Internet surfing has taken the world by storm. Today, smart phones and tablets have replaced computers for many people. With the ability to surf the Internet, check email, chat, check social media, take pictures, read books, and even edit Microsoft Office documents on the go, many have chosen not to be encumbered by a desktop. While the first smart phone, the IBM Simon, was created by BellSouth in 1993, the first viable smart phone was the Blackberry, which was released in 2002. However, it was in 2007 that the world of mobile communication would be changed forever by Apple's iPhone.

The iPhone made it possible to have an actual PC Internet experience, complemented with a high-end camera and phone, all in your pocket. People were hooked. Then the iPad followed, and Internet surfing would experience a paradigm shift of its own. There was a decrease in PC sales and an increase in tablet and smart phone sales. Mobile Internet surfing began to overtake traditional PC Internet surfing. It's reasonable to assume that the PC may be seeing its last days as the major form of electronic commerce and communication.

What does this mean to you as an entrepreneur and inventor who will need to promote a product to the masses? First, since a smart phone is always in someone's pocket or purse, you will achieve greater success reaching people with your message. Furthermore, you need to make sure your website is mobile ready. Since you don't know whether your visitor will arrive via a monitor, laptop, tablet, or smart phone, your website has to be able to adapt accordingly, so you don't lose any traffic.

eBooks

I remember when I couldn't afford an electronic reader, I would say, "I love the feel of a real book and the smell of the paper and ink. It doesn't feel right to read on an electronic device." While I still love a good old-fashioned book, once I got my Google Nexus 7 tablet, I was easily converted to a lover of electronic books. And, what's not to love? You can carry a library of books on your smart phone, tablet, or e-reader.

As a matter of fact, print book sales are down and e-book sales are up. What does this mean to you? One of the best ways to promote a product or brand is a book. As my friend Marsha Friedman would say, "It's the new business card." Imagine telling your story or sharing your expertise while building your credibility. A book can do all that and act as a marketing vehicle to get people to your website, and, therefore, to your invention. When it's all said and done, your website should be the goal of your marketing efforts. Why? Quite simply, your website is the hub of all your business.

YOUR WEBSITE

While there are many new innovations and ways to reach the public, you want everyone to wind up eventually at the same location: your website. Think of it. What has become part of our vernacular? "Google it!" When someone reads, sees, or hears about a product that grabs her interest, the first thing she will do is look for a website to do homework on it before making a purchase. When was the last time you heard or saw something on TV or radio, or read about it in a newspaper article, or even found it posted on social media, and went straight to the product's website and purchased it? Maybe once or twice in your lifetime? If you're like most people, probably never. What most people do is look at a website, and if it draws them in, they peruse it and glean information to see if they are still interested. Even if they are, they will probably bookmark the website and never return. You see, most people will forget they saw and bookmarked it until they decide to clean up their bookmarks. Then they will wonder what the bookmark was for and click on it. However, if they have already purchased elsewhere what the website is offering, or they are no longer interested because they forgot what got them excited in the first place, they will delete the bookmark and move on. A good website will make sure this does not happen.

If your website was designed with marketing in mind, this scenario was anticipated, and you will be able to keep your website, product, and message in front of your public, so when they are ready to buy, they will remember what got them excited in the first place and provided all that wonderful information. You do this with a blog.

What Is a Blog?

The term "blog" is short for "web log." So what is a web log? Well, imagine you were a journalist who had to provide a weekly article on your invention. You would consider the process of creating your invention, what purpose your invention serves, the many facets of your invention, what areas in life it helps to improve, how much money it can save your customer when used properly, and so on. These are all topics for short articles you can write to share information on your invention with your audience. These short articles make up your blog.

Some people get intimidated when they hear the word "blog" because they think it means creating an entire newsletter with multiple articles and ads, and they believe they don't have the time to dedicate to such an endeavor. In reality, all a blog has to be is one article, 350 to 750 words in length, written with passion and expertise to entertain, inform, and help your audience. Sound familiar? These are the three reasons why people use social media. This is how you connect the dots to make sure you have an effective marketing machine that will promote and sell your invention. Plus, a blog will provide you with four huge benefits. While these four benefits are powerful, they are not the only ones you will receive; they are just the most prevalent. To explain, a blog may do the following:

- **Shorten the sales cycle.** Since you will be sharing information on an ongoing basis through your blog, people come to learn what you do best. They will also learn the reasons your invention is a good fit for them, how they should use it to achieve maximum benefit, what its many uses are, and any other information you wish to share. I call this "drip marketing." Drip marketing is about sharing information a little at a time to keep your public's interest. In doing so, your potential customers will learn everything they need to know to sell themselves, so when it comes time to buy, you have little explaining or selling to do. They already know who you are, why your product is their best choice, how to use your product, and that there is no one better than you to buy it from. The only thing now is the price.

- **Earn your trust and credibility.** As mentioned above, since the customer has learned who you are and what you know, the only reason she is now buying is because she trusts you and believes you're credible. After all, people buy from people they like and trust, so it's safe to assume if they are contacting you to buy, they've come to like and trust you.

- **Drive traffic to your website.** Your blog will reside on your website. I do not recommend opening blogs with third-party providers because they may take people to some places other than your website. Plus, since the domain will belong to the provider, it's not the best search engine optimization (SEO) strategy. SEO is how Google and other search engines rank you, so when people look for what you offer, you come up near the top of the search results. When you post your blog on social media, you will post the headline, a brief description, and a link back to your article on your website. Whoever wants to read it has to come to your website to do so, thus driving traffic.

- **Become a referral tool.** Humans have what is known as a "herd mentality." We tend to congregate with like-minded people. The same occurs online. So, people reading your blog and following you will know other people who might also need what you have to offer. When they get questions from friends or family members regarding your field of expertise, they will frequently refer the friends or family members to your article, which will be linked to the original blog post on your website, taking them to your product.

Your blog, however, is only a portion of your website. There's still the core part to be considered, which is made up of your home page, about page, services page, product page, and shopping cart (if applicable). If these pages are not done well, your visitors may not stick around on your website to give you a chance to educate them on your invention. So, you need to make sure you have a good website.

WHAT MAKES A GOOD WEBSITE?

Not all websites are equal; if they were, everyone would be successful online. It's important that you choose the right person to create your website for you, or if you are creating it yourself, you need to think it through and get marketing input whenever possible. You see, just like with social media, there are individuals out there calling themselves website gurus because they know that most people know very little about building websites, and these individuals will try to sell you their services at a premium price. By the time you figure out they are not working out, you will have paid a lot of money. Since a designer is not necessarily a marketing professional, she may design a beautiful website that, at first glance, inspires awe, but in the long run, pulls in and converts no one. So, let's look at some very important things you need to consider when building your website.

Aesthetics

This is where designers with little to no marketing experience may fool you. When a designer doesn't know what's effective, and since you are depending on her to show you what is effective, she may present a website template with eye-popping effects and snazzy graphics, which you will love simply for the look of it. However, as time goes on, you will likely realize the website is not really working—no one is signing up for your blog, buying your product, or following you on social media. It could be that the designer was overzealous in her work and created a distracting and eventually annoying experience instead of a truly attractive and helpful website. Your website will be all eye candy and no substance. There's a difference between an image that portrays your message and one that does it with the proper impact. Use the right images and avoid the others.

Space

Once you've chosen your graphics and overall look and feel, how you lay everything out is crucial. You want balance and proper flow. You want to guide the reader naturally. Poor layout looks cluttered and choppy, and makes the reader struggle to find what she's looking for. Plus, you want to make sure your home page is used properly. The home page is not meant to overload the visitor with info; it's meant to guide the visitor where you want her to go, taking her deeper into your website.

Layout also includes proper use of typeface. Avoid serifs (Times New Roman, et al.), unless there is a well-considered purpose for them (financial or legal service, for example). You want to use 125-percent to 150-percent line height, and when it makes sense to do so, use earth tones. You see, if you make the environment soothing, people will want to read your content. However, if it's tight, black and white, and lacks good flow, it will irritate the eyes and readers will leave your website.

Content

While this point should have been first, I chose to make it third because if the aesthetics and layout don't pull your visitor in, she certainly won't read the content. The content is your message; it's what will persuade the reader, meet her where she is, and take her where you want her to go. If the content has not been written professionally, with passion and marketing insight, nothing else will matter. The reader will have been pulled in only to decide that the website is boring, tedious, and/or overwhelming.

Remember, it's not what you say, but rather how you say it. Moreover, saying too much is just as bad as saying too little. Whenever possible, try to hide information in plain view. How? Use tabs and drop-down boxes that people can use if they want the information, but make the page look like there is less to read. Everyone has two or three minutes to spare, but if it looks like it will take some time to get through the website, they may choose not to hang around or even bookmark it for later.

Lastly, you already know how important a blog is to your website, but I must remind you of this fact yet again. Please consult the earlier section regarding blogs if you need a refresher.

Conversion Form

A conversion form is how you capture your visitor's information. Once visitors arrive at your website, you will need to learn who they are in order to communicate with them in the future. If there is no conversion form, visitors will not be able to contact you with questions or subscribe to your blog. You will lose the valuable opportunity to keep your company on their minds.

There is no way to measure with certitude what persuades a person to buy. If a potential customer needs what you have to offer now, she'll buy it now; but typically a person will do her homework before making a purchase. So, when it's time to buy, you need to make sure she does not forget it was you who helped her, thanks to your great info. This is how to ensure future sales.

Bribery

If your content is very good and your articles are worth reading, people will subscribe to your blog easily. However, since most people tend to think their writing is great, even when it is not, you are the worst person to judge your blog and decide that it will pull in the reader. So, you need to tip the scale in your favor. Put together a free download or some sort of free offering for the subscriber. It could be a white paper on your expertise, a training video or podcast, a software tool—whatever. Just have something that would make the reader think, "I want that information and all I have to do to get it is sign up for a free subscription." Follow this advice and watch your subscription numbers increase substantially.

Functionality

Since social media is how you use your blog to drive traffic to your website, understand that if someone likes what she reads and wants to share it with her friends on Facebook, Twitter, Pinterest, or any other social media website, you need to make it as easy as possible to do so. Make sure you have buttons that not only allow people to follow you on your different networks, but also for them to post, tweet, like, and share your content through their social media websites of choice.

PRO OR DIY?

Now that you know what you are looking for and what you need, the question is, "Should I hire a professional or should I do it myself?" If you have the resources to do so and have no background in marketing or design, then outsourcing your website to a professional is recommended. When you consider the time it would take to write your content creatively, choose your platform, figure out software, and find your graphics and prepare them for your site, you may realize that your time could be better spent in other areas of your business.

If you choose to hire a professional web designer, do not look for one on bulletin board listing services (Craigslist, Elancer, etc.). While I applaud people who want to enter into this industry by trying to promote themselves on these websites, you don't want them learning their craft on your project. While design is important, design experience with no marketing strategy to guide you is sure to result in lost sales. So, make sure the designer you hire is either a marketer or works with a marketing firm. In addition, ask to see a portfolio of her previous projects. See what she's done and ask other people you know for their opinions on her portfolio.

Always ask your potential designer to walk you through her plan for your design. Based on your goals, she should be able to explain how she intends to achieve them, and why the methods she uses will accomplish them. Ask her what kind of after-sale service you can expect. For example, once she turns over the site to you, will you be on your own? Will she charge you for support? If yes, then how much will this support cost? If free support is available, what is it and for how long? Will you need a webmaster, or will you be able to manage the website yourself? And, of course, before hiring a professional, ask for references from previous customers.

Unless you need a highly complex site with extensive database capabilities and a back office, stay away from complex platforms like Ruby, Pearl, or Joomla. You don't want to be locked into any one particular company, should you choose to move on. While there are always new things to consider, these suggestions are a good guide to ensure you have flexibility and get a website that will perform well. After all, if it's done correctly, your website will provide a return on your investment.

Doing It Yourself

Now if you want or have to do it yourself, then you want to make sure you have the best opportunity to create a site that will work properly and pull in readers. Look at other websites—not just inventor sites, but product sites. After all, your invention will be a product. Look for the very best and see what was done well, and look at some that are not so good to determine what was done poorly. Learn from the good as well as the bad. If you have any friends who are marketers or designers, ask for their input and guidance. If you know anyone who has already gone through this process, ask her how she did it, what went well, and how to avoid any pitfalls.

Use a simple system. I highly recommend WordPress. WordPress also offers a free stand-alone version of its software, which you can use to build a custom website with your domain name. The platform is intuitive, simple, and has plenty of flexibility; you will be able to create a fully functional site without a webmaster. Shop around for a good web hosting service. Do an online search for reviews and make sure you choose one that has been in business for at least ten years.

Your website is just the beginning. During the design process and after you've published it, you'll have to maintain it. This means weekly blogs and other content will have to be written, and graphics will need to be added and refreshed. You need to keep it current and original, so repeat visitors don't get bored and search engines rank you highly. You see, search engines such as Google look for new content constantly. The more you refresh your site and post new articles, the more Google "bots" will update your ranking. Sometimes called "spiders," these bots (short for "robots") scan the Internet to index everything they find. When they see a website with articles, images, comments, testimonials, or other content refreshed on a consistent basis, they consider this website relevant. So, if someone searches for your topic, Google will make you one of the top results displayed. Consistency will be rewarded over time.

Unless you are a professional, chances are you don't have software programs such as Adobe Photoshop or Acrobat. You may or may not have MS Office. Fortunately, there are free options out there to help you with your website's content.

Stock Photos

Unless you are a professional photographer, limit any photos you've taken yourself to your website's photo gallery or "About" page. Why? We've all seen websites with amateurish photos; they look bad and have little to no impact on the reader. You want to pull the person in with great images. Do not use Google or another search engine, however, to find images to use for free. Those images belong to someone else and if you grab the wrong one, you can wind up with a lawsuit from either the photographer or distributor to the tune of five thousand dollars per unlicensed image. It's not worth it, especially when you can find images and own licenses for their use for about one or two dollars at most. 123RF (www.123rf.com) is a royalty-free stock photography provider with images that cost as little as one dollar. On this website, you will find high-impact, professional photos that will allow you to deliver your message.

Keep photos and images in their proper aspect ratios. Avoid the temptation of skewing images out of proportion to make them fit. This looks worse than unprofessional and will hurt the image of your website. When necessary, crop your images and resize them to fit, maintaining their proper aspect ratios.

Photo Editing

One thing you will find yourself doing often is manipulating photos—not necessarily in a professional capacity, but doing simple things like resizing or adding text over photos for effect. These are very simple processes. You want to make sure the resolution you use is no more than 72 dpi (dots per inch), and that you make the image the actual size needed to fit the spot in which it is to go. PIXLR (www.pixlr.com), which looks very similar to Photoshop, has a soothing and inviting feel, and will allow you to do all these things and more. As you get familiar with the program, you may even find yourself getting bold and adding special effects.

Documents

To create documents, if you don't have Microsoft Office or Word, then either Google Docs (https://docs.google.com) or LibreOffice (www.libre office.org) are great choices. If you work remotely and don't always have access to your own computer, Google Docs is the way to go. However, if you work mostly from the same computer, then I recommend LibreOffice. Why? LibreOffice will offer more features, and you won't be dependent on Internet access, since it will be loaded on your computer. LibreOffice also offers PC-, MAC-, and Linux-based versions, so no matter what kind of computer you own, you have an option.

Due to Adobe Acrobat's popularity and ease of use, PDF files have become the de facto standard for ensuring there will be no layout issues when a document is opened on other computers, and for sharing a document that needs to be protected. As you develop whitepapers, reports, or premium content to share with your subscribers, you may want to do so in a PDF file. This way you can make the information available for download with ease. To do so, you will need a program to create PDF files. With CutePDF (www.cutepdf.com) you will be able to do so free of charge.

Text Editing

Finally, nothing kills a job well done more than poor editing. Typos, misspellings, redundancy, and bad grammar can be death blows to your website. But let's face it, not everyone is a writer. This doesn't mean you're not intelligent, just that you are more focused on developing other talents. The ability to write is like a muscle. It is weakened by lack of use. If you don't write regularly, you will not write well. You may be able to get your point across, but your writing would not be publishable. Don't worry; you're not alone!

Unfortunately, people will judge you on the way you write. So, you want to make sure you have tools to help you compensate. While most good word-processing programs contain built-in spell checkers, they may not be the most robust. It is very common for MS Word to report a misspelled word simply because it doesn't recognize it. Moreover, if you are using technical terms related to your expertise, it may not recognize any of these words. Therefore, you want to make sure you have access to a current dictionary. In addition, it's easy to get stumped and use the same word too often, so a good thesaurus is a must. Merriam-Webster (www.merriam-webster.com) is one of the best in both categories, and it's free.

Grammar and punctuation are two other considerations, separate from vocabulary and spelling. So, if you're not familiar with comma rules, when to use a colon or semicolon, whether "I" or "me" is correct, or countless other rules, access to a good resource on these topics is a must. Although there are many other helpful options online, Grammar Girl, available on the Quick and Dirty Tips website (www.quickand-dirtytips.com/grammar-girl), is a pleasant, easy-to-use free online guide. You can check grammar and punctuation by entering a question or key words into its search engine.

CONCLUSION

The Internet is here to stay. It will continue to evolve, adding more and more innovations and resources. Social media will grow into a necessity and not an option. I believe customer service will eventually become the biggest use of social media for businesses, as good customer service also means great public relations, which result in sales. Smart phones and tablets will probably become the main method by which people engage in commerce and computing, making a company's access to the public much easier. After all, how many people can avoid the jingle of their phones when they receive messages? Very few. So, whether they mean to or not, when you post to your blog or comment on social media, those connected to you will hear a jingle and grab their phones to take a look. However, even with these innovations, one thing won't change, and that's where you want these people to go after they've received your message: your website.

9. Sales Reps

Don Debelak

Grant Koppers was a fishing guide on Lake Ontario. He came up with the idea of a better fishing lure that actually looks like a live fish. In 2011, his product was featured on the cover of *Field and Stream* as one of the thirty best lures, and now his lures are sold in much of the northern United States and across Canada. How did Grant go from an inventor with an idea to a successful entrepreneur? He did many things right, but one of the most important steps he took was to get sales representatives involved in his project early. These reps provided major help and support, including the following:

- Injecting seed capital.

- Suggesting how to package, price, and promote the product.

- Playing a key role in determining which lures would be bestsellers in order to hold down inventory costs.

- Helping to locate the major investor that was needed to launch the company.

Don Debelak is a new product marketing specialist who has been involved with inventors and inventions for over thirty years. Don has experience working with all types of products, from small novelties to medical innovations. He has also been a columnist for *Entrepreneur,* and has authored several inventor books. He is a registered patent agent, using his wealth of experience to help his clients with intellectual property protection.
dondebelak34@msn.com
www.onestopinventionshop.net • www.patentsbyDonDebelak.com

- Making the initial introductory sale rounds and promoting the product to major Canadian retail outlets.

- Finding other reps to represent the product in other territories.

An independent sales rep is a person who takes on a variety of products from different manufacturers, typically with a minimum of ten product lines, though they can carry up to one hundred lines. Reps may be independent or they may work in a group with other reps. Reps and rep groups typically make money on commission, getting a percentage of the sales they make from manufacturers. They make money first and foremost because they know and treasure their customers and their markets. And they know how to sell their customers. This is why they may be valuable to you.

Reps have strong connections to their suppliers (or principals, as they are usually called), who pay them their commissions. Some principals may be ideal licensing prospects. If reps like your idea, they just might be willing to take your product to the companies they know and see if they can get any interest in it.

FINDING REPS

So, when should you start looking for a representative to help you develop your product introduction? Show your product to one or two sales representatives as soon as you can, even if it is just a prototype, model, or drawing. You want to find these one or two helpers, preferably in your area, to help you determine features that your product may need, price points, competition, introduction strategy, key contacts, and packaging strategy. If a rep likes your product, he may invest in your product. You might also offer the rep a master rep commission of about 2 percent for all the distribution that he sets up after the product has been launched. So, if you offer a 10-percent commission to sell your product, then your initial or master rep will receive a 2-percent override on the sale, meaning that you are paying an overall commission of 12 percent.

Before finding additional reps after you've acquired one or two reps, you should wait until you have sufficient inventory or the ability to get more inventory quickly. Reps have a lot of lines they could carry, and they will drop you if you can't deliver. Remember the representatives get paid only on commission, so if you don't have inventory that can produce sales, they are working for nothing. One or two representatives early in the process can produce enough sales for you to prove your product will sell. This proof will help you line up manufacturers, investors, or banks to support product growth. Your initial reps will be hoping for big eventual paydays due to their investments or their master rep agreements. They will wait through a slow start in your sales. But reps who receive a standard commission will typically drop a company when its work doesn't pay off immediately.

Locate leading trade magazines and trade shows for your industry. If possible, attend these trade shows, go to booths with complementary products, and see if they have reps. These booths may even be run by reps. When attending trade shows or other industry events, network with other inventors and ask them if they know any good reps. Subscribe to industry trade magazines and send away for information on complementary products. When you receive the sales literature, see if names of local reps are included. Talk to these reps and see if they know others. Sometimes industry trade association websites have lists of reps. *The Encyclopedia of Associations* by the Gale Directory Library is also helpful, and may be found in most large libraries. Internet searches should be enough for you to find industry trade associates. Also check out manufacturers' sales representatives directories such as the Manufacturers Agents National Association (MANA).

If you are having a hard time finding reps or you don't have the time to find them, you can purchase a sales rep list at One Stop Invention Shop (www.onestopinventionshop.net).

Reps are always interested in finding new lines, but that doesn't mean it will be easy for you to sign them. Reps are only interested in your line if it will make them money and add to their reputations. Be prepared to create your best opportunity for success when approaching them.

SIGNING REPS

Before you attempt to sign a rep, you should be aware of a few general points. Reps will want to make at least $10,000 a year selling your product. They will want an exclusive agreement in their territories for the markets they serve. For most consumer products, they will want a commission of 10 to 12 percent. Reps consider their customers to be the keys to their businesses, so you must realize that they will side with customers on most issues. If reps aren't finding success with your product, they won't spend time on it. You need to be prepared to change reps if they don't produce revenue for you.

To sign a rep, you have to start by getting his interest. Reps in your area, or reps recommended by retailers in your area, will often ask for some information before talking to you further. The best way to respond is by email, but don't overload your email with a lot of attachments. Instead, have one or two pictures and at most 300 to 500 words to highlight the big selling points of your idea. Remember, your goal at this juncture is not to convince a rep to carry your product; it is to get them to continue talking to you. I find a short, simple email gets you the best results. Try to cut down the file size of all pictures, so your email opens as quickly as possible.

Your email should include a short statement that lets the reader know you have a new product, what your market is, and the fact that you are looking for reps to sell into this market.

It should also have a picture of the product and its packaging, if possible. State the product's suggested retail price, a short list of the product's benefits, a rundown of major sales achievements to date, and how to receive a product sample from you.

Once you have a representative interested, show your professionalism by asking the following questions:

- What are your target accounts?

- How many products are in your line?

- What are these products?

- How many sales people are in your organization?

- How long has your organization been in business?

- What was the last new product you took on?

If the rep looks promising, then you have three options. Give out additional information on the phone or through email and send a sample. Answer all of his questions and then send a complete package of information that he can use to decide if he wants to carry your product. This package should include a sample product, pricing packages, store displays and brochures (both for store owners and to be used at small regional shows), and literature the rep can use to present your product to retailers. Also supply a list of frequently asked questions and details about where your product has been sold to date. If you don't currently have sales, show whatever research you have.

Offer to work with the rep to create a special package to present to his three top customers. This package should help generate sales at their stores. It could be an in-store demonstration, special interactive display, contest of some sort with a meaningful prize, or package sale in which you offer a complementary product—from you or from another vendor—to generate sales. You might also decide to guarantee sales, which means that you will take the product back if it doesn't sell to the first three retailers.

As you probably already know, the more steps you take to land a rep, the better off you will be. Reps can sell a product for you for years, and the upfront costs to get them started are very important. Most of the work can be done over the phone, but if at all possible, I recommend you visit your first one or two potential reps in person. You may be doing something wrong, you may have items you have neglected, or there may be steps you could take to improve your chances. These issues might come up in a personal visit but not in a phone call. The other reason for a personal visit is the fact that reps are often reluctant to take on a product line when you don't have any other reps or an established network of retailers. A personal visit gives you a chance to build rapport with reps, which could help you land your first rep.

SETTING UP A REP NETWORK

You may have started with a rep from the beginning, and if you have, you can use your rep to help you set up your network of sales representatives. If not, you can still set up a rep network on your own. Setting up a sales rep network is one of the most cost effective ways to start selling regionally, nationally, or internationally. Don't start until you are ready to start selling and shipping products, though, otherwise you will quickly lose the interest of your reps. Expect sales reps to take a 10-to 12-percent commission, but for inventors starting out, this is much cheaper than trying to hire, train, and motivate hired sales employees. Sales reps bring with them expertise, experience, industry knowledge, and many contacts within the industry—all things that you'll need to succeed. Additionally, while stores will buy from anyone, they prefer fewer vendors, so sometimes being an inventor with one product makes it difficult to get into retail stores. Having sales reps that already sell to your target market benefits you as an inventor, as many of your stores may already buy from your rep and can add a new product without much hassle.

Before you start contacting sales reps, you'll want to have a manufacturer's rep agreement ready, in case they are interested. You can find a sample manufacturer's representative agreement on the Internet or at your local library, or you can have one prepared by an attorney. There are many particulars in the agreement that you will see in samples that you find. The main thing you should expect is to pay a commission of 10 to 12 percent.

Having great materials for your rep mailing is the key to success. You need to let reps know you have a hot new product, are running a professional and serious business, and are ready to do all it takes for your product and your reps to succeed. The reps will be extremely interested to see the type of materials you have to help them sell your product to retailers. Your literature should include sales flyers, price lists, stories, and testimonials. You should offer samples, list your web page, and include info on manufacturing capabilities. Discuss marketing support, ads being run, trade shows you will attend, PR efforts, and other support. Offer information on sample policies, consignment or guaranteed sales for new customers, and co-op advertising programs. Also include what reps will receive in terms of promotional materials, sales materials, and samples.

You need professional-looking materials so the reps know you mean business. If your mailing looks like it was put together by a fly-by-night company, it is unlikely to attract talented and experienced representatives. Initially, send your package to between ten and fifteen reps, then call them up and see if any are interested in your line. If not, try to discover why they are not interested. You may need to make some changes in your package. If your first mailing doesn't go well, make changes to your package and send it to another ten to fifteen sales reps. Call them up, and if they are not interested, find out why. Keep doing this until you know you've gathered the right mailing materials. At this point, do a larger scale mailing to all the reps on your list. When sending out your mailing, don't send the contract, but have it ready in case someone is interested.

If a rep is interested, make sure you ask him a few questions to make sure that he is really the right rep for you. Reps should have complementary lines. For example, if you have a new style of backpack for camping, you want the rep to have other outdoor product lines for the same market. You also want a hungry rep. Selling a new product can be hard, so you want someone who is ready to go out and give it his all. The best reps are ones that have worked for another rep agency and then started their own and are anxious to build sales. Also check that the rep has taken on other new lines successfully over the last two years.

The rep needs to believe he can make at least $10,000 or $15,000 with your product. If he can't make that much, it is unlikely he will support it for long. The rep has to have the technical knowledge to represent your product properly. This doesn't apply to all products, just ones that have a technical or scientific nature. For instance, if you have a chemical product, you need reps that can intelligently and understandably talk about how your product works and answer questions of a technical nature. They don't need to be chemists, but they should have a basic understanding of the technical side of things.

REPS AND LICENSING

Two heads are better than one, so if you are trying to license your idea, why not get a partner? Often the best partner is a sales rep that is already in the industry. He will know the market, many of the major players, and what kind of deal really makes sense. For inventors, this partnership doesn't mean you have to give an equal share to the partner; often just a 10- to 15-percent share will be enough if you have a "works like, looks like" prototype and a marketing plan. You might need to increase the sales rep's share if you need money that he may contribute or help raise, but typically you will pay a modest amount to the rep for all the value he can offer you.

Besides just licensing an idea straightaway, the rep can help you take other steps that might be important to land a licensing deal. An example is a partnership with a manufacturer who will help design the new product, build prototypes, and eventually produce the product. This relationship can be important if you are licensing to a company that outsources production, or if your product is too expensive for you to produce on your own. Inventors form alliances or partnerships with sales reps because they don't have established contacts in the industry, or because they need a partner to help foot the bill. Most inventors think they just need an idea or patent to get a license, and in some cases this is true, but there are some additional steps that an inventor can take to improve his chances of landing a license, and to land a higher royalty. Sales reps can help with all of these steps. One thing to note is that it is not just the rep's contacts that can help you. You will also receive a major boost with everyone you talk to once they realize you have an industry professional backing your idea.

Improving Your Chances of Licensing

Have a patent or patent pending. An inventor typically does this step on his own, often finding an engineer or designer to complete design work on his invention. Sales reps typically know industry people with the right expertise to do this, and know contacts who might work for a percentage of the idea. Find a manufacturer to make the prototype and possibly set up a small production run. Again, the rep may know people who can do the job, and might do it for a share of the product rather than for an upfront fee. Set up a sales test at a key retailer or end user to get market feedback. Reps will have contacts for a wide variety of market tests.

Get conditional purchase agreements from manufacturer sales rep agencies, other marketers, retail chains, or other key target customers to prove your product is viable. Arrange for the product to be shown at a trade show to get market feedback, which you can use to show potential licensors that your product has a high chance of creating strong sales. Line up other industry people as investors or supporters of your idea.

What You Need to Succeed

Sales rep partners, or any other partners, look for a significant benefit when they decide to team up with an inventor. Typically, they are only interested in your product if it can increase their annual incomes by 15 to 25 percent. The perfect product, from their perspectives, is one that has considerable market impact. But inventors have another card to play with sales reps, who likely want to differentiate themselves from all other reps who seek profitable lines from major companies. Working with inventors is a way for a sales rep to increase his value in the market and make a mark in the industry. This is important, and it is a key factor in why a rep might help you.

From an inventor's point of view, perfect products for a joint venture are ones that he doesn't have the resources to produce, or the marketing network to launch. A partnership with a rep allows inventors to move quickly to improve and finalize their products for licensing with much less financial risk. The key to success is finding the right reps to approach.

Money Matters

Other than key contacts, the main advantage of a partnership is that you get funding from your partner. For example, you may have identified a big market opportunity, but lack the money to create prototypes. Reps can help you with the money, or help you find an engineer or a manufacturer to help you develop your product.

Protection

You don't really need a patent to strike up a partnership agreement with a rep, but it does improve your negotiating position and helps ensure that your product's intellectual property rights belong to you.

Prototypes

Many inventors choose a partnership because they don't have the experience or the money to finalize a "looks like, works like" prototype. But a drawing often isn't enough to get a positive response from a potential partner. Having a prototype is important and helps in getting a better deal from a rep, but don't spend too much money creating a rough prototype. Take it far enough so the partner can see your product's sales potential.

Research

You won't have any trouble finding a partner if you uncover a product that satisfies the needs of a large market. The reps often know the market, but I feel it helps your negotiating position if you can show that you know the market is there. Your research should show that customers need and want your product, and that they're willing to pay a reasonable price for it.

Dos and Don'ts

Don't be greedy. The sales rep will make you a lot more money in the end, so don't be afraid to agree to his terms if he can do the job for you. Do give yourself an out. Tell the rep you will offer the percentage only if he spends twenty to forty hours every three months to help promote your idea. State that if you are unsatisfied with the effort, you will let the sales rep know you are unhappy and give him sixty days to rectify the situation or your agreement will be terminated. Don't approach a potential partner without at least some market research from target customers. Your position is more favorable if you have survey results from at least fifteen to twenty potential users. Don't be a pain. Sales reps won't proceed with a partnership arrangement, no matter how profitable, if you appear difficult to work with. Don't call constantly with questions, revisions, or suggestions. Limit your contacts to one or two per week, at which point you can mention any major concerns.

IS A PARTNERSHIP RIGHT FOR YOU?

A partnership with a rep may or may not be right for you. One of the advantages of a partnership is that it allows you to introduce new products that are beyond your reach in terms of either resources or experience. A partnership may also help you gain market experience that you can use in the future. It speeds up the introduction and market penetration of your new product, allows you to improve your odds of landing a licensing agreement, and lets you introduce your new product when you can't afford a "looks like, works like" prototype.

On the other hand, a partnership doesn't give you total control of your product. You will also be forced to depend on another party to do his job effectively for your product to succeed. In addition, you won't be able to withdraw your product to start a company on your own. A partnership may not even establish you as a market force capable of launching your own company. Finally, your input may be overridden by your sales rep partner.

INVESTMENTS FROM REPS

Inventors do best with a rep that helps the company grow by investing money (or time and effort) in return for stock. But this concept is full of pitfalls. What if the rep stops working? He will still own the stock, and you might need to take on other partners. If you need to sell more stock, will the rep's share of the business stay the same? If it will remain at the same level, your percentage of ownership will go down.

I feel the best way to proceed with early sales reps is to take the following steps when discussing a possible invention investment. You will need to have a lawyer draw up the agreement once you agree to terms.

- At the beginning, set all shares at a certain value. Typically $1 or $2 is a good starting point. State that your company will have one million to five million shares once all paperwork has come in. Explain that most shares are not issued now, but will be available later, both as a reward for "sweat equity" and to new investors.

- State how many shares you have for your idea, and start with your shares being worth at least $100,000.

- Tell the rep he can buy up to a certain number of shares for the value you set on them. If you set the value at $1, and you own one hundred thousand shares, you might let the rep buy up to ten thousand shares.

- Explain clearly that you will receive a certain number of additional shares each month that you work more than twenty hours on your invention. For example, you will earn three thousand shares per month.

- Explain that a rep can earn up to one thousand additional shares for each month that he works more than ten hours on your invention.

- Explain that you might later need to take on additional investors. The shares purchased by these investors will probably reduce the rep's percentage of ownership in the company. This is a key point. The rep buys ten thousand shares, not 10-percent ownership of the company. The rep's percentage of ownership will vary depending on the overall number of shares owned.

- Offer the rep the right to buy shares at the same price as the next investor. Explain that the number of shares the rep can buy might be limited in order to keep your ownership percentage high.

- If the rep stops actively promoting your invention, or his or her time drops significantly, you should have the right to buy back the rep's shares at the price paid for them.

MASTER REP AGREEMENT

Although it is far better to have your initial representative be an investor in your company, you may need to have a master rep agreement instead to get such a rep involved. You should consult your attorney for this agreement. Some key points to include in this agreement are the following:

- A contingent clause. This agreement is contingent on the representative continuing to help you, typically for a minimum of five to ten hours a month, until the product is successfully launched. You don't want to have a commitment to the rep if he doesn't continually help you.

- A clause paying commission only on sales generated by the rep. The master rep override commission is only for distribution networks and other representatives that the master rep finds for you.

- A clear statement declaring that this agreement is not setting up a joint venture or partnership.

- A clear definition listing the commission rate, when commissions will be paid, what the commissions are paid on, and how commissions will be paid.

- A clause stating how you can cancel this agreement.

- A standard mutual confidentiality and non-disclosure clause.

- A clear listing of the duties you expect the rep to perform, which should include helping to develop your product, developing your product introduction strategy, landing your initial company sales base, and developing your nationwide sales network.

- A limitation that states the rep cannot commit the company to any action or pricing structure; these decisions remain with the inventor.

- A limitation of liability for both parties.

CONCLUSION

Reps aren't perfect. Their main drawback is that they will consistently put their own interests ahead of yours. They won't hesitate for a minute to drop you when they have better deals in place. They won't follow your instructions if they feel there is a better way, and they will almost always take the customer's side in disputes. Despite these drawbacks, I believe that reps are a viable option for inventors. They know the market, have developed a list of key contacts, and are a low out-of-pocket expense to get your product off the ground.

ONE BIG IDEA

Designed and marketed by Apple, the iPod's exclusivity to Mac computers and high price tag resulted in slow sales when it was first introduced in 2001. By the middle of 2002, a PC-compatible version of the portable media player became available and new models began to be sold at different price points, boosting sales and making the device the most popular digital music player in the world. The brand has since branched out into a line of players, offering a number of sizes and features.

10. Retailers

Karen Waksman

You have a product that you think would be perfect for big box retailers. You've either been selling to retailers for a while or you're just getting started. Either way, you want to ensure that you have the best possible meeting with that buyer. What should you say in the meeting? How should you prepare in advance? How should you present to the buyer? Most importantly, what fundamentally matters to the buyer so that she will be more inclined to buy from you?

In this chapter, I will address key tips and strategies related to a successful buyer meeting. It took me years of interaction with chain store buyers, and plenty of trial and error, prior to understanding some of these fundamentals. I'm hoping that wherever you are in the process of selling to chain stores, this information provides value. If you are a newbie in the world of retail, then my goal is to support your interest in successfully closing that first dream account. If you've been selling to retailers for a while, then I'm hoping this information reminds you to get back to basics. If you've been in the business for a long time, you might have forgotten some of the fundamental decisions that brought

Karen Waksman is a manufacturer's rep turned author, speaker, and consultant. She has sold millions of units to the world's largest retailers and now teaches her proven sales strategies to thousands of product companies across the country. She is the founder and CEO of Retail MBA, which provides a step-by-step plan on how to approach and pitch to chain store buyers effectively.

karen@retailmba.com • www.retailmba.com

you retail success in the first place. The following information can reinvigorate your business and support your existing retail customers.

GO SHOPPING

If I can give you any advice on having effective chain store buyer meetings, it's that you should always go shopping and walk their stores prior to the meeting. And I'm not talking about the stores that you checked out months ago. I'm talking about going within a week or two of your buyer meeting. Buyers absolutely hate it when you don't walk their stores prior to a meeting. Not only does it show that you are not serious about doing business with them, but buyers will almost always ask you the last time you checked out their stores, so it's to your benefit to do so.

This especially goes for those of you who have been selling to retailers for years. It's so easy to get busy and complacent with doing simple tasks such as walking stores, but sometimes getting back to basics will help elevate your business tremendously. Buyers love it when you take initiative, so walking their stores can only help.

By the way, for those of you who don't live anywhere near the retailer, I highly recommend finding a way to examine it, regardless. Fly in a few days early before your meeting to make this happen.

What are you looking for while walking a store? You are looking at the section of the store that the buyer is responsible for. You are wondering if your pricing is comparable, better, or worse than your competitors' products. You are considering if your current packaging will fit well in the store. You are asking whether your product is different, better, and more interesting than what the buyer has on the store shelves today. Will your product add value to the current product assortment? Does it fill a need that isn't being addressed by the retailer?

There are many other things to think about while walking stores, but these are some of the key points. Reviewing a store prior to a meeting and then offering valuable suggestions and input as to how you might help increase revenue for this store is absolute heaven to buyers.

They are looking for partnerships and collaboration with their vendors. So go shopping, walk their stores, and prove to these buyers that you are serious about doing business with them.

VENDOR PORTALS

One of the things that most people don't do prior to meeting with a chain store buyer is review the retailer's vendor portal. What's a vendor portal? Most chain stores have a separate website that outlines their vendor requirements for new and existing vendors. In other words, it's a website where the retailer explains what you need to set up in advance prior to working with it. This website includes valuable information, including instructions on how much business insurance you are required to have, how UPC codes need to be handled, how to set up a D&B number effectively, and what certificates the retailer needs. I mention this vendor portal because if you can review it before your meeting and let the buyer know you've already prepared yourself to do business with her, then you are on your way to a more effective buyer meeting.

Buyers love companies who are organized, truly care, and show initiative. And you can easily display these traits by following their instructions and setting your business up according to their requirements—information that's included in their vendor portals. Another thing to note about these vendor portals is that sometimes you can find really valuable information about a retailer that you didn't expect to find. For instance, when I was digging around the Walgreen's vendor site, I found a list of all the names, titles, and phone numbers of its category managers, or buyers. I find interesting stuff on vendor sites all the time. The problem is that most people don't take the time to look.

How do you find a retailer's vendor portal? Well, if the buyer has not given you this information, then just do an online search. Type "vendor relations" or "vendor" or "supplier," along with the name of a particular retailer, into a search engine and you should find your information pretty quickly. If you would like to see an example of a retailer's vendor portal, check out Macy's vendor website at www.macys net.com. The bottom line with vendor portals is that chain store buyers want to be able to work with product companies that are ready to start doing business with them quickly. So, help these chain store buyers by reviewing their requirements and fulfilling them in advance, or at least research all you need to know prior to your meeting.

YOUR "MONEY" STORY

I've taught classes and workshops on the subject of selling to chain stores to thousands of product companies across the country, and the one thing I consistently notice about why product companies aren't selling more products to stores is their lack of good "money" stories. When I say "money" story, I'm talking about truly convincing the buyer that the product will sell well in his store.

If a buyer truly believed at her core that your product would blow off her store shelves, then she would find a way to put your product in her stores. Buyers will jump through hoops to make it happen. Yes, there are always exceptions to the rule, but the majority of buyers are hungry for the next successful product. Why? Because buyers are responsible for generating revenue for their retailers. So, if you approach a buyer with a great product and a story regarding why your product will make her money, then you will absolutely pique her interest. The problem most product companies have in buyer meetings is that they focus the majority of their time on the features and benefits of their product rather than their "money" story. Features and benefits are great, but that's not enough to tip the buyer's decision as to whether they will buy from you or not.

Buyers get calls all day every day from product companies that have similar products and want to sell to them. The ones that differentiate themselves and focus on revenue are the ones that ultimately win. So, what needs to be included in your "money" story? The following are a few suggestions to help you get started. Ask yourself these questions while writing your story:

- What other chain store retailers are currently selling your product?

- Can you show proof that you are currently selling products to the retailer's ideal customer base? For instance, women between the ages of thirty-five and forty-five.

- How many units of your product have already been sold overall? Were they sold through small retailers, online retailers, or some other venue?

- How are you going to help the retailer sell your product once it is in the store?

- What other products can you introduce to the retailer later on so he or she may continue to generate revenue with you on a long-term partnership basis?

There are so many ways to develop your "money" story, but I'm hoping you get my point. Buyers love to know that your product will generate revenue for them, and they want you to tell them why you think your product will be a success. So, come up with your "money" story prior to meeting with a chain store buyer.

By the way, if you are now panicked as to how to answer these questions, have no fear. There is always a way. I've had students who have had zero proof of sales and only one product, or SKU, that has gotten into chain stores, but who have been successful nonetheless, so I know it's possible to come up with a "money" story at any point in your product's life cycle!

MARKETING COLLATERAL AND SAMPLES

One of the most common questions product companies ask me is what to bring to a buyer meeting to make the most effective mark. In light of this, I want to talk about marketing collateral and samples. First of all, a buyer wants to touch, feel, and experience your product while in a meeting, so be sure to bring your product in its packaging for the buyer to review. This may sound obvious, but I've heard plenty of stories of people who brought product samples to buyer meetings but no packaging, which is a big no-no.

Buyers actually want to see what your product will look like in their stores. The only way to do so is to show them your product in its packaging. So be sure to bring a few packaging options to your buyer meeting. The other thing to mention is that effective marketing collateral can be tremendously useful when trying to close a deal with a chain store buyer. For a buyer, this means that your marketing collateral explains visually what your product is and does in five seconds or less. Buyers are too busy to read an endless supply of words about your product on marketing collateral. They are visual and want answers fast. Buyers want to know the key features and benefits of your product, as well as your "money" story and what your product looks like, and all in as few words as possible. Does this all sound impossible?

Check out one of my students' marketing collateral as an example. Just follow the link http://retailmba.com/sample-sell-sheet. This is her one page sell sheet. Her product, packaging, and quantities sold have significantly changed since this initial example, but she was nice enough to let me share. Notice that you can tell visually what this product is and does in five seconds or less. This is what buyers want—quick and efficient bullet points and visuals to explain what your product will look like in their stores. Here are some key takeaways from this example:

- The product and packaging are deliberately included in the marketing collateral, so the buyer can visually see the product in action.

- It has been done in a one-page format, so it's easy for the buyer to review the information.

- It includes simple bullet points that answer how the product will make the buyer money.

- It shows the features and benefits of the product, so the buyer gets a feel for why the product is different or better than its competitors.

Buyers are inundated with marketing material for products all day long, so if they receive simple yet effective marketing collateral from you they will be thrilled. The bottom line is that less is more when it comes to marketing collateral with chain store buyers.

DO NOT OVERWHELM THE BUYER

If you want a great buyer meeting, you must make your time with the buyer as efficient and effective as possible. This means that you'll need to craft your story for the buyer in such a way that you don't overwhelm her. Walking into a chain store buyer meeting and dropping several products on the table for the buyer to choose from is not an effective meeting. A buyer will want you to walk into the meeting and tell her exactly which product she should buy, why you think she should buy this particular product, and in what order she should continue to buy your other product options, if you have any.

Buyers expect you to come to the meeting with unshakable confidence about your product, and the way to do this is to show them which product they must buy first while explaining all the reasons this product will be successful in their stores. This means that you need to show them your bestsellers, or products that you know will do well for them, and then tell your story about future product options towards the end of the meeting.

As I've mentioned, buyers like doing business with product companies that are organized, truly care, and show initiative. If you go into a meeting chaotically, the buyer will not be excited to do business with you. So, tell a story in the meeting. Focus on the product that the buyer should purchase first and the reasons she should do so, and then focus on other product options when needed. This strategy will help ensure an effective buyer meeting.

CONCLUSION

If you want effective chain store buyer meetings, you must take the time to think about what truly matters to these buyers. And the only way to do this is to shop their stores, review their vendor requirements, come up with your "money" story, and effectively present your product with visuals and information that get straight to the heart of why they should buy your product. If you focus on these things, you will truly be on your way to chain store success.

ONE BIG IDEA

The jockstrap, also known as an athletic supporter, was invented in 1874 by C.F. Bennett of the Sharp & Smith sporting goods company to support the genitalia of male bicycle messengers, or bicycle jockeys, as they rode over cobblestone streets. In 1927, a hard cup was added by Guelph Elastic Hosiery to prevent injury during sports and other physical activity.

11. Licensing

Joan Lefkowitz

Many inventors dream of securing million-dollar licensing deals for their products. Getting a product licensed involves a lot of hard work, persistence, and vision. So what is licensing? According to Barron's *Dictionary of Marketing Terms,* licensing is defined as a "contractual agreement between two business entities in which the licensor permits the licensee to use a brand name, patent, or other proprietary right, in exchange for a fee or royalty." So, why do so many inventors want to take this path? In this chapter, I will discuss why inventors choose to license their products and what it takes to get your product licensed.

WHY LICENSE?

Licensing enables the licensor, or inventor, to profit from the financial resources, manufacturing capabilities, distribution channels, or other capacity of the licensee, or party who licenses it from the inventor. For example, if an inventor has a product in the category of hair tool

---

Joan Lefkowitz is the president of ACCESSORY BRAINSTORMS, Inc, a licensing, sales representation agency, and consultancy for inventions in the fields of fashion, beauty, and intimate apparel; accessories; and lifestyle. Based in New York, the agency licenses inventors' products to major corporations, and markets to mail-order catalogues, TV shopping programs, and retail outlets. Its products include Topsy Tail and Hairdini.

web@accessorybrainstorms.com • www.accessorybrainstorms.com

accessory, he may license it to a well-known hair accessory manufacturer under its brand name to give the product instant brand recognition, exposure, and sales in the marketplace. If a product is a good fit for direct response television, or DRTV, such as a kitchen gadget or an exercise device, then licensing it to a company with a successful record in that field could position it to be profitable for both the licensor and the licensee.

This chapter covers many aspects of licensing, and is geared to basic consumer use products, not those that are highly technical or scientific. Because there are different types of licenses, the focus will be on the universal aspects of licensing inventions. There are many variables as to why inventors might choose licensing as the best route for their products. An inventor might want or need to stay in his current occupation, or he may not have sufficient funds to launch a product on his own. He might like the idea of earning royalties and not have a need to control every detail of his product. Many inventors are non-entrepreneurial. These inventors want to spend time coming up with their next inventions, not running a business.

PREPARATION FOR LICENSING

A licensor is a party that licenses, or "rents" out, the use of a patent or intellectual property to a company for the purposes of manufacturing or distributing a product in exchange for a monetary percentage of sales. There are general industry protocols that need to be followed by an inventor prior to introducing his product to companies for licensing. An inventor needs to complete many steps before making any presentations, including:

- Inventing a product and making an initial prototype to evaluate if it works.

- Doing a preliminary patent search to see if the product is on the market.

- Checking retailers for competition.

- Securing a non-disclosure form to use prior to revealing the invention to the trade.

- Getting a professional patent search and opinion done.

- Applying for a provisional or non-provisional patent, if the product is potentially patentable.

- Having a professional prototype made, if feasible.

- Selecting a product name and doing a trademark search.

- Doing some market testing and using focus groups to gauge consumer interest.

- Researching manufacturing costs in the United States and Asia.

- Achieving sales, if possible.

Qualities of a Great Product

To make a licensable product you must start with a great product. Topsy Tail and Bumpits, both hair tools, each sold over 100 million dollars' worth of product. The market wanted or needed these products. Topsy Tail was the first hair invention to appear in a TV commercial. Bumpits was already well known through sales to the professional market before it was licensed to a company that sold it on TV and to mass market retailers. Both of these products had all the following qualities:

- Uniqueness and the ability to solve a problem.

- Patent or patent-pending.

- High perceived value (up to ten times greater than the cost to produce).

- Wide market appeal.

- Cost of $29.99 or less.

- Ease of operation and a pleasant look.

- Elements of magic.

If your invention has all of the above, then you have started your journey towards securing a license for your product.

Licensing Agents

Many inventors use a licensing agent to advise them in the licensing of their products, and in securing the right deals. A licensing agent can help save steps, locate qualified licensees, get to the right people who will consider your product, steward your product through the company review process, help negotiate the terms of the agreement, and maintain contact with the licensee to assure that it is upholding these terms.

Inventors need to locate licensing agents who handle products within the categories or industries of the inventions. Another advantage of using licensing agents is that they understand the needs of the company as well as those of the inventor. The agent can present your invention in the most efficient manner, and can bring an unbiased view to negotiations that will benefit both parties. These considerations are often more attractive to a company than dealing directly with an inventor.

On average, licensing agents charge between 25 to 50 percent of fees, both advance and royalty fees, that the inventor earns as a result of the license. The percentage may vary from industry to industry, and may be affected by the amount of assets an inventor brings to the table. For example, if an invention already has brand recognition, a useable mold, inventory, or an established customer base, it would be simpler for the agent to secure a licensing deal. The agent might charge the inventor of the product a lower agent fee than if there were only a working prototype that required further development by the licensee.

A licensing agent should help negotiate the license based on familiarity with and norms in specific industries, but inventors should have attorneys work out the language and fine points of the terms of the agreement. A lawyer, however, is not a substitute for a seasoned licensing agent who is closely attuned to what is happening in the marketplace.

Royalty Rates

Royalty rates for licensed inventions may differ by a number of variables. Factors such as if a product is utility or design patented, patent pending, or not patentable, as well as if the product has properties useable to the licensee such as molds or tooling, a customer base, or brand name will affect royalty rates. Whether a product is licensed exclusively to a company or if it is licensed to multiple companies may influence the royalty percentage.

Not all industries offer the same royalty rates. In my area of expertise (fashion and beauty accessories) the royalty norm is 3 to 5 percent— 3 percent if the product is unpatented, and 5 percent for patented products. Sometimes a manufacturer will offer 3 percent to patent-pending products and increase it to 5 percent when the patent has been issued. I have even seen some licensing rates go as high as a 7-percent royalty with large companies, and a 10-percent rate when licensing to smaller manufacturers, which typically do a lower volume in sales.

According to Kris Hudgens, vice-president of America Invents, in the consumer and electronics category the norm for licensing is a 3-percent royalty for non-patentable products, which may have existing assets, and a 2- to 4-percent rate for a DRTV license. To license patented products, the norm is a 5- to 7-percent royalty. For short-form DRTV licensing on patented products, the inventor can expect a 2.5- to 5-percent royalty on direct-to-consumer sales, with a higher percentage of 4 to 8 percent on wholesale sales, as wholesale prices are lower than retail prices.

Prospects

A licensee is a party or company that licenses or obtains the right to use a patent, intellectual property, or product from a licensor for the purpose of manufacturing or distributing a product to generate revenues. Basically, a licensee is a company that licenses your product from you. When selecting licensee prospects, be prepared to spend a great deal of time researching companies that license products from the outside. Look for companies that have established manufacturing or distribution of products that fall within the category of your invention.

Evaluate what is important to you. Are you looking for brand name recognition or the best deal? Do you want to sign with a company that sells to retailers, or one that sells directly to the public? Or do you prefer selling your product to the professional market?

Based on your financial goals, select what size company to approach. Keep in mind that larger companies have specific criteria, so research the specifications and evaluate if your product is what they want. For example, Proctor and Gamble's website has specific guidelines for those interested in submitting their inventions to the company. If a larger company does not suit your needs, smaller more specialized companies may be a better fit—better equipped to give your invention proper attention.

To locate potential licensees, you can go into the marketplace to search for manufacturers of products in the category of your invention. Visit various types of stores, attend trade shows, research the Internet, and review databases such as Hoovers, Thomas Register, and Manta.com.

Approaching Companies

After you have established which companies license products, you'll need to find out who the people are that evaluate new inventions for them, and what their procedures are for product presentation. Typically, before a product is licensed or rejected by a company, it goes through a variety of evaluations. For example, the initial evaluator may like it and take it to a team for review. The team will then show it to the decision maker. Keep in mind this process takes time, and it may take months to get an answer. Companies may tell you a specific amount of time it will take to review your product, but if they let it hang indefinitely, you should withdraw it from consideration. If they decide to take on the invention, they may want to put it through various types of testing before committing to putting it on the market. This can include focus groups and small test runs.

Many inventors become frustrated when they are not able to make contacts within companies. This is the reason that inventors hire licensing agents. Agents prequalify potential licensees. They know how to get products reviewed and placed. Many inventors make the mistake of overselling their products, while others may feel uncomfortable presenting to business people. Companies frequently prefer working with licensing agents rather than individual inventors for these reasons.

LICENSING PRESENTATION

When the time comes to present your invention to potential licensees, it is important that you include certain elements in your presentation, if applicable. You should have put together what I call a "presentation book." The book should be created as a hardcopy and digitally, so it will be available to send electronically. Your presentation book should consist of the following:

- Attractive cover with the name of the product and its trademark status.

- Introduction, which includes the title of the product, what the product does, and why the product is needed.

- Inventor's goal for the product.

- Instructions for use.

- Pictures of the product, photos of the product in use, professional drawings or website to demonstrate the product, or a CD demo.

- Technical drawings.

- Need for the product in the market.

- Target market, demographic and size of market, potential sales.

- Competition (include pictures if available), and benefits versus competition.

- Marketing strategy.

- Focus group results.

- Testing.

- Costs to produce the mold as well as the final product domestically and internationally.

- Patent information.

- Contact information for yourself or your licensing agent.

The presentation book reflects your professionalism and how much care you put into researching the subject of your product prior to the professional presentation.

CONTRACTS

A licensing agreement is a written agreement between a licensor and a licensee that allows the licensee to manufacture and distribute the licensor's product as its own. It addresses the specific terms and conditions incumbent upon the licensee, and identifies the arrangement of financial compensation to the licensor.

Negotiating contracts is one of the most challenging parts of licensing. Each party has its own needs and goals. Coming to a consensus is vital to ensure that everyone wins. Prior to working out an agreement with a potential licensee, you should consult with your professional licensing team, namely your licensing agent and contract attorney, to review your questions relating to the terms of the contract. It is especially important to keep flexible, so that they are able to negotiate effectively on your behalf. Negotiations are a sensitive part of getting the contract done. A licensee will expect to negotiate with experienced professionals in order to get a contract completed in a timely and efficient manner.

Negotiations should be used as a method of establishing a great relationship with a licensee in order to work well together over the life of the license and in the future. There are aspects of licensing contracts that are particular to licensing inventions. The following are some specific terms that you should evaluate with your agent. Include them in your agreement as they apply to you and your invention.

A licensing contract or licensing agreement, like any other contract, holds the parties, namely the inventor and the licensing company, accountable to a set of mutually agreed upon rules and circumstances. A licensing contract should provide an arrangement that is both desirable and practical.

Royalty

A royalty refers to the money earned by the licensor from the licensee as a result of allowing the licensee the use of a product, patent, or intellectual property. What makes licensing so attractive is that after recouping initial expenses for items such as prototypes, patents, molds, and so on, the rest of what an inventor earns from royalties is residual, or passive, income. It flows to you automatically, while you are free to create other income streams. Negotiating the royalty rate of a contract is not something that should be handled lightly. My suggestion is to work with your agent on the royalty percentage and other specifics of the contract. Working with someone should help you avoid mistakes, and may save you money in the long run.

Royalty payments should be based on a percentage of the price for which a licensee sells your product, whether be it to retailers or directly to consumers. It should not be based on a percentage of the profit that a licensee makes on the sales. Most companies pay royalties to inventors on a quarterly basis. The amount is generally based on how much money a company has received as a result of sales of your product in the prior quarter. Some smaller companies pay out royalties on a monthly basis.

Royalty Advance

A royalty advance is money that is paid to a licensor by a licensee at the beginning of a contract period, prior to sales of the product, against future royalties to be earned as a result of sales. Depending on the product and company, it is possible to get a nonrefundable advance payment on products in certain categories, such as juvenile products, toys and games, personal care items, fashion accessories, and some housewares. Certain DRTV companies will pay an advance on licensed products. Since there can be many months between the time that a licensing agreement is signed and the time that a licensed product generates royalties due, royalty advances are advantageous to inventors.

In industries that pay an advance royalty to an inventor, the amount paid is ordinarily in the range of five thousand to twenty thousand dollars. An advance is paid prior to the first year of contract, or it may be paid prior to additional years, depending on what is agreed upon. It is paid as an advance on future royalties to be earned by a licensor on sales of a licensed product by a licensee.

Territory

A territory is a geographical area in which a licensee is permitted to sell a licensed product. The term is a clause in a contract that specifies geographical areas (countries, states, or regions) in which a licensee is allowed to sell a product. In granting a territory to a licensee, an inventor needs to be careful in the way that it is detailed in the contract. For example, some contracts will use the general term "North America" to describe the territory. This region is sometimes meant to imply the United States, Canada, and Mexico. Your wish, however, may be to secure a separate license for Canada. If you are going to allow licensees to sell in a specified area, make sure you state in which countries they will be allowed to distribute your product.

Territories cover geographical locations, but may also cover market segments or specific types of accounts. The market may be segmented by mass market stores, such as Target and Wal-Mart; small enterprises, such as boutiques and hair salons; or TV shopping programs, such as HSN and QVC. These segments reflect different customer bases with different purchasing patterns.

Term

The term of a licensing contract is the fixed period of time after which the agreement ends. Most invention licenses are made for a term of between one to three years. Licensees will most likely request that a period of from six to nine months be included in the term to give them time to develop the product and prepare marketing materials. Keep in mind that the longer the development period, the less excited the licensee may become to produce and sell the product. So, yes, have a development period, but only one you deem to be a fair amount of time.

Mary Sarao, inventor of Ask The Inventors!, suggests to include provisions that allow you to renegotiate after a specified number of years, and to address what would happen if the company to which you have licensed your product were to file for bankruptcy or go out of business.

Renewal

If a licensee is satisfied with the sales that a licensed product has achieved during the time of the licensing contract, the licensee will want to renew the contract with the licensor. Terms for renewal are written into licensing contracts. Renewal terms can be written in a few different ways. Most licensing contracts will offer the licensee the opportunity for automatic renewal if the product sales achieve a specific dollar amount during the course of the license. In this scenario, if the licensee does not make a minimum amount of sales, there will be no renewal of contract, except if both parties agree to a renewal or a new contract; but there is no money owed the licensor if the dollar amount of sales is not achieved. All advance royalty payments should be non-reimbursable to the licensee.

The licensee and the licensor set the figure for the product sales required for automatic renewal. If the amount is not met, the licensee is required to pay the licensor royalty based on product sales, to make up the difference between what was sold and the amount at which the minimum guarantee for automatic renewal was set.

Another type of guarantee can be set in which a required amount of royalty is due the licensee each year of the contract. If the royalty payments per year do not meet the minimum guarantee, the licensee is required to pay the licensor the difference between the amount paid and the amount guaranteed at the end of each of the years of the contract. In this type of agreement, a separate high figure for product sales can be set for automatic contract renewal. In any case relating to contract renewal, there should be a provision in the original contract that allows for either party to request adjustments of the terms in the new contract.

Stephen Key of InventRight (www.inventright.com) suggests that you set up a "minimum guarantee" that you think the manufacturer can meet, and that you will be comfortable with, if the manufacturer does not sell more than the minimum.

TYPES OF LICENSING

The type of licensing contract can be referenced by the territory it covers and the level of exclusivity the licensee receives. The territory and levels of exclusivity are distinct from one another, and distinguish exclusive licenses, limited exclusive licenses, and non-exclusive licenses from each other. These licenses share characteristics, but differ in other ways. It is important to be aware of the fine points.

Exclusive License

An exclusive license is defined by the geographical territory in which only one licensee can sell your product. When a licensee requests an exclusive license, the licensor has the best chance of receiving an advance royalty as well as a higher royalty rate, based on the norm for the industry of the invention. An annual minimum royalty payment should be agreed upon by both parties. With this type of license, even the inventor does not have the right to sell her product in the territory.

Limited Exclusive License

The limited exclusive license, like the exclusive license, is defined by the geographical territory, but it is defined also by the market segment in which a licensee can sell your product. In this type of agreement, there is an allowance whereby the inventor and other licensees are permitted to sell the product in specific market segments in the territory. As an example, in the hair goods industry a licensee may require exclusivity in selling to the mass market and department stores, while allowing the inventor or other licensees to sell to professional hairdressers and boutiques. In this type of agreement, an annual minimum royalty payment may also be set.

Non-Exclusive License

A non-exclusive license gives a licensee permission to sell your product in a specific geographical area or territory and market segment. The inventor and other licensees can also sell the product in the same territory or market segment.

LEGAL FEES

In a licensing contract, it is necessary for one of the parties to take responsibility to pay any legal fees required to protect the patent or other proprietary information covered by the contract should it be infringed by a third party. No party other than you should be making money from the sale of your product, except where a license has been issued to allow it. If a licensed patented product has been copied by another company without permission, the patent holder can take that company to court and sue it for infringement. On the other hand, you may be sued if another company claims your product infringes its patent. Be aware that court costs are very expensive and may never be recovered.

The licensee should always be the party responsible for legal fees, as it has the financial advantage over the inventor. If the licensee recovers expenses from infringement by a third party, and also recovers additional monetary damages from lost profits, the inventor should be paid a percentage of the recovered lost profits.

If you do not have the money to pay for a patent, it is possible to get your licensee to pay to obtain one. In such a case, however, the licensee may want to control the patent. You are named as the inventor on the patent, but the licensee will own all rights to the patent. If you want to use the rights either for yourself, or to license your product to another company, you would not be allowed, unless the licensee agreed to it in a contract.

It is also possible to negotiate with your licensee to pay for a patent in which you are named owner and allow the licensee use of the patent. In order for the licensee to agree to this arrangement, it would most likely require the inventor to sign a long-term exclusive agreement.

EXPECTATIONS

Many inventors are in love with their products and may not be willing to recognize the realities of the marketplace or the innate potential of their inventions. Although an invention is useful and can solve a problem that many people may have, the marketplace will determine whether your invention will be a success. Some key factors to consider include:

- Acceptance from the marketplace.
- Market size.
- Competition.
- Strength of the licensee.
- Distribution strength.
- Timing.

Keep in mind that even after a product has been licensed, manufactured, marketed, promoted, and packaged, there is still no guarantee that it will sell. In the end, the consumer may not find a need for your invention, or he may be satisfied with another product he owns that solves the same problem yours does. If a deal seems good, check it out thoroughly and go with it. Many inventors will sit on potential deals thinking they can get better ones. By then their products may have become obsolete or no longer attractive as a licensed product. Trust yourself.

Many inventors have unrealistic expectations about the money they will make from their licensing deals. You are not going to make millions of dollars as an advance royalty, or in the early stages of the distribution of your product. Inventors can make money beyond an advance royalty if the market responds. If a licensing agreement satisfactory to both parties has been signed, you have a good chance of financial success.

An inventor can be an influence in the success or failure of his product. Clear communication of your expectations, attention to legal detail, and research and preparation for presentation all play major parts in helping you reach your goals. Sharing your expertise on your product with your licensor can affect how she manufactures and markets it.

CONCLUSION

Having been in the business for over three decades, the best recommendation I can give you is to hire a licensing agent. Agents understand the licensing industry and are best equipped to guide you, help you land the right deal, and consult you on how to avoid the pitfalls that can come from the licensing journey.

Licensing is a great avenue for inventors to make profits from their products, but the process is complex. Regardless of whether you are preparing a simple prototype or a completely manufactured product, you must have a commitment to excellence. The more you know about licensing and the better you prepare your invention for presentation, the greater the likelihood that you will find licensing success.

12. Public Relations

Marsha Friedman

Whether you plan to sell your invention directly to consumers or hope to catch the attention of a manufacturer that may take it on, you'll need to get the word out about your product. You may have the most innovative idea since the paper clip, but if no one has heard of it, no one will come looking for it. Launching your own public relations campaign can be an affordable and effective means of promotion. Publicity is free. Unlike advertising, you don't have to pay journalists, talk show hosts, or social media followers to help spread your message—you just have to get them interested in it. And how do you do that? By "celebritizing" yourself! That's my term for branding yourself as an expert. It's how you make yourself a go-to source for the media by providing journalists, show hosts, and social media users with information and insights that they find useful. In return, these sources will provide you with a mass media audience.

Have no doubt; as an inventor, you are very much an expert. If your innovation solves a problem, you've likely devoted a good deal of time studying that problem. Maybe you've researched other attempts to

Marsha Friedman is CEO and founder of EMSI Public Relations, a national agency that has been providing publicity services for twenty-three years. She has helped thousands of entrepreneurs, inventors, professionals, and authors gain exposure and credibility through appearances on radio and TV shows across the country, editorial coverage in newspapers and magazines, and social media. She is the author of the best-selling book *Celebritize Yourself: The Three-Step Method to Increase Your Visibility and Explode Your Business.*
info@marshafriedman.com • www.marshafriedman.com

solve it. You may have looked into the problem's consequences, and the benefits of solving it. Do you have other, less obvious areas of expertise related to your invention? Is your product green or sustainable? Is it affected by politics or the economy? Does it have ramifications for a particular industry, group of people, or geographic area? These are all ideas to consider as you look for ways to plug yourself into newsworthy topics and national conversations and gain media exposure for yourself and your invention. You don't have to be a Hollywood star, a university professor, or an elected official to get the media interested in you; "regular" people do it every single day. However—and this is critically important —you do have to provide valuable, engaging content. A sales pitch does not qualify. When you give a radio, TV, or print interview, or post on social media, you will not engage audiences by saying, "Here's why my gizmo is fabulous and why you should buy it!" By providing content that helps people solve their problems, you'll gain exposure in a more subtle and valuable way.

While the do-it-yourself approach requires minimal—maybe even zero—financial investment, it will demand your time, energy, and patience. Given all you've already put into your invention, are you ready to be just as tenacious in telling the world about it? Here's a step-by-step guide to getting started, including identifying your audience and crafting your message, creating a website, and pitching yourself to the media, along with tips for using social media to spread the word.

YOUR AUDIENCE AND YOUR MESSAGE

First things first: You have to figure out who your audience is because that will influence the message you convey and the media you use to publicize it. Unless you have a truly niche product, consider your potential audience in terms of ever expanding ripples. For instance, your collapsible coffeemaker may be just the thing for a college student's tiny dorm room. That's your initial target audience. But his parents and grandparents, who are helping outfit that dorm room, might also be audiences. In fact, now that the kids are going off to college, these folks may be downsizing their living quarters, so they might just want one for themselves, too. How about others who live in small spaces? Campers? Boaters?

Once you know your audience, you will have a better idea of where to find it. Is your audience older adults? The bulk of people reading newspapers, online or in print, are forty-five or older. Are they men? Slightly more men than women listen to talk radio. Women? More women than men watch TV talk shows. Do they use social media? Facebook, Google+, and Twitter are the largest social networks. As you consider your audience, think about who these people are, and what types of problems they have. What mother with young children isn't looking for ways to save time? Retirees may be frustrated by the learning curve involved with using new technology. These insights can help shape your communications. People want to solve their problems.

Now it's time to work on crafting your message. To do that, you'll need to identify:

- **Your expertise.** Did you develop an app that creates a grocery list based on your family's favorite meals? Or did you come up with a handy household tool? A better box? Those inventions might mean you're a cook or an efficiency expert, experienced with household repairs, or have a knack for packaging. What expertise led to your invention— or was it the other way around?

- **Your passion.** What is it that got you this far—that made you want to spend the time and effort developing your invention? Maybe you want to make life easier for other parents. Maybe you want to make our planet cleaner. Maybe you're a fitness buff and your tool will inspire more people to get off the couch. Identify what it is that makes you passionate about your invention—that's what you'll love talking about. Your enthusiasm will not only be contagious, it will also energize you and fuel your drive to get your message out.

- **What others need from you.** What sort of useful information relevant to your invention can you provide to audiences? If you invented that grocery list app, perhaps you're a master at efficiency who can offer valuable information about other ways people can streamline their lives. Or perhaps you developed your app because you've got a smorgasbord of family-favorite budget recipes. In that case, you probably have lots of money-saving tips.

Combine the answers to these questions about your expertise, your passion, and the information that your audience needs and add this information to your message. For example, the message for my company, EMSI Public Relations, is, "At EMSI, we create visibility and credibility for our clients using a pay-for-performance model that guarantees media exposure and sets us apart from our peers."

YOUR WEBSITE

A website is a vital marketing tool for a number of reasons. It gives people a place to go to learn about you and your invention. They can find out about events you plan to attend and other projects you're working on, and ask you questions. And it's your shop—where you will sell your invention, whether you're selling to consumers or manufacturers. In either case, there's a lot riding on a website. It has to convey your professionalism and brand, communicate your message, engage visitors, and make it easy to convert them into customers. Every detail plays a role, from the logo to the text to the design and functionality. Your website should provide all the information people need to know, and make it easy for them to find that information. It should include testimonials and links to the newspaper articles and TV and radio interviews you've done, which shows that you're not only credible, but also that the world is interested in you and your creation.

If you're going to spend money, this is a good place to invest. Your website is that important. However, there are a number of services that provide the tools to design and publish your own small-business website for free. These services will often also host your site for free, or for a very low monthly fee. Just a few of the many good options available are Moonfruit.com, Weebly.com, Jimdo.com, and Yola.com. The other option—and I recommend this—is to hire a professional web designer and a web developer to do the work for you. Proceed with caution, though. To avoid a potentially expensive mistake, you must do the kind of research you'd do before making any big purchase, whether you're hiring a roofer or a lawyer, or buying a car.

A web designer is the person responsible for the look and feel of the site, how the user navigates it, and how the information is presented. A web developer writes the code that implements the designer's ideas.

Ideally, the person you hire will be both developer and designer, or a developer who works closely with a designer. When looking to hire someone, ask people you trust for recommendations. This helps narrow the field of candidates and provides a small degree of assurance that the person or company has performed well in the past. In addition, visit your candidate's website. Is it easy to navigate? Is the copy professionally written? Do the graphics and text convey a message about her? Do you like the look? If a candidate's website doesn't impress you, then move on. Explore the site for a portfolio of other sites she has designed, information about how long she has been in business and whether she has handled clients like you in the past, where she is located (if you prefer someone local), and testimonials (how old is the business?).

Talk to current and former clients. Ask how satisfied they were or are with the work provided? How's the customer service? Were deadlines met? Did your candidate meet, exceed, or fall below expectations?

Most importantly, know your goals. Before you interview a designer, have a clear idea of what you would like. A good professional will explain what you need and what she can do to get it. You may have goals that aren't within your candidate's purview. For instance, it is not the job of a web designer or developer to put you in the top Google search rankings; it is her job to provide you with right tools to achieve that goal.

PUBLICITY

By definition, publicity is not advertising; it's coverage by the media of people, events, and issues deemed to be of interest to audiences. Getting publicity may be one prong of your marketing plan, which might also include doing speaking engagements, gaining followers on social media, and, yes, buying advertising.

What can publicity do for you? A colleague of mine who is a former newspaper reporter has a story about a savvy attorney that may answer this question. He'd tip her off whenever he had a particularly juicy case, but only if she promised to include his name alongside that of his client in her story. He'd figured out that having his name in the paper bought him something no amount of advertising could: credibility. Whether he won the case or lost it, people remembered his name.

The endorsement of traditional media, even if it's simply mentioning your name, is marketing gold to anyone trying to sell an invention. Thanks to the Internet, the value of that gold is through the roof. Potential customers have more than ever from which to choose. They also have more scammers and con artists to worry about. What makes one product more trustworthy and appealing than another? The endorsement of TV and radio shows, newspapers and magazines, and now bloggers, news websites, and followers on social media, too.

When the media recognizes that you have something important to say, you gain credibility. When you have hundreds or thousands of people following you on Twitter, Facebook, or LinkedIn, you have a stamp of approval from the general public. Both forms of recognition give others confidence that you—and your invention—are as good as you claim.

But the return on investment usually isn't immediate, which can be frustrating to people who expect a surge in website visitors or sales with every media interview. That used to happen more often in the old days—way back in the 1990s—when a radio talk show host might chat with you for thirty minutes, and newspapers had twice as many pages to fill. Sometimes, when the timing of an interview aligned perfectly with an urgent public problem, the person's expertise, and her solution-oriented content, that person could hit the jackpot.

More often today, marketing through media exposure is a strategy that pays off over time—with effort from you. So, how do you grow your investment? You display your endorsements prominently on your website—"As seen on CBS," "featured in the *Louisville Gazette*," "heard on WTUT radio." Don't forget to mention your twelve thousand Twitter followers, and all those Facebook fans, too. You also attract visitors to your site by continually posting new, useful, and entertaining content, perhaps via a blog. Keep building contacts and allowing people to get to know you by interacting with them on Twitter, LinkedIn, and other social networking sites, and look for more opportunities to be an expert source for TV, radio, and print.

YOUR MEDIA PITCH

If you can get a journalist or talk show host interested in your invention or story idea, you might be interviewed for an article, asked to write an article for publication, or invited as a guest on a radio or TV show. A media pitch is your written communication to reporters, editors, bloggers, and TV and radio producers and talk show hosts, telling them what you have to offer their audiences. Depending on what your invention is, you might write a press release or short story in newspaper style describing it. Once again, this is not a sales piece. Avoid adjectives that make your pitch sound like a product review. Instead, remember your message. What's your expertise? What's your passion? What problem can you solve for people? Describe the problem and how your invention addresses it. You might include a testimonial or two, studies that demonstrate its effectiveness, and what sets you (and your invention) apart from the crowd.

Be objective, factual, and concise. You could also include bullet points highlighting other related information or tips on how readers can address the problem with or without your product. You may also pitch the media with a story or show segment ideas that are relevant to your expertise and not focused on your invention. This is the "celebritize" method I discussed at the beginning of the chapter, where you gain exposure as "Joe, that really smart guy who invented the barking mailbox," for example. With either approach, you'll have more success if you pay attention to timing and the news.

Timing

What are the seasons, holidays, national anniversaries or events that might be relevant to your invention or expertise? The media will be looking for fresh new ways to tell these recurring stories, and you might just hold the key. If you invented that collapsible coffeemaker I talked about earlier, you could send your pitches to the media in July, just before parents and college kids start serious off-to-college shopping. You could send out one pitch about the difficulties of trying to live in a tiny dorm and how your coffeemaker solves that problem. And you could follow up with a short pitch about your five best space-saving tips for dorm life. In the spring, you might offer up your camper-oriented pitches, and as summer approaches, address boaters.

News

Mass media, including trade publications (if you're hoping a company, manufacturer, or investor buys your invention), are focused on issues and events in the news today, so you're much more likely to get publicity if you can speak to something going on now. That's not as difficult as it sounds, but it does require creative thinking. If you've invented a foolproof new door lock, and home invasions are in the news, you might suggest an article or talk show segment about the safest doors, locks, and other home security measures. If you are the inventor of a device that helps expectant parents, you may also be the perfect person to talk about tricks for easing labor pains when a celebrity's pregnancy makes the headlines.

When you send your pitch, be sure your contact information is clearly visible and accurate. Don't weave it into your pitch, and don't rely on your recipient hitting the email reply button. Include a telephone number that you can answer at any time, or one for daytime and another for evenings and weekends. You may get just one call from an editor or producer interested in your pitch, and if you don't answer, she may very well lose interest.

Make sure your email is free of typos, grammatical errors, and other mistakes that make you appear less than authoritative. Never write a pitch and hit "send" without carefully re-reading it to be sure it's clean, makes sense, and is as concise as possible. If there's no urgent need to send it immediately, wait twenty-four hours, and then look it over again before sending it.

SOCIAL MEDIA

For many people, launching a personal social networking account on Facebook, Twitter, or Google+ and then firing off some posts is pretty basic stuff. Even the technologically challenged among us find that, with a little help getting started, it's not so difficult. But using social media to market your invention can be a lot like learning to play golf. The game appears simple: Put a ball on a tee and whack it towards a little hole. Then you discover all those pesky nuances you have to learn, like mulligans, handicaps, bogeys, and hooks. In social media marketing, if your goal is to develop followers, friends, and connections to promote yourself—and by default, your invention—there are some things you should do and others you should not.

With social media, like traditional media, the goal is always to give the listener, viewer, or reader content that is of value to her. With all the competition for the user's attention, if she can't quickly answer the question, "What's in it for me?" in one place, she'll head somewhere else. So, what should you do? You should provide content that is informative, useful, entertaining, and engaging. And avoid the five common mistakes a lot of people—even some social media veterans—make:

- **Over-posting.** People who send a flurry of tweets and status updates in brief bursts will get less response than those who measure out their posts over time. Posting once or twice a day, at different times of the day, allows people time to respond and doesn't overwhelm them. It's a marathon, remember, not a sprint.

- **Inconsistency.** Update your social media on a regular basis. If there's an event or news related to your topic, make sure to share or discuss it on a timely basis. If there's nothing going on in the news, don't allow your account to sit idle for long periods. Share a personal experience, an observation, or a photo. If you forget about your audience, they'll forget about you.

- **Lack of interaction.** When people comment on your post, ask a question, or take the initiative to share something with you, respond to them. Too often comments and compliments go unacknowledged and questions unanswered. If you spoke to someone at a party and he ignored you, would you walk away and find someone more courteous and engaging to talk to? Of course you would.

- **Forgetting to tie in your topic.** It's perfectly fine to share an anecdote, observation, or commentary that appeals to a broad audience, but don't forget to bring the post back to your message, if possible. If you invented that collapsible coffeemaker, for instance, you might share a funny comment about your family vacation, wrapping it up with, "Good thing I had my collapsible coffeemaker along! Our little hotel room didn't have room for anything! Much less five kids and a coffeemaker!"

- **Not sharing your mainstream media exposure.** If you're getting coverage in traditional media, share it! Let your social media followers know you have an upcoming TV or radio interview, tell them when and where to check it out, and share a link to it after it has aired. Post links to articles written about you. This not only increases your exposure, but also tells people you're a credible source of information and someone journalists trust.

If you do it right, you can use social networks to build your audience and drive traffic to your website. When you are posting, remember your audience's first question: "What's in it for me?" If the majority of the content you're sharing is pleas to "Visit my blog!" or "Check out my cool collapsible coffeemaker," the answer will be, "No thanks."

CONCLUSION

Public relations and sales are not the same thing. A sale is what happens when you convert prospective customers into buyers. PR is about developing relationships and gaining the visibility that brings you those prospective customers. Depending on how much you're willing to spend on professional help, a lot of that work may be up to you. And it requires the same creativity, persistence, and focus you put into conceiving and developing your invention. But it doesn't have to be drudgery. Becoming a media "celebrity" is a lot of fun. It's gratifying to help people solve their problems, it feels good to be recognized as an authority, and the relationships you develop can be deep and meaningful.

To be successful, remember these critical elements:

- **Create a great website.** Your website is not only your "store," it's your face in the world. Definitely not a place to skimp! It is where you convert prospective customers into buyers, so make sure it provides them with all the information they need in a way that's easy to navigate—and easy to make a purchase. Make sure it appeals to everyone in your audience.

- **Know your audience.** If you're appealing to manufacturers or investors, your audience is not just those who manufacture or invest, it's also the people who consume products and inhabit the market. Think about everyone who has a stake in your invention, identify their problems, and tell them how you can solve their problems. That way, you will reach your target audience—and those who have their ears.

- **Give the media what they want.** Be creative about tying into seasons, news, and anything timely or topical. The media are hungry for fresh angles, sources, and great information. If you move quickly, you can be the person who fulfills these needs.

- **Share your publicity on your website.** Links to radio and TV interviews and mentions in print publications give you credibility. The implied third-party endorsement by journalists and talk show hosts is marketing gold. It makes you stand apart from the competition, and tells visitors, "This is someone the media go to for information. She must be trustworthy and knowledgeable."

Remember, the subjects discussed in this chapter make up only one prong of your marketing campaign. Speaking to groups is another. If your invention solves a problem or captures the imagination, and you expose it through the use of PR, you'll be successful.

ONE BIG IDEA

Kitty litter was invented by Edward Lowe in Michigan in 1947, when a neighbor came to Lowe's home to ask him for some sand to use as litter for her cat. Lowe made his product available to the public in 1948, eventually creating the Tidy Cat brand in 1964.

13. Direct Response Television

Gil R. Tatarsky

"**B**ut wait, there's more," "Set it and forget it," "Call in the next ten minutes and we'll double your offer!" We have all heard these sayings on infomercials while watching late night television. We see so many of them that we think it must be easy, and that everyone is cashing in. The truth is that only about one in twenty infomercials tested, including long-form (thirty minutes) and short-form (one to two minutes), actually roll out and become market successes. The other nineteen products die on arrival, never to see the airways again after the initial media testing. So, if you wish to sell your product on TV, you have a 5-percent chance of being successful. With such small odds, why do people do it? They do it because it may lead to selling millions of units and being in every retail store across the country, if the product happens to be the previously mentioned one in twenty. Also, the glitz and glamour of seeing a product marketed on TV is very appealing.

Gil R. Tatarsky has a wide range of business experience, from developing raw ideas into market opportunities to working with multibillion-dollar global companies. Since 2001, he has been actively involved in the direct response television industry through the creation, introduction, and marketing of several products. Gil formed Distinct Creations in 2011 to help inventors get their ideas to market by structuring licensing deals between inventors and direct marketers. Gil is a CPA and a graduate of SUNY Albany's Business School.

gil.tatarsky@verizon.net • www.yourideastolife.com

There are several ways to market your product on TV. They include a typical thirty-minute infomercial, a one- to two-minute spot campaign that primes your product for mass retail distribution, and a segment on a home shopping program (QVC, HSN, ShopNBC, among others). I have experience in all of these areas, and I am going to share my knowledge and experiences to help you market your product on television. There are basically two methods of going about it—do it yourself (DIY) or license your product to a TV marketing company. I have experience in both, which I will share with you. I am also going to discuss what criteria make for a successful television product, as well as some general information about the TV marketing industry.

ORIGINS

It all started with pitchmen like Ron Popeil. These people would go to county fairs, boardwalks, and tradeshows with products to sell directly to consumers, doing the same pitch over and over again to different crowds. This would involve a long day's work to sell to a few hundred people. It was a good day's pay, but how about if you could reach millions of people with only one pitch by recording it, editing it, and then broadcasting it? You would reduce your investment (because you wouldn't have to give the pitch more than once) and increase your return (because you could pitch to millions of people at once). This method was made possible in the mid 1980s as part of television deregulation enacted by President Ronald Reagan. All the cable channels needed to fill their programming with something during those late night hours, and people who were up watching TV were more easily sold on new products. Today, infomercial marketing has become common throughout the day because consumers see the value in buying products they see on TV.

Some of the most successful infomercials of the past thirty years include Sweatin' to the Oldies, Ginsu knives, Blublocker sunglasses, Topsy Tail, George Foreman Grill, Tae Bo, ShamWow, Snuggie, and Oxi-Clean. Product categories that haven proved themselves good for TV marketing include kitchen gadgets, pet products, tools, fitness programs, and toys.

LICENSING VS DIY

I am a big supporter of licensing, especially for the novice inventor who doesn't have experience in television marketing. You may ask, "Why should I license my product instead of marketing it on television on my own?" The answer is very simple. Venturing into any business is quite risky. It is hard to achieve success, but trying to handle direct response television, or DRTV, on your own makes it even harder. Because a product must fit into a very narrow profile on TV, the failure rate is much higher than traditional retail. This makes the experience needed to find a hit that much more important and valuable.

Television marketing involves producing a product, producing a commercial, performing a media test of the commercial, and seeing if you have a winner. As an inventor doing it yourself, you may not know these steps or how to maximize them, and it could end up costing hundreds of thousands of dollars to produce and manage a TV campaign, which, in the end, has a 95-percent chance of failure.

When you license your product to a TV marketing company, the odds increase in your favor. By using experienced people, you increase your chances because you benefit from their years of experience. In essence, by licensing your product, you are doing the following:

- **Increasing your chance of success.** These are the experts with deep pockets and long track records of success. They have all the money and human resources to make your invention a hit.

- **Limiting your investment and risk.** Once you license your product, you don't have to do anything else besides collect a check. You don't need to keep investing time and money while exposing yourself to a high level of risk.

- **Making sure you get paid first.** If you license your product, you get paid first, and on sales not profits. So, the project doesn't have to be extremely profitable for you to make money. If you DIY, you are the last one to get paid, after all your vendors and investors.

The DRTV market has grown significantly over the last few years, and there has been no shortage of vendors willing to sell their services to DIY inventors, but they offer only individual parts of the whole process. As you look into launching your invention on DRTV, be sure you understand each part of the process, and find the right vendors to meet your needs. Of course, you may instead license your product and partner with a DRTV marketer who knows the business and has the capital to increase your chance of success.

I also recommend getting a licensing agent to help you to obtain a licensing deal. The benefits of having a good licensing agent to help find and negotiate a licensing deal for you are many. They provide one-stop shopping. They can match you with the best marketer for you and your product. They can get your product in front of a large network of marketers, allowing you to find the best deal. They are familiar with how a deal works and what a good deal is. They can help you negotiate the right deal for your product. They are familiar with licensing contracts and can help make sure the agreement is fair, and they will protect your interests.

Since licensing agents bring marketers a lot of products and not just yours, you will receive favorable treatment from marketers and encounter fewer problems, as these marketers are used to managing relationships.

CRITERIA

Before deciding to sell your product on television, you need to determine if it meets certain criteria for a successful TV product. A good product for television is unique, demonstrates well, solves a common problem, is easy to use, and appeals to a mass audience. Remember, niche products are difficult to sell on TV because they make it difficult to target the media.

An appropriate invention for TV should appeal to women between the ages of thirty-five and fifty, or even older. (At a minimum it should not exclude this group or be something a woman would buy for a man.) A good TV product has an average retail markup with enough of a margin to make a profit after production and media costs. Usually the suggested selling price is five to ten times the cost of the product. So, if a product costs five dollars to make, you may sell it for twenty to fifty dollars. If the product appears on a thirty-minute infomercial, it should sell for closer to ten times cost. If it is shown in a two-minute spot, it should sell for closer to five times cost.

You should have a prototype of your product to demonstrate how it works. Preventative devices, such as fire extinguishers and burglar alarms, do not work well on TV. Your product should fix a problem, not prevent one from happening.

The SciMark Seven

A good weekly round-up of new DRTV products and analysis of what's working and what's not may be found at the SciMark Report (www.sci-mark.blogspot.com). This website features what it calls "The SciMark Seven," which refers to the seven aspects that make a successful product on television.

The first three aspects deal with the product. The product must be:

- **Needed.** Is the product needed enough to generate an impulse to buy? For example, does it solve a problem?

- **Targeted.** Is the product designed for a big enough buying group? Is that buying group known to be DRTV-responsive?

- **Different.** Is the product different enough to get people's attention or change the fate of an established product?

The next aspect deals with the category of the product, which should be:

- **Uncrowded.** Will the category be relatively free of competition? Or is it already dominated by big brands with big ad budgets and a few decades of consumer loyalty behind them?

Finally, the remaining aspects refer to the commercial itself, which must be:

- **Engaging.** Does the commercial grab the audience's attention and hold it throughout? Specifically, does it have the right opening, pacing, and demos?

- **Motivating.** Does the commercial feature an offer that will motivate people to pick up the phone? Specifically, does it display an attractive value comparison, price, bonus, and guarantee?

- **Clear.** Does the commercial communicate clearly? Or is it confusing, raising questions or objections that are left unanswered?

These are the major elements to remember, but the success of your product will ultimately hinge on the consumer—if they like your product and see its value, they will buy it.

SHOPPING FROM HOME

Home shopping started in the early 1980s. A Tampa radio station owned by Roy Speer was owed money by an advertiser. The advertiser didn't have the money, but could barter with the station for can openers to satisfy the obligation. Bud Paxson, the general manager of the station, sold the can openers at a special low price to his local audience in an effort to get rid of the product. The can openers sold out, and home shopping was born.

Paxson thought that other products might sell on the radio, so he tried selling other items and experienced the same results. He then realized that this might work on TV, where you can actually demonstrate products live while people watch. This was first done on a local show in Florida, and people would have to go pick up their purchases at a warehouse. Then the home shopping show started to broadcast in other cities.

Shortly after the Home Shopping Network (HSN) came to be, Joe Segel (the entrepreneur who started the Franklin Mint) formed a new shopping network called QVC which stands for "Quality, Value, and Convenience." QVC is now the biggest DRTV network and generates almost twice as much as HSN in revenues per year. It is designed for a more upscale audience.

As I mentioned earlier, along with airing segments on home shopping programs, other effective DRTV marketing approaches include infomercials and spot campaigns. I would like to share some helpful information on each of these strategies now.

Getting on a Home Shopping Program

As I am most familiar with QVC, I will focus on it here; but the following advice may be applied to any other home shopping channel. The biggest advantage of marketing your product on QVC is that it has a built-in audience of loyal customers that have purchased many items from the channel. This differs significantly from an infomercial or spot campaign in which you are fishing for sales from a market of people watching TV, but not necessarily interested in buying anything at that time.

In business, it is not what you know but who you know, so the best way to get on QVC is to know someone there, especially one of the buyers. There are several other ways you can get your product on QVC, though. QVC usually runs a best product search event around the United States. You can sign up to attend in a city near you to present your product to the buyers. Similarly, the channel has a web program called *QVC Sprouts* for new products. You can find out more on their website www.qvc.com. You may contact a manufacturer's representative who already deals with QVC. Make sure you check out the reputation of the rep before making any commitments. A rep will usually charge between 5 and 15 percent.

If you have a successful infomercial, it is easier to get on QVC, as the buyers realize that there is a correlation between a successful infomercial product and a home shopping product.

There is a vendor manual that explains each step in the process. The process for getting your product on QVC generally begins with you presenting your product to a buyer via a video demonstration, if possible. If he is interested, the next step might be to come to his office and present the product in person. Thanks to today's technology, this step may be taken by phone or via Skype.

You would next provide a sample to the buyer. If he likes the sample, he will discuss pricing. Usually, QVC takes 50 percent of the retail price, so if it sells a product for twenty dollars, it will pay you ten dollars per unit sold. You will then be asked to sign up for the QVC vendor program. If you are using a rep, he should have an account with QVC and would be the "vendor of record." QVC will then ask for samples to put through its quality assurance, or QA, review. It will test your product's functionality, and check your instructions for accuracy and safety among other things. In other words, it will make sure what you deliver is packaged, produced, and presented to the consumer properly. If there is one little problem, it will be rejected and you will need to fix the problem and resubmit the product for approval.

QVC will then issue a purchase order, or PO, with the amount of units, expected delivery date, and price. Typically, it will be looking to sell between $30,000 and $75,000 worth of merchandise on the first airing, so the price it pays you will be about half that, as mentioned. The product is then presented to the planning department, where the timing will be solidified. Of course, QVC will not put your product on air unless it has been shipped and logged into its warehouse. QVC will then assign you an on-air date and time. If you are not using a rep, you will need to be there to present on air, so make arrangements as far ahead of time as you can. QVC also has on-air training courses that you will need to attend. If you use a rep, he will probably handle the airing and presentation. Make sure he knows everything about your product and previews a mock-presentation before letting QVC present your product on television. The good thing about being on air is that you can see the sales results live while sitting in the green room. If you sell out, the buyer will invite you back to sell again. If not, you will get your unsold merchandise back. QVC will usually cut you a check within sixty to ninety days of airing.

Buyers are important people at QVC, and they will be your key contact, so make sure you treat them with respect. It's hard to get on QVC and stay on QVC. Once you are on one shopping network, you can't be on another.

Preparing Infomercials

When people refer to the term "infomercial," they are really referring to the thirty-minute program whose goal is to tell a story about a product and sell that product. This is also called a long-form commercial. A one- or two-minute commercial selling a product is called a "spot," or a short-form commercial.

Products that cost more money and require more time to sell are sold on infomercials in the thirty-minute format. Within this time frame, you need to tell a great story, keep people entertained so they keep watching, create an emotional appeal, and motivate and inspire people to buy your product. It typically costs anywhere from $150,000 to north of $500,000 to produce an infomercial. It is used to sell high-priced products so you can get a higher return on your investment. The goal in an infomercial is to stay on TV and make money that way. By saying that your product is not available in stores, you are keeping demand up and improving your ability to sell on TV. A spot campaign is completely different, whereby you are usually losing money on TV or breaking even, with the idea of driving retail sales with this "free" advertising. You have to have retail distribution to capitalize on a spot campaign. Without it you will lose a lot of money. A short-form initial testing could cost you $50,000 to $100,000 for the production of the commercial, production of the product, and media testing.

As mentioned, with an infomercial you do not have a customer base of people who have bought from you before. You are entering the mass market to find people who are willing to buy your product. This process is a lot more expensive than having a loyal customer base, as with QVC.

A thirty-minute infomercial is usually divided into three segments of ten minutes each, which contain the same message, call to action, and closing.

Required Elements

A successful infomercial requires certain elements, some of which are complex, which is why I don't recommend the DIY route. The first element is product development, including establishment of intellectual properties (i.e., patent and trademark). This also includes designing and developing packaging for TV and retail. You must also determine the unique selling features of the product and develop a project budget to make sure you have enough money for the entire infomercial campaign. As mentioned, the most common reason for failure is insufficient capital.

A very important element is the selection of a production company to shoot, edit, and produce the infomercial. In order to have a successful show, you will most likely need good testimonials. If you don't have them already, you can hire a company that performs testimonial trials.

You must also coordinate a review of your product and its marketing claims by FTC legal counsel. In some cases you will need to have the FDA review your product as well, such as with supplements. There must be media testing and evaluation. The main determining factor is the media efficiency ratio, or MER, which refers to sales generated per media dollar spent. Then you need to determine breakeven, which shows all costs and compares them to all your expenses. Media could cost you 50 percent or more of revenues generated.

You must also handle manufacturing for the test and, if successful, for the roll-out. You may have to tweak the show to increase its performance, or for a national media roll-out. There will be ongoing development of media scheduling and evaluation of media results. You may need to develop premiums (giveaways) for the campaign.

Of course, you will require a website to capture Internet sales. As much as 50 percent of your sales could come from the Internet, so you need to have a strong web presence. In terms of sales, the selection of your inbound order call center and the training of your sales agents are both vital.

Make sure to keep these important elements in mind as you attempt to launch your infomercial campaign through its testing phase. Addressing each issue will help give you an idea of the complexities and challenges in setting up and launching a TV campaign. Again, the complex considerations recently listed are the reasons I recommend the licensing route.

Preparing Spot Campaigns

As previously described, the spot campaign is a format of one to two minutes in length. It is geared towards identifying a problem, helping the audience to identify with that problem, and then showing that your product is the best solution at the best price. The goal of a spot is to drive at least $5 million to $10 million in media exposure at breakeven, which will provide the exposure necessary to drive retail sales. All major retailers have an "As Seen on TV" section dedicated to these products.

If you are going to do a short-form campaign, it is critical that you have a retail partner to capitalize on this advertising to drive retail sales. It would be a big mistake to go into a spot campaign without having a retail distribution partner. You can go to YouTube and search for nearly any two-minute spot. I recommend watching spots for products such as Snuggie, Ped Egg, Pedipaws, Wax Vac, Instahang, Pajama Jeans, and Perfect Tortilla.

DRTV SUPPORT TEAM

If you are going to go the DIY route, the good part about the DRTV business is that there are vendors out there that handle each component of the business—from producing the commercial, to running the media, to taking orders and shipping product. You can leverage the success of these companies to build your business. You also need to make sure you use the right companies. The Electronic Retailers Association (www.retailing.org) puts out an annual buyers' guide called *The Gold Book* that includes the names of relevant companies and their contact info. It should help you find the right companies. If you come across a company that interests you, research that company on the Internet and ask for three references from its clients before hiring it for your project. When looking for companies with which to build your support team, the main categories necessary are:

- **Production.** A company to produce the commercial.

- **Media.** A company to buy media for your campaign.

- **Financing.** A company to provide funding for a successfully tested infomercial. You will require funding because you will need to pre-pay for media before the infomercial runs and generates sales (i.e., cash flow).

- **Telemarketing.** A company to take incoming orders.

- **Web.** A company to design the website and manage the website order process.

- **Merchant accounts.** A company to set up credit card payments from the customer.

- **Fulfillment.** A company to process, pack, and ship incoming orders.

CONCLUSION

I hope this information is helpful to you as you endeavor to find success in the TV marketing business. As mentioned, it is a very tough business, and you should take advantage of all the help you can find. I especially recommend taking the licensing route and finding a good licensing agent to help you. Best of luck.

14. Trade Shows

Deb Hess

In real estate, the three most important words are location, location, location. In new product development, they are networking, networking, networking. And what better place is there to network with people in the industry than a trade show? Trade shows give you direct access to individuals who can help you determine if there is a market for your invention. Even in this internet-driven, social media world, it is still important to build strong business relationships through face-to-face human contact.

If participating in a trade show is part of your marketing plan, you need to prepare yourself to meet your marketing objectives. Why attend? Because it is a great place to meet people in the industry, see what is selling, receive inspiration, find out what's new, and determine if you have market-ready products. You may even take orders for your new product at a trade show.

So, should you attend a trade show, or even exhibit at one with your latest product?

It depends. I am willing to bet that as an aspiring inventor you have heard the same short answer to a number of your questions about the

Deb Hess is the acting Program Director of the Minnesota Inventors Congress (MIC). She uses her marketing and management experience to teach inventors how to develop marketable products. Deb has been involved in the coordination of the MIC Inventing Success Workshops for thirty years. She is a certified trainer, coach, and facilitator, fostering the creative and innovative spirit of entrepreneurs.

deb@minnesotainventorscongress.org • www.minnesotainventorscongress.org

product development process. But it really does depend in this case. It depends on what your reason is for attending the event. If you don't know why you will be attending, how will you know if you've accomplished your goal?

It depends on where you are in the product development process, and on the purpose of the show. It depends on whether you are in the process. Perhaps you are just starting the process and really don't know if there is a market for your product, or maybe you are further along down the road and have market-ready products and can fill orders. It also depends on your financial resources.

Let's look at a few of the reasons behind when you should attend a trade show, either as an attendee or an exhibitor.

WHEN TO ATTEND

When do you participate in an industry trade show as an attendee? I believe it's when you're at the stage where you want to identify companies that produce similar products, see what is new in the industry, attend educational seminars, and network. Be cautious of how much time you spend with vendors. Respectfully use their time wisely. Have your questions in mind, take notes, and ask if you can follow up with vendors after the event.

When do you test market your product at an inventors' trade show? There are events hosted by inventors' groups across the country that provide the opportunity for you to test market your idea. They can give you a chance to gain new information about what it really means to showcase your idea. You should test your product at one of these events when you want to polish your pitch and receive feedback on your product from attendees and other inventors. You may connect with people who can introduce you to the right person to take your product to the next level.

When do you participate in an industry-specific trade show with your market-ready product? According to my research, the best answer I can give you is, "When you are ready to fill orders." Industry-specific trade shows can be very expensive. The majority of attendees at these shows are buyers. They are there to place orders for their businesses and are under the assumption that everything in the exhibit hall is ready to be shipped to their stores. Aspiring inventors have set up booths at these events and have had some successes. But the reality is that they are exceptions, not the rule. That is why it is so important for you to make sure you are making the best business decisions, for you and your advisors, about participating as an exhibitor at a show. What works for one inventor may not work for another. You want to be taking calculated risks as you develop your idea. Ask yourself if this is the best format for you and your product.

When you begin to gather advice, you will learn that there are differing opinions on every topic and exceptions to every rule. One exception is when an inventor doesn't have market-ready products, but decides to register for an industry trade show and exhibit in a special section on the show floor for new products. The reason this exception makes sense is that the stage is set for the attendees to understand that this section is different from other areas on the show floor. What a great way to connect with the people in your industry!

TRADE SHOW TASKS

Once you have determined that a trade show is a good match for you, there are many tasks you need to complete. At this point you will want to create a spreadsheet that includes all the decision-making tasks relevant to each event. This list will help you develop your budget. Be sure to add a few extra dollars to the bottom line for unknowns, which always pop up.

The first few lines on top of the spreadsheet should list the name of the event, where it is being held (city and state), the event facility, and the hours of the event, including set-up time. Break your task list into seven categories: registration, booth, marketing, preparation, accommodations, shipping, and wrap-up. Then add a column down the left side of the page for each of the line items listed below each category. Your list should include a row for your timeline, one for who is responsible for completing each task, one for checking off the completed task, and one for how much money you have budgeted for the task. Place a separate row for additional notes.

Registration

Make sure you read the registration materials. Then read them again! Go online and search through the event organizer's website and learn everything you can about the event to make sure it is a good match for your goals. Don't be afraid to contact the event organizer. Her goal and yours should be to make the experience a very worthwhile venture. Minimize your challenges by taking time to ask questions.

Be sure you gather all the information you need before you begin filling out the registration form. If your product is market-ready, find out if you can sell from your booth. Complete the registration form and make a copy for your records. Keep track of your expenses. If possible, select your location on the show floor. Make your deposit or pay the required fees and submit the additional forms required by the event planners. Be sure to take advantage of the early bird rate, if one is offered. Make any additional payments by their due dates.

Booth

Your booth should be appealing to the eye and designed to draw people into your space. Make a mental note to keep it neat and organized. Consider setting it up in a way that invites people into your space instead of blocking the entry with a table. Many exhibitors turn their tables and move them to the side to make them open and personal. Do you know where your booth will be located on the show floor? Find out if you have the option of choosing a location on the show floor that takes advantage of the flow of traffic.

Find out the size of the space. Know what comes with the booth and what you might be required to rent from the host or facility. Does the trade show provide a table? If it does, then what size is it? What table covering would be appropriate? Does the show provide chairs? If it does, then how many? Is electricity included in the booth cost? Find out what the floor is made out of because standing on a concrete floor all day can be challenging. You might want to purchase a pad to make things easier on your feet. Do you need additional space? Do you or your staff have special needs?

As you begin the design phase of your booth, make sure you keep in mind future events you may attend. So many inventors have told me that they invested a great deal of money on a trade show display unit for a specific event, only to learn that it did not fit in many of the booths they were in after that initial one. They then had to spend more money to adapt the booth appropriately.

Do you have a trade show display unit designed for your target market—the audience you are hoping to attract? What equipment will you need in your booth? Will you need a laptop, WiFi, PowerPoint projector, television, or lighting? Will you need to register for electricity to power the equipment? Do you have the right length of extension cords?

Have you put together a mini office supply container and toolkit? Include items like pens, scratch paper, tape, packing tape, duct tape, extra flash drives, hooks, string, scissors, stapler, screwdriver, wrench, and other tools needed for your equipment? Also, are there spare parts you might need to have on hand for your product?

Identify the signs you need for your booth. When having a sign made for your booth, be sure to consider other uses for the sign. If you create an eight-foot sign to fit in a ten-foot booth and the next show you attend has an eight-foot booth, your sign might not look right in that space. Make your sign eye-catching and include your product name and what you are offering. Be concise. Have at least one form of contact on the sign, preferably your website or phone number.

Marketing

Each vendor at a trade show has to work very hard to draw people into its space. Before the event, you should make every effort to let your target market know that you will be there, and why you want everybody to stop by to see you. Create a "buzz" that will make your target audience want to be there. Once you get these individuals in your booth, what will you do to meet their needs? What materials will you have in hand to answer their questions? Have you notified the media that you will be there?

Trade shows provide a great opportunity to conduct a survey. Consider having one for the people who stop at your booth. Include a section for their contact information, which will help you build your database. Limit it to five to seven simple questions, such as:

- Do you currently own or use products that are similar or competitive to the invention?

- How would you compare this product to similar or competitive products?

- Does this invention solve a problem you've experienced?

- Would you buy one today?

- Compared to similar products, what would you consider paying for this one?

- Do you have any safety concerns regarding this product?

Create questions that will help you address your unmet market needs. Your literature should include a one-page document that includes the product name, a sentence that explains the benefits of the product, the product's features and benefits, testimonials (if you have any), a photo or two, and contact information. If your goal is business-to-business contact, explain that you are looking for manufacturers or interested in licensing your intellectual property. If you are connecting directly to the end user of the product, offer a show special and be sure to include a way for your customer to order the product after the show.

What kind of pre-show marketing are you planning? Make sure it reaches your target market. Have you designed your media kit? Is it available on your website? Do you have the appropriate marketing materials, literature racks, and order forms? Are you hosting a drawing or awarding door prizes? Have you made the ballots and signs for the drawing? Do you have an attractive container for the ballots? Are you giving away any items in your booth? Be sure to order enough items for the length of the show.

Is there an option to advertise in the show guide? Do you know the criteria for submitting an ad? What is the deadline for submission of artwork? Have you developed a lead form to follow up after the event? Include on the form a place for names and contact information, and describe why you will be following up with them. If you will be taking orders, be sure you have plenty of order forms on hand. Be sure to add an item on your list to thank your sponsors, if appropriate.

Presentation Preparations

Presentation is important. Whether they are manufacturers, product scouts, competition judges, or members of the general public, trade show attendees want to feel as though you are well informed and excited about your invention. Write down your story, and tell it well and with enthusiasm. Design a welcoming space to bring people into your inner circle. Make a good impression. I have read that 88 percent of a viewer's memory of your booth is based on how you behaved in the interaction. Be prepared to exchange contact information, discuss your invention's advantages compared to the competition, explain its importance to the market, and answer questions.

Dress in a manner that appropriately complements your invention, and dress the booth with fitting accessories. For example, if you have a hunting product, wear camouflage and add outdoor features to enhance the atmosphere you are trying to create. Prepare yourself for the show. How would you feel if you walked up to a booth and someone was sitting in a chair making you feel like you just interrupted her nap? Make sure you do not give that impression at your booth. Are you prepared to stand for hours on end? Stand in a comfortable position so you can greet everyone who enters your space with a smile on your face. Trade show days can be very exhausting. You want to maximize your energy. Learn how to stand, and rotate your balance from one foot to the other. Learn how to move from one side of the booth to the other and change your stance without looking nervous.

How would you feel if the person was too busy eating her lunch or talking on her cell phone? Same goes for you. No food, no cell phones, no newspapers. Take a few minutes and move away from your booth, but work very hard not to leave your booth empty at any time. How would you feel if no one was there to greet you at a booth? Not good, right? If you have no other choice but to leave your booth unattended, leave a note that says you had to step away momentarily and will return shortly. If possible, have at least two well-informed people at your booth at all times. Three is best, as this number would allow you to schedule time for each person to participate in the show, attend education classes, and take breaks. Create a schedule for the show hours.

You want one person to be the demonstrator that will showcase the invention. A separate individual should be the salesperson that meets and greets, distributes literature, and, when appropriate, points out the benefits and features of the product. Friendly, well-informed personnel in the booth are essential. Make sure you select the right people with the right personalities to help you accomplish your goals.

Write and practice your pitch, or what is known as your "elevator speech." It should clearly describe the benefits of your product in one sentence. Make sure you craft your pitch so it is clearly meant for the people who will be stopping by your booth. You may write your pitch differently depending on whether you are talking to a manufacturer or the consumer of your product. A manufacturer will want to know how your product will make her money; the end user will want to know how your product will help fulfill a want or need she may have. I can't say it enough: Make sure your pitch is designed for your target market. Rehearse your pitch out loud. Stand in front of a mirror and practice it as though you are talking to an audience. Be sure to change your tone and inflection to keep the audience's attention. Practice your pitch, and then practice some more. Practice makes perfect.

Be there when the doors open up and when the event closes. It isn't fair to the attendees who pay to participate in the show to see your empty booth space. Learn how to be assertive and move people along by asking direct questions about their needs, and commit to getting back to them after the event. Write down everything you've agreed to do, so you can follow up properly.

Accommodations

When you are preparing your budget, don't forget about all the travel arrangements required for you and your staff. Be sure you have confirmed reservations for lodging. Identify all the transportation needs for each member of your staff, such as airplane, rental car, taxi, shuttle service, or personal vehicle. What meals not covered by the registration fee will you need to include in your budget? Finally, will there be any special needs to address?

Shipping

If you need to ship your booth display, products, and resource materials ahead of time, be sure to review the event organizer's policies about shipping, handling, and storage carefully. There are some facilities that have very strict policies about how materials are handled within their walls. The event organizer should provide this information in the registration material.

Select an appropriate carrier if you need to ship materials to the event. Determine your pick-up date. Make sure you have a box on your spreadsheet to mark with a check once the event organizer has received your shipment. If anything needs to be returned after the event, be sure to note your required date of return as well. Print any appropriate labels and complete all the necessary forms.

Wrap-up

Don't skip this important step! Evaluate your experience at the event shortly after you return home. The return on investment for participating in a trade show should be carefully analyzed soon after the event to help you determine the pros and cons of participating in that show. Make sure you ask the tough questions about why you attended and whether you accomplished your goals, and keep good notes. Schedule a time to visit with the people who were with you in the booth to review the successes and challenges of the show. Write down recommendations for future use. Send hand-written thank you notes to those who helped make the event possible and to anyone else you wish to acknowledge for the show's success. Make your list as long as possible.

Complete the event planner's evaluation form. The feedback received by event planners is essential to the success of future events. It is how they take a step back to see what they can do differently to improve outcomes for exhibitors. It is also how they learn what they are doing right for their clients.

Lastly, ask yourself these questions: Have all the orders been processed? Who is responsible for verifying the leads and following up on them? Is there any other correspondence you need to address?

CONCLUSION

Being prepared is the best gift you can give yourself. Not every trade show will require every item on your checklist, so you should adapt it to meet your needs. Attend trade shows that clearly meet your marketing needs. In doing so, you will know are spending your time and money wisely.

In closing, the best advice I can give anyone who chooses to participate in a trade show is this: The passion you have for your idea is critical to its success, but you have to make sure you are balancing that passion with objectivity. In other words, don't let your enthusiasm overpower common sense. Don't let your fear, greed, or ego get in the way of good business decisions.

15. How I Did It

Maureen Howard

Before I tell you how I did it, I would like to explain why I did it. Most things are created or invented to meet a need or solve a problem. My story is no different. I had a problem that I needed to solve. At about three months old, my baby stopped sleeping for long stretches because he could no longer be swaddled. He would kick and squirm out of the swaddle, which would wake him up and leave him in his crib with a loose blanket, which I knew was not safe. I, too, stopped sleeping for long stretches, as I had to hold and rock my baby throughout the night and day. We were both constantly tired. I also felt like a failure as a mom because my baby was tired and unhappy, and not getting the sleep he needed to grow and develop properly.

Desperate to fix the situation, I read a lot of books on the subject, and tried many products and techniques designed to help, but nothing worked. What I noticed, however, was that my baby slept well in his

Maureen Howard is a wife, mother of four, and pediatric physical therapist. Maureen's educational background includes a BA in Biology from the University of Delaware. After completing her bachelor's degree, Maureen accepted an invitation to attend Temple University's College of Allied Health Professionals and earned a Master of Physical Therapy degree. She has worked at the renowned Children's Hospital of Philadelphia and Children's Seashore House.

After the birth of her first son, Maureen began experimenting with methods to improve the quality and duration of his sleep, which led her to invent the Magic Sleepsuit and start her own company.

info@magicsleepsuit.com • www.magicsleepsuit.com

stroller when bundled in layers of clothing. After our walks in the stroller, I would roll him into the house and leave him in his stroller in the living room, where he would sleep for hours. This was great, but I knew it was not a good permanent solution. He was not learning how to sleep on his own, and I wanted him in his crib and on his back, with no loose blankets. I tried to think of ways I could duplicate the feeling of coziness and security for my baby. I used my instincts as a mom, and my education and training as a pediatric physical therapist, to start experimenting with sleepers that would provide it. It took some time, but after a number of tries I created a sleeper that had some fabric weight (layers), which would provide the cozy and secure feeling my son needed. I also designed it with features such as a scoop neckline to keep the fabric away from his face, two zippers to make it easier for diaper changes, and I also left the feet exposed so that my baby would get some additional ventilation and heat dissipation, so he would not overheat in the sleeper.

To my great joy, my baby loved his sleeper and would nap two to three times a day for up to two hours at a time. He would also sleep eight hours or more at a stretch at night. My husband and I were thrilled because we were better rested and our baby was much happier when awake. My husband and I used to say, "It's magic!" Hence, we ultimately called the sleeper the "Magic Sleepsuit." By about ten months of age, my baby's startle reflex had diminished and was not waking him as often. He had also learned how to sleep on his own in his crib and self-soothe back to sleep if woken, so I knew it was time to transition him out of the Magic Sleepsuit. To my great relief, he continued to sleep well. I found that he had learned how to sleep soundly on his own, which was really my ultimate goal.

I put the sleeper in the closet and forgot about it until my second child was born and started having the same sleep problems. So, I pulled out the Magic Sleepsuit and tried it again. To my great surprise and relief, my daughter experienced the same great results as my son. I then really started to think that I had created something unique and effective. I also felt compelled to share this belief with others. I made a few more Magic Sleepsuits and started sharing them with friends and relatives. When they began to tell me that their babies loved the Magic Sleepsuit, I became convinced that I had created a truly special product. I decided to look into starting a business selling the Magic Sleepsuit, and my journey began.

After my initial decision to create a business, it took several more years to launch a market-ready product. It was a much more difficult and time-consuming process than I had ever imagined, but it was also more rewarding than I had ever imagined. Today, tens of thousands of babies and their parents enjoy longer or more restful sleep because of the Magic Sleepsuit.

Now that you know why I did it, I will explain how I did it, covering the steps I took to develop my product and business into successes.

BUSINESS PLAN

After deciding to start a business, I first wrote a business plan. Having no business background or education in business, however, I needed help. So, I decided to take small business startup courses offered at a local university. Thanks to these courses and some basic mentoring from my instructors, I was soon able to write a comprehensive business plan and start my own business. The plan gave me direction and served as a guide throughout the process of creating my business. The plan I ultimately wrote included a detailed product description and a detailed business description. It listed the business's objectives and goals, and outlined a business strategy. It contained information regarding the baby sleepwear industry, pricing, costs, financial feasibility, market analysis and sales strategy, target market, market size, and competition.

It also dealt with product safety regulations, consumer product safety standards, international standards, industry trade associations, testing, and manufacturing. Finally, it included the résumés of the management team, a conclusion, and possible recommendations.

I certainly did not have all the answers, but my business plan allowed me to focus on the most important aspects of the endeavor, including my business's goals, market, product, and competition. Moreover, it allowed me the opportunity to demonstrate the focus, strategy, and financial feasibility of my business to investors, if necessary. Since then, my business plan has been revised and updated a number of times, forcing me to maneuver and change as the business has grown.

PATENT AND TRADEMARK

Once I had my business plan in place, I knew that I needed to protect my idea before I took it to market. At first, I researched the market to see what similar products were already being sold. I found a lot of sleep aids, books, and other products, but I saw nothing quite like the Magic Sleepsuit. My research furthered my belief that I had a unique product, and that there was clearly a need in the market for it that was not being met. I also learned that there was a very large market for my product.

At the time of my research, more than 4 million live births occurred each year in the United States alone. Not all babies have sleep issues, but it appeared that enough did and were not being helped by the current products on the market. I knew I could grow a successful business selling the Magic Sleepsuit even if I captured a small percentage of this market.

After determining with some confidence that I had something different, I wanted to protect my idea by obtaining a design patent. I considered writing my own patent or utilizing one of the many generic patent programs, but ultimately decided to spend the money to do it right and hired a knowledgeable and experienced patent attorney to navigate the process, write the patent application, and submit the application to the United States Patent and Trademark Office.

I had self-funded the business thus far, but it was really just sweat equity. Hiring a patent attorney was going to be a very big financial step. I wanted to find someone I could trust. I talked to friends and relatives to see if they knew of a patent attorney they would recommend. One good friend told me of a competent patent attorney and suggested that I meet him. When I met him, we really hit it off. He seemed genuinely interested in me and my product, and wanted to help me achieve success. He was not, however, cheap, charging more than $350 an hour. Nevertheless, I decided to go with him.

When it came to writing the patent, I provided the attorney with a copy of the business plan and wrote most of the application myself. He took what I had done and put it into the proper patent application format, with claims, evidence, and so on, so it would be structured appropriately. In the end, I will say, I think I could have probably written the patent application myself and saved a ton of money, but by the same token, I did not know better, and I was not familiar with the process and procedures. I would not have done as good a job with all the filing and other steps of the process. I knew the application was too important to risk making a big mistake.

As I completed the patent application, my attorney completed the research and work to obtain a trademark on the Magic Sleepsuit name. Again, this was a lot of paperwork and cost a lot of money to obtain, but now I will always have the registered trademark on the Magic Sleepsuit.

INCORPORATION

I wanted to protect my assets and company, so I turned again to an attorney for advice on incorporating my business. We decided the best strategy was to form an S corporation. I processed all the paperwork and incorporated, becoming President of the Baby Merlin Company. My husband, who continues to be instrumental in all facets of the company and product, became Vice President. We share in all company decisions to this day.

PROTOTYPING

As part of the patent process, I needed to create drawings and a true product prototype. While I had the concept and a rough prototype, and I knew what I wanted the Magic Sleepsuit to look like, I actually required drawings for the patent, size charts, and a professionally created prototype. I created another homemade Magic Sleepsuit to show the manufacturer, as the one I had made for my children was so worn-out. I then searched the internet and spoke to a number of small factories and manufacturers. Ultimately, I found a small manufacturer in Missouri that could create a professional prototype, provide drawings, and get us started with a few samples.

It was many months of back and forth with this group, which was located halfway across the country. I continued to tweak the product's size and features until I felt satisfied with the prototype.

What I thought was a fairly simple concept turned out to be rather complicated. For example, I wanted three color options: blue, yellow, and pink. What I had not realized was the amount of different shades of each color. I also discovered that what pastel blue meant to me might not be what pastel blue meant to a manufacturer. I then discovered Pantone color selections. Pantone is an international color guide that lets you pick colors, each of which has its own number code, in order to get that exact color from any manufacturer in the world. When it came to fabric, I also discovered that there are thousands of fabric weights, textures, etc., from which to choose. I needed to be consistent. The Magic Sleepsuit consists of three layers of fabric, each different from the other, which made the process even more difficult.

Deciding on thread colors, thread material, and labels proved equally complicated. Even choosing a zipper was tough. Ultimately, I decided to use YKK zippers, probably the most commonly used clothing zippers in the world. The thread color was important, so I went back to using a Pantone color selection. Even more important was the structure of the thread. It had to be strong enough to withstand seam tension tests, but also safe for use in infant clothing. Monofilament thread, I discovered, was not acceptable to be used in children's wear. Again, what seemed simple ended up being very complex.

Once I had the all the materials, I had to put everything together and get the sizing and features correct. I researched sizing and found that each manufacturer had a somewhat different sizing chart for infant clothing. I was back to trial and error. It certainly helped that I had another baby at the time, which meant I had a baby model to work out the sizing issues. In addition, many of my friends were having children, and they offered to try my product and give me feedback.

FOCUS GROUP

Finally, I had the prototype, size chart, and patterns required for the patent. I also hired a company to create a small batch of Magic Sleepsuits so that I could give them to others, which would allow me to continue my research. I decided to use a small batch to test the product with the help of a select group. This "focus group" consisted primarily of friends and family with babies. I took about ten to twelve Magic Sleepsuits and shared them with my focus group. I asked the parents of the babies to critique the product. I wanted them to use the product, wash it, abuse it, and tell me what to change or improve. To my surprise and delight, they had recommended very few changes. A few minor tweaks were suggested, but generally they were very pleased with the product. Thankfully, they were surprised with how well it helped their babies sleep. I asked the focus group to fill in a questionnaire about the product. Questions included:

- Which of this product's features did you like?

- Which of this product's features would you change or eliminate?

- Would you purchase this product online?

- Would you prefer to purchase this product in a store?

- What price would you pay for this product?

- Did this product help your child sleep better at naptime? At bedtime?

- Did the duration of your child's naps and nighttime sleep improve with this product?

- What length of time were your child's naps prior to using this product?

- What length of time were your child's naps after using this product?

- What temperature is your child's nursery?

- Did your baby get warm while wearing this product?

- Had you ever swaddled your baby prior to using this product?

- Would you recommend this product to others?

This focus group became my first true, live test of the final prototype. I asked for both positive and negative comments. It provided me with a lot of insight into what people liked and disliked, what they would pay, and where they would buy the product. It gave me great information that I could use as I began my business.

DESIGN EVALUATION

Once I made the final changes to the product based on the focus group comments, I wanted to get a design evaluation completed to insure that the product was safe and met all requirements for children's sleepwear. I turned to an international testing agency called Bureau Veritas to complete the design evaluation. With offices all across the world and an excellent reputation, I knew I could rely on this company to provide a solid evaluation.

I sent a package of information along with the latest prototype, sample hang tags, sample packaging, and sample labels. I ordered a specific evaluation designed to identify any potential concerns with the product and provide a review of labels, hang tags, and packaging. A design evaluation should also take into consideration applicable United States regulations and standards. In my case, it was the United States Consumer Products Safety Commission standards for infant sleepwear. Today, these standards are part of what is known as the Consumer Product Safety Improvement Act, or CPSIA.

The design concerns and proposed improvements of my product stated that the zipper needed to be strong enough to pass torque and tension tests, the thread should not be monofilament, and any metal pieces should not have sharp edges. They also said that all metal pieces should be coated to prevent corrosion and oxidation, and that the use of lead-based paint on any metal pieces was prohibited. Finally, I found that labels must list fiber content, instructions for appropriate care, and country of origin. Fortunately, these were fairly small requests with which the manufacturer could easily comply.

Bureau Veritas recommended that the final product in production (mass production samples) should be tested to ensure compliance with product safety standards and the recommendations of the design evaluation. Recommended tests included:

- **Colorfast testing.** To ensure that the fabric does not stain or discolor when exposed to water, perspiration, urine, saliva, light, or excessive rubbing.

- **Seam strength.** To ensure that sewing and seams will not rip, tear, or separate.

- **Mechanical hazards.** To test sharp points, sharp edges, small parts using torque and tension tests (for metal pieces).

- **Flammability.** To ensure the product complies with flammability requirements, making sure flames do not spread if the garment is exposed to fire.

- **Lead content.** To ensure that all components comply with limits on lead content.

- **Labeling requirements.** To ensure that care instructions and fiber content are in compliance with US regulations.

- **Packaging warning label.** To ensure that all plastic bags contain appropriate warnings to keep them away from babies and children to prevent suffocation.

Ultimately, I had to make a few changes to the prototype to comply with the recommendations, but really did not need to change the overall function of the product, which made me really happy. My company continues to use Bureau Veritas to complete pre-production testing for each batch in the manufacturing process. A batch once failed the zipper strength test because the manufacturer ordered the wrong zippers. Fortunately, as a result of the pre-production testing, this was discovered and changed before mass production. The value of the tests was well worth their cost.

OFFSHORE CONSULTANT

While the small batch of prototypes was great, when I asked for a larger scale production, the cost was such that I would have had to charge much more than I had hoped if I wanted to make a profit. I didn't want to charge more, so I began the process of looking for other manufacturers. I was stuck between and rock and a hard place because I needed small batch production, but wanted a professional manufacturer at a good price.

After researching and interviewing a number of manufacturers in the United States and Mexico, the recurring theme was that my company needed to source the product with a factory in China. Of course, I knew nothing about this type of sourcing, did not know how to speak Chinese, and was overwhelmed by the idea of manufacturing overseas.

Through another contact I had made I was given the name of Edith Tolchin of EGT Global Trading, who, I discovered, had many years of experience sourcing various products in Asia. I spoke to Edie over the phone and via email, and ultimately met with her. I thought she was a good fit for my company, so I decided to move forward and have her source the product in Asia. She chose China because of her previous dealings there, the number of textile manufacturers in the country, and the ability of these manufacturers to meet my need for small scale manufacturing at a good price. As it turns out, fleece, which is a large component of our product, is made in China. Therefore, the country has great prices and tons of capacity to get the material to manufacturing facilities.

Initially, Edie sourced the product to about four or five manufacturers in China. I received three bids to manufacture the Magic Sleepsuit. Each manufacturer and bid had its good and bad points, but ultimately I relied on Edie's expertise and my gut instinct to make my choice. Edie and I spent a lot of time communicating with my chosen manufacturer, getting samples made and making sure everything was just right for the first shipment. The company had a young, aggressive sales manager who was a great communicator via email. Ultimately, he got it all done with Edie and the initial batch was shipped.

The sales manager left my first manufacturer after the second order and went to a new manufacturer. I ended up following him to the new manufacturer, which ended up being a mistake. The third order we placed had some issues in both timing and delivery, as well as a few errors in the product. So, I went back to Edie to find a new manufacturer, which I have used ever since. Volume has increased tenfold from the first order, and my manufacturer is able to handle the increase. Timing is still an issue, however, as manufacturing in China must factor in approximately one month for the shipment to get to the United States. The Chinese New Year holiday also shuts down manufacturing for a month, so if your production is scheduled around this period, you may lose an additional month.

All in all, I am happy with the product, service, and price of manufacturing overseas. I would highly recommend, however, that you have a consultant such as Edie Tolchin to help you navigate the process.

WEBSITE

I had a product to sell, and now I had to sell it. I knew I could not open a storefront with one product. I also did not have the time to run around trying to get my product into shops and boutiques. So, I ultimately decided to sell through a website. Designing a website was a really exciting part of the process. It really felt like it was my storefront. I had place where people could see and purchase my product. It looked quite simple, but ended up taking months to complete, which included lots of back and forth with my web designer.

My biggest suggestion when looking for a web designer is to find someone who understands your audience. My initial designer had some great, creative ideas, but the ideas did not match our audience, so it was a bit of an artistic struggle. The designer was a little inflexible when it came to understanding what we wanted, but in the end, I got the website, though I've changed it a number of times since the first design. I know a lot more now, but wish I had received better advice at the outset, as it would have saved me the time and money involved in redesigns.

I wanted our site to be attractive and eye-catching, not too busy or confusing, easy to navigate, and user-friendly when it came to making a purchase. Perhaps most importantly, I wanted it to be the informational portal of our product.

I had ideas for the look, but found many variables to consider, including:

- **Color palette.** I wanted the color scheme of the website to be soft and whimsical, representing a fun and exciting time for my audience. Again, I had to go to Pantone colors to maintain consistency, and to be sure the designer used my color palette. What I found interesting was that the Pantone color library for fabric is different from the collection for text and paper. So, the colors I picked for the product actually had different Pantone color codes than the ones I used for the website.

- **Typeface.** I wanted something that was not too business-like, not too crazy, but just right for babies and new parents. I was amazed with the number of typefaces there are out there. There are hundreds if not thousands to choose from, and lots of websites that allow you to investigate typefaces. Some typefaces have to be purchased, while others are free. Eventually, I decided on a fun, appropriate typeface suited to my primary audience of moms between ages twenty-five and forty-five.

- **Photos.** I wanted to show babies and the product on the website. I looked at lots of stock photos, which can be purchased online, but in the end, nothing really fit. Instead, I hired a photographer to take photos of the Magic Sleepsuit, and of babies wearing the Magic Sleepsuit. Taking pictures of babies is tough enough, but doing it with babies wearing the product and trying to get everything perfect was a real challenge. In the end, I used the babies of a few friends and had tons of pictures taken, from which I was able to find several to use on the website.

- **Store.** There are many websites that process orders for online storefronts. Using this method, the customer actually leaves the product's company website and enters a separate website to make a transaction. The buyer doesn't always notice this transition, but some stores look different from the main website. This was true in my case. While it was a seamless maneuver on my website, with a click of the mouse that moved the customer to the store, the store itself looked different from my website. The capabilities of online stores vary tremendously, and my initial store was pretty basic. I could change only a few things and my options were fairly limited. For example, I had few choices when it came to shipping costs. I had to use the same shipping cost for all orders, whether the product was shipped within my state or halfway around the world. As a start-up, this method was economical and worked with my design, but it became impractical and was changed in time.

- **Payment processing.** I also incorporated into the website an application to transfer online payments to my bank account. Known as merchant services, these applications vary in capability and cost. I chose PayPal, which is a great processor and quite safe. It processes each order at a flat price, regardless of payment type (credit, debit, etc.). Some applications charge different prices for different payment selections. I wanted to use a processor that was recognizable to buyers, making them feel safe in their purchases, with no privacy issues compromised. PayPal is, however, not cheap. One thing I quickly discovered was that PayPal and all merchant services hold transaction funds for a time, and that you have to transfer the funds from PayPal to your bank account manually. So, in addition to the fees you pay, processors also earn money during the "float" period before your funds are transferred to your bank account.

PURCHASE ORDER

I had a prototype of my product, a manufacturer to make my product, and a website designed. All I needed was to place a purchase order with my manufacturer in China. Edie Tolchin, my offshore consultant, helped me create my first purchase order. It had to spell out exactly the product, shipping instructions, payment terms, and so on, so that everything I wanted would be delivered as expected. The main elements of the purchase order included:

- Buyer name and address
- Seller name and address
- Product name
- Product quantity, including style (size) and color breakdown
- Product price
- Shipping terms and date
- Material and fabric components and description
- Description of labels and packaging
- Payment terms
- Shipping documentation required
- Testing requirements
- Pre-production and mass-production sample requirements

- Inspection instructions for final product inspections

- Customs broker information for importing goods into the United States

- Other notes necessary to the shipment and goods to be sent

A purchase order is usually four to five pages long and provides details on each of the previously noted elements. The down payment is typically 30 percent of total order value. It is sent with the purchase order, with the balance being due after inspection but before the shipment leaves China. I hire an independent inspector to take random samples of the product and match them to the test results. So far, this has been a great way to ensure that the manufacturer complies with both the tests results and my expectations.

From the purchase order to my door, the process can take as many as four to five months. A bit of inventory management and planning is necessary to ensure that you'll have your product to sell.

SALES AND MARKETING

The most important piece of the process is driving traffic to the website and finding buyers. From the beginning, I knew that I was a small outfit with a new and unique product and a small marketing budget. I wanted to rely on word-of-mouth advertising. I wanted my product to be successful because it worked and was recommended by one happy customer to another, solving such a universal issue with babies—sleep. I have never done a lot of traditional marketing or advertising. Sales of the Magic Sleepsuit have grown almost exclusively from one mom or dad telling another about my great product and service.

Once my customers had the product and it worked, I knew they would tell their friends. What I did not realize is that much of the discussion is now done on websites geared towards new parents and babies. The Bump (www.thebump.com) and Baby Center (www.baby center.com) are two of the more popular websites. Anyone can join. As a new parent with lots of questions, these are great places to get answers and look for advice. Discussion boards on these websites talk about everything from prenatal care and birth to raising your children from infants on up. Thousands of parents are on discussion boards looking for answers, asking questions, or responding to others who may be in similar situations. This type of website drove my company's sales in the early years. It is a great marketing tool that is also free.

I have engaged a number of sales reps, but few have worked out, as they were typically moms who used and loved the product. They sometimes had some sales or marketing experience and were looking to do something on the side as they raised their babies. I almost teamed with a large retailer whose products were in about 800 stores nationally. Unfortunately, this company was having some financial difficulty and the partnership did not last. As it turned out, the company ended up in bankruptcy and would not have been a good partner.

I received a call one day from an Amazon (www.amazon.com) rep who indicated that he wanted to make me a preferred seller. Within three weeks of joining Amazon, the company called again. Sales were so good that they wanted to feature the Magic Sleepsuit as a "Daily Deal" and begin fulfillment by Amazon directly. My company actually ranked in the top 25 percent of all sellers on Amazon within a few months of sales on the website. Amazon recently asked that we ship directly to them from China, allowing them to fulfill all orders.

A real factor in my company's growth was my tremendous emphasis on customer service. I have a no-questions-asked thirty-day money-back guarantee, eliminating any risk involved in trying my product. To my delight, I have received very few returns.

CONCLUSION

I feel very fortunate to have been able to build a successful company in just a short period of time. I have taken no outside funds, which has allowed me to control the direction of my company from the start. I measure success not only by the growth of the company, but also by the number of emails, phone calls, and testimonials I have received from customers who seem genuinely happy to have found a product that can help their babies, and them, get some sleep.

ONE BIG IDEA

The Rubik's Cube was invented by Hungarian architect and professor of architecture Ernő Rubik as he was attempting to address the design issues associated with a structure having independently moving parts. The 3D puzzle was initially called the Magic Cube, for which Rubik obtained a patent in 1975. The toy's name was changed to Rubik's Cube in 1980 when Rubik licensed the product to Ideal Toy Corp. The Rubik's Cube went on to become one of the best-selling toys in history.

16. What I've Learned

Bonnie Griffin Kaake

The single biggest source of frustration between inventors and those who provide them services is unrealistic expectations. The second biggest is a lack of adequate communication between parties. Managing expectations on both sides can accelerate progress towards a successful product licensing or product launch. Too often service providers do not fully explain what they are actually providing, thereby leading inventors to come to their own conclusions and assumptions, which are often misguided. In addition, many of these services do little to further the success of an inventor's product. This problem is compounded by the fact that inventors don't know the right questions to ask to get straight answers. As an inventor, you need to know the basics that will help you receive what you need at the point when you actually need it. I hope to dispel some myths about inventing by focusing on marketing as it relates to commercialization through licensing or launch.

Bonnie Griffin Kaake has thirty years of experience working with innovative product-based businesses and inventors. She enjoyed a long career with General Electric, where she was the recipient of many awards for her marketing expertise. She holds a BS in Business Administration, and is a graduate of GE's Technical Marketing and Management Program. Bonnie is also the founder of Innovative Consulting Group, Inc., which provides consulting and out-sourced marketing services that accelerate product commercialization. Recently, Bonnie introduced Inventors' List, a website with a growing list of providers of inventor services and reviews of their services.

bgkaake@biz-consult.com
www.icgproductmarketing.com • www.inventorslist.com

OUT OF THE GARAGE

My father was an inventor. He was very creative and mechanically oriented. He would often work three jobs to support his nine children, and his garage resembled a small factory. Many innovative, creative, and probably patentable inventions came out of that garage, as well as many of my family's toys and gifts for birthdays and Christmases. Unfortunately, he made all the mistakes inventors still make today. Although he earned many rewards for his inventions, the rewards were meager compared to the money his inventions made for the companies that employed him. As I remember, the largest incentive he was given for his creative endeavors was fifty dollars in the late 1950s. In addition, often the engineers where he worked, who were more educated than he was, would file and be granted patents on my father's genius in their own names. Unfortunately, he didn't know how to protect or capitalize on his inventions. Nor did he know what the possibilities were once he developed an invention to the best of his ability.

As a female pioneer in the area of technical product marketing, I enjoyed a long career with General Electric. Creative like my dad, I was the recipient of many awards for significant marketing contributions in the areas of sales, national sales forecasting models, and competitive analysis. For the past seventeen years I have excitedly pursued the entrepreneurial world, starting my own companies or partnering with others to passionately promote and support the successful commercialization of inventors' products. It has been a wild ride working with inventors. There have been many wonderful twists and turns, learning experiences, and successful and not-so-successful products. The biggest challenge has been finding a balance between providing quality services to inventors at reasonable costs and managing their expectations.

Most inventors start their journeys into the unknown by focusing on problems, frustrations, or challenges they have either experienced or observed. Being problem solvers, they diligently work on providing a solution to the perceived problem. Far from their minds are issues relating to how likely they are to be compensated for their ideas. They naïvely think that somehow proper compensation will follow if the product concept is good enough. This is simply not true.

FOLLOW THE MONEY

Over many years of marketing new products, what I have learned can be summed up in two words: financial motivation. This is true whether you are an inventor, patent attorney, agent, retailer, wholesaler, manufacturer, or anyone else who provides services to inventors. Each of these individuals understands her own financial motivation. Nevertheless, it is far more difficult for inventors to understand and appreciate where the money motivation is for others. At the same time, it is to every inventor's advantage to have a firm grasp of this fact in order to maximize her chances of success. Most importantly, following the money allows you to separate the providers of valuable services from those whose only motivation is to profit from your lack of information, unwillingness to listen, or naïveté.

Don't get me wrong; it is healthy to want to make decent money and live in comfort. This applies to inventors as well as those who provide them services. Earning the minimum wage or working for someone else rarely, if ever, secures the lifestyle of one's dreams. It is critical that you are aware of some important concepts as you proceed on your journey. The following information is meant to help you lift the fog in front of you, so you don't get run off the road before arriving at the end of the rainbow.

You are not a charity. Never tell anyone, "I'm looking for someone who will take my idea and run with it." When an inventor uses these words, the person on the other end of the conversation often struggles to maintain her composure. Most service providers hear this statement and translate it as, "I am naïve and cheap." They also know that, if they allow you to, you are likely to waste a lot of their valuable time. The unethical, sleazy service provider will hear this as a bullhorn bellowing out, "Please take advantage of me." The ethical service provider will direct you to free educational material or nonprofit educational inventor organizations to cure you of your ignorance. Don't be offended. Ignorance is curable with education. Stupidity is permanent. Look for local inventor groups that are not for profit but rather educational in nature with outside speakers on topics of interest. You can find educational inventor organizations by typing "inventor organizations" or "inventor organizations + (your state)" into an Internet search engine.

Some questionable service providers will send you a form to fill out and request that you pay them to look at your idea. Some won't even advise you to explore intellectual property protection before they take your money. Some "submit your idea" companies generate high six-figure revenues every year by collecting nonrefundable fees in exchange for looking at inventors' ideas. Although charging a small fee to review your product concept may sometimes be justifiable, I would recommend you secure some intellectual property protection before submitting your idea to anyone. At minimum, you should have a comprehensive nondisclosure agreement. I acknowledge that there are some costs associated with employing a qualified person to review paperwork, especially when most ideas are not worth pursuing for a variety of reasons that are not always obvious to the inventor. Nevertheless, if a company is truly generating revenue by making inventions successful in the marketplace, reviewing new possibilities might be considered the price of doing business.

Some companies operate on the fringe, sending you form letters that look personalized because they have included your name and patent number, enticing you into their offices for a little arm-twisting by their salespeople. Before you know it, you have committed anywhere from $900 to $15,000 on mostly worthless "services." They may even offer you financing and, only if you commit today, a "special deal." Kiss your savings goodbye!

DO YOUR HOMEWORK

Don't spend one cent before you do your own research. You will need an Internet connection and a note pad. You'll also need to take a few trips to both brick and mortar stores and online shops where you hope to sell your product. A camera may come in handy, too. When doing your homework, you will want to find out what is already patented that is similar to the idea you have for your product. Use different words to describe your product concept while searching websites such as www.google.com/patents or www.uspto.gov. Write down the patent numbers of anything that comes close or is similar. You will need this information later. Don't avoid adding one to your list because it is just close; the patent examiner will find it and use it against you to deny your patent after you have spent a lot of money with a patent attorney or agent.

Use more than one search engine. Don't limit yourself. You will be amazed at how the search results change depending on which search engine you use. This is due to the fact that many search engines list only those websites that pay for a spot at the top of the list associated with a particular search term. You have probably wondered why you get seemingly unrelated results from searches. Keep looking beyond the first page; most people do not. Try common terms that someone might use to find your product. Look for competitive products and make notes listing the retail prices of the products, how they are packaged, and how and where they are sold. You will need this information later.

Go to a store where you would expect to find your product on a shelf or in inventory. Look for similar products or competitive products that may also serve the same purpose or function as your product. Make notes about packaging, pricing, and anything else that could be helpful, such as where the products are manufactured. Once you have finished your homework, proceed to the professionals.

Interview Legal and Marketing Professionals

Make appointments to see a patent attorney or patent agent and a marketing professional familiar with launching new products in your industry or a complementary industry. When you call to schedule an appointment time, make that first call brief. Remember, you are calling to schedule an appointment, not to convince the agent you have a "million dollar idea." Most professionals will meet with you in person, over the phone, or on the Internet without charge for an initial conversation to get you pointed in the right direction. Some service providers are familiar with Internet video-conferencing services such as Skype, and using one of these applications would allow you to demonstrate your idea or prototype live. You will not need a nondisclosure agreement with a patent attorney or patent agent. You will want to have one signed to discuss your product concept with anyone else. Although not legally required, have your children sign a nondisclosure agreement as well. It will be an excellent time to educate your kids about the importance of intellectual property.

Gather and organize your research to bring to your meetings with legal and marketing professionals. You will receive better guidance with the information in hand. Avoid "diarrhea of the mouth," though. Briefly explain or show what you have done and learned so far, and then be quiet and listen. Of course, you should ask questions regarding a service provider's fees, how she works with clients, her successes and failures, and what she would recommend as your next step.

Manage Your Expectations

A patent attorney or patent agent will charge you for preparing and filing legal documents to secure a patent or other intellectual property on your behalf. A good patent attorney or agent will thoroughly explore prior art (using your search results and a professional search) and prepare well-written claims that will increase your chances of securing a patent and give you the broadest coverage possible.

Depending on your industry and the complexity of your idea, your initial legal fees may amount to $3,000 for a well-written provisional patent application to over $20,000 for a utility patent on a complex product in certain industries. Also, remember that a patent does not protect you; it gives you the right to prevent someone from duplicating what you have patented. The job of a patent attorney is to provide her best effort to secure a patent for you, not to help you decide whether your idea is marketable, or whether it can be manufactured. Although patent attorneys may have some knowledge about marketing and manufacturing, these are not aspects of their training. You would not ask your accountant to create a piece of fine art for you, so don't expect your attorney to give you credible advice on marketing or manufacturing. She may be able to refer you to an appropriate party for additional services, if necessary.

Your patent may or may not be granted. In the best case scenario, it will likely take as long as three years or more to be granted. Approximately 95 percent of patent applications are rejected upon first examination. Furthermore, even when a patent is finally issued by the U.S. Patent and Trademark Office, it does not in any way mean the idea or product described in the patent is viable in the marketplace, or that the patent will not fail if challenged in court. Less than 25 percent of infringement cases are won in court by patent holders. Infringement cases rarely cost less than $600,000 to prosecute.

There are warning signs that you need to be aware of when talking to a patent attorney/agent. The first red flag is a patent attorney/agent that works for or directly with a marketing company of any kind. This is not in your best interest. Also, avoid a patent attorney/agent that offers to take an equity position in your company in exchange for part or all of his/her fees. You want your legal representative to represent you directly. And, you want to retain the power to discontinue working with that attorney/agent if the performance is less than what is expected of a provider of legal services. Like any profession, there are good ones and bad ones.

Your product's success or failure in the marketplace is primarily dependent on how well it is marketed. The term "marketing" literally means "creating the perception of value." The key word here is "perception." We have all seen bad, bad for you, or mediocre products succeed, and great products fail. It is all about the marketing. Do not underestimate the importance of good marketing. Unfortunately, most inventors do just that, and pay the consequences. Understanding how complex marketing issues may affect your ability to commercialize your product is absolutely critical.

As you explore intellectual property protection in the form of a patent, you also need to meet or interview marketing professionals. This is the time to discover whether you can reasonably pursue the commercialization of your product. There are four up-front considerations when determining commercial potential.

Product Is Patentable and Marketable

A product that is both patentable and marketable is extremely desirable and has the highest probability of commercial success. It gives the inventor the strongest position in the commercialization process.

Product Is Marketable but Not Patentable

This scenario is very common. Consider the fact that approximately 75 percent or more of the products that are commercially available for sale are not patented. The key in this situation is to out-market your competitors or provide a product in a small niche market. It is more about entrepreneurial expertise and success than it is about patenting. Nevertheless, there may be additional opportunities to leverage different types of intellectual property protection, such as trade secrets, trademarks, and copyrights. Be more observant the next time you are shopping for something.

Product Is Patentable but Not Marketable

This situation is a trap for inventors who tend to place too much emphasis on patenting without sufficient consideration of marketability. For example, a gentleman in his late seventies broke his right leg and was in a cast. Living alone and without a vehicle, he could not drive to the grocery store, which was only a block away. Since he was on crutches, he could not comfortably carry a grocery bag and manage the crutches at the same time. Once his leg had healed, he went to a patent attorney with a custom-machined prototype of a hook that allowed a person to carry a bag while using crutches. He was granted a patent. The potential liability and cost of manufacturing the custom hook made the product not viable in the marketplace.

Another example of this scenario occurred a few years ago when two women came to me with a novel idea for manufacturing disposable diapers. Before meeting with me, they had hired a large downtown legal firm to file a patent on their behalf and secure the opportunity to patent internationally, which cost them over $25,000. The patent was granted. Unfortunately, they did not have the capital needed to commercialize their unique diaper. Most importantly, due to the existing diaper manufacturers' focuses on mass production, there was no interest in licensing a product with a lower profit margin, regardless of how great it was for the consumer.

A final example may be illustrated by an inventor who spent $70,000 patenting and prototyping a bicycle product. I had the unfortunate task of telling him that what he had created was not suitable for the industry and would not sell. Avid bicycle enthusiasts, who would be the prime target for the product, want lightweight accessories that are designed in such a way that they won't scratch the bike's frame. A total redesign of the inventor's product, new patenting, and a commercial product launch generated some sales, but the market opportunity soon passed him by. The bike manufacturers changed their frame designs and made his products no longer viable. A new product's viability in the marketplace is usually a short window of about five years from the date of product launch. Due to the delay caused by his initial efforts, the inventor missed the biggest window of opportunity for the best return on his investment.

Remember, it is not the job of a patent attorney or agent to know if the product concept you are patenting is commercially viable. In addition, it is a rare industrial designer or product designer that has even a little knowledge of product marketability, unless she is a specialist in a particular industry and has been working with marketing professionals directly.

Product Is Not Marketable and Not Patentable

It is better to know if this describes your situation sooner rather than later. It allows you to move on to your next great idea without incurring the expenses involved in following a dead end.

LICENSING

From my thirty years of experience in product commercialization on a national and international basis, I recommend that inventors do not waste time looking for someone to license their ideas, provisional patent applications, or issued patents, unless licensing is the only option. The probability of securing a licensee is slim at best, and most likely just a dream. You may be better off buying a lottery ticket. Furthermore, never hire the same company to do or manage your intellectual property protection, as you would for marketing services.

Some companies run contests, sell books and CDs, or say what you want to hear in their marketing materials. Many offer some value, presenting options you may not have considered. You may gain some knowledge by participating or purchasing information. The manufacturers that promote contests or contract other companies to offer contests for them do so for several reasons. They may be pursuing new products that can minimize their research and development costs and reduce the amount of time needed to get a product to market. They may also be gathering ideas to develop better products of their own, without giving any compensation to you. Often the goal of a contest is to enhance a company's public image through the advertising and publicity that surrounds such an event.

Some investors and promotional companies launch contests to find products for development and relicensing to manufacturers. In most cases, they require you to assign your intellectual property rights to them as part of the process. This may be done in an attempt to avoid the requirements of the American Inventors Protection Act (AIPA) of 1999. Even if they try to convince you otherwise, or maybe they have found a way to circumvent the law, ask them to provide the information in writing anyway. If they refuse, there is a reason they don't want you to know, and you should avoid doing business with them.

ENTREPRENEURSHIP

You have a significantly better chance of being successful with your invention if you think of yourself as an entrepreneur and act accordingly. If this idea intimidates you, or you simply think you don't have the skills, gather a team of competent people with complementary skill sets around you to make it happen. It is easier to start a business today than it has ever been. It is exciting and immensely profitable for those who are not frightened by the thought of owning their own businesses, and who are willing to listen to advice and do the work.

One of the two biggest keys to success with a start-up is to first start small. The second is to have a written marketing plan of action with an associated budget. You may need some professional guidance, but it is not necessary to spend a lot of money or a lot of time to put a marketing plan in place that is action oriented.

A good marketing consultant or agency will usually offer consulting services at an hourly fee after an initial free consultation. After that, you'll want a firm written proposal for the services the company intends to provide or are recommending. Make sure the proposal is detailed sufficiently, so you know what to expect as a result of the work. One of the very first services that you should be looking for is a marketing plan for product commercialization. This plan needs to include industry and product research that is specific to your product, a list of tasks that need to be accomplished, a timeline for implementation, a projected budget, and the person or company that will be responsible for the completion of each specific task. My recommendation is that this marketing plan be developed for a period of six to twelve months. The plan will need to be flexible, as circumstances may change and new information may be revealed along the journey.

Today, all marketing efforts have to be integrated to be effective. This requires a carefully considered plan of action. With a plan, you have a clear vision of where you are going, what needs to be done, when it needs to be done and by whom, and what the estimated costs will be. A good product launch plan that integrates the different methods of commercializing and promoting your product in a focused manner will result in a positive outcome. Unfortunately, most inventors and entrepreneurs spend too much money and time in one area without realizing the benefits associated with creating an integrated plan beforehand. The typical example is the person that knows she needs a website to start a business and hires a website developer. She often seems totally unaware of the need for graphic design to make the website attractive enough to hold the interest of visitors, the need for a copywriter for content development, and the need to market the website after it has been developed. Website developers are glorified mechanics; they make websites function. In my opinion, 95 percent of websites do not produce desired results because they are not well integrated with the other marketing needed to generate revenue.

BE CAREFUL

If you do not understand certain terminology, ask a qualified individual to interpret it for you or, better yet, seek legal counsel. What you think a contract says and what it actually obligates you to do can be two quite different things. Realize that any company that has worked with inventors long enough has learned to protect itself. Inventors don't like bad news, tend to have unrealistic expectations, and too often are willing to "shoot the messenger" by stubbornly refusing to pay the bill for services rendered. If you want a provider of services to treat you fairly, you have to conduct yourself in a businesslike manner.

It is your responsibility to ask questions and make sure your expectations match what is being delivered. If all a contract says is that the company will market your idea or patent, that company is not really promising to do much of anything. Ask for specifics about what a provider will do, what its methods are, and get this information in writing. Do not be intimidated by attorneys or other service providers, or those with more education than you. You are in the hiring position, and you have the right to receive answers to your questions. Ask for case histories of successful work and samples of the type of communication you can expect from a service provider. Better yet, ask for a written proposal before committing to a contract or agreeing to use any company's services. If the written proposal is not clear or the contract is not understandable, be sure to request clarification, additions, or corrections in writing. Perform an Internet search for information pertaining to the company's reputation. Enter the company's name into a search engine along with terms such as "fraud," "scam," and "complaints." Contact the Better Business Bureau for complaints. Look for blogs mentioning the company and read what others have had to say. If you cannot find information on the company or its owners or partners, be extra cautious.

You can also check out websites such as Angie's List (www.angieslist.com) and my new website, Inventors' List (www.inventorslist.com), to find information and reviews on providers of services to inventors.

CONCLUSION

Do not spend any money until you have done your own preliminary patent and marketing research. Consult with a patent attorney or agent and an experienced marketing person to get an opinion about your product's probability of being patentable or marketable. Once you have done this work, provided the feedback is positive, begin pursuing intellectual property protection, look into having professional marketing research done, and devise your plan of action. Do not hire or contract with the same company to do your intellectual property protection and your marketing.

Your dreams of success as an inventor will have a better shot at becoming reality if you are willing to acknowledge what you don't know, understand the value of planning, have a healthy balance between the need to get everything right and the need for action, value the work of others and the importance of teamwork, and appreciate that getting a patent or patent pending status is only the tip of the iceberg.

Understand that nothing is free, and that many services are not worth what you pay for them, although others are worth far more than their costs. It is up to you to ask questions and be sure that you receive written agreements detailing the services offered. Be teachable and listen with an open mind, even if someone recommends that you stop pursuing your dream. They may be right. Manage your expectations and conduct yourself in a professional manner. Everything will cost more, be more complex, and take longer than you think. It is up to you to make your product a success. And remember, time is of the essence.

Conclusion

While this book is geared toward the novice inventor in the United States, its information is valuable and pertinent to any inventor, anywhere. I would, however, recommend that anyone living outside the United States do a little extra research and check the laws of his or her particular country regarding small businesses and issues such as patenting, importing and exporting, licensing, and customs.

The journey that lies ahead can prove to be both exciting and rewarding. If you proceed carefully, armed with the knowledge and tools presented in this book, you can successfully turn your idea into a marketable product. Chances are, you will even find yourself mentoring other novice inventors along the way, sharing some of the experiences you've had and the lessons you've learned.

During your journey, I urge you to always be vigilant in researching industry associations and service providers before making any commitments. Doing your homework will prevent you from getting involved with people who are more interested in dollar signs than they are in you and your idea.

After reading the words of wisdom and advice found in this book, I hope that the mystery involved in bringing an invention to the marketplace is no longer so mysterious. It's not a trick; it is simply a matter of dedication and a commitment to hard work. I wish you success!

Resources

Taking your invention from inception to a finalized product in the marketplace can be one of the most rewarding experiences of your life. The following websites can provide you with a large resource of information on everything from inventors' groups, prototyping, and packaging to patenting, marketing, licensing, and much more.

INVENTORS' GROUPS

Ask the Inventors • www.asktheinventors.com
Sister-inventors Barbara Russell Pitts and Mary Russell Sarao provide a website full of free information on inventing, which includes useful articles and many other resources.

Edison Nation • www.edisonnation.com
This website has an online forum that provides assistance in bringing new consumer products to market.

Inventors Society of South Florida • www.inventorssociety.net
This group of inventors meets monthly in Delray Beach, Florida, to share ideas. It offers fellowship, valuable guest speakers, expos, and formidable information.

The United Inventors Association of America • www.uiausa.org
The United Inventors Association of America is a registered 501(c)3 nonprofit educational foundation for inventors.

PROTOTYPING

Applied Rapid Technologies • www.artcorp.com
This company provides rapid prototyping for products within such industries as consumer electronics, toys and games, sporting goods, and aerospace.

Job Shop • www.jobshop.com
Job Shop is an extensive network of contract manufacturers and skilled craftsmen in the United States.

MacRae's Blue Book • www.macraesbluebook.com
Since 1893, MacRae's has been America's leading industrial directory, helping industrial buyers find the products or services they require.

Suburban Artworks • www.suburbanartworks.com
This company assists inventors in bringing their conceptual ideas to life with state-of-the-art 3D software.

Thomas Net • www.thomasnet.com
Originally Thomas Register, this website lists trustworthy manufacturing sources.

PATENTING

IP Watchdog • www.IPwatchdog.com
Founded by IP attorney Gene Quinn, this website has everything you've ever wanted to know about intellectual property. It contains numerous tabs, each of which contains an abundance of information.

Service Corps of Retired Exectutives (SCORE) • www.score.org
A resource partner with the U.S. Small Business Administration, SCORE is a nonprofit association dedicated to educating entrepreneurs and helping small businesses start, grow, and succeed nationwide.

U.S. Patent and Trademark Office • www.uspto.gov
This government agency deals with all things patents and trademarks. It is a great resource, especially for novice inventors.

U.S. Small Business Administration • www.sba.gov
This government agency supports the development of small businesses throughout the United States.

CROWDFUNDING

CircleUp, Indiegogo, Kickstarter, Launcht • www.circleup.com, www.indiegogo.com, www.kickstarter.com, www.launcht.com
These are four leading crowdfunding websites.

U.S. Patent and Trademark Office
www.uspto.gov/patents/resources/types/provapp.jsp
The United States Patent and Trademark Office website provides a provisional patent application.

U.S. Securities and Exchange Commission
www.sec.gov/divisions/marketreg/tmjobsact-crowdfundingintermediariesfaq.htm
The SEC website includes an informative article on frequently asked questions concerning crowdfunding intermediaries.

PACKAGING

Communication Arts • www.commarts.com
This website is the online companion to *Communication Arts,* a magazine devoted to creativity and visual communications.

The Dieline • www.thedieline.com
Established in 2007, this website is a comprehensive online package design directory.

HOW • www.howdesign.com
Starting as an award-winning design magazine in 1985, HOW has branched out to become a design brand that includes books, online courses, competitions, and a website.

LogoLounge • www.logolounge.com
This website is an online logo database, offering information on logos and branding.

Josh Wallace • www.joshwallace.com
A contributor to this book, Josh Wallace shows his extensive background in graphic arts via an online portfolio of his creative and colorful works.

Packaging Diva • www.packagingdiva.com
JoAnn Hines, aka the Packaging Diva, has many years of experience with packaging solutions.

MANUFACTURING, IMPORTING, AND PRODUCT SAFETY

EGT Global Trading • www.egtglobaltrading.com
EGT Global Trading is the brainchild of Edith G. Tolchin, aka the Sourcing Lady, who has over thirty-five years of experience working with factories, sourcing and manufacturing in Asia, importing, and consumer product safety, and holds a U.S. Customs and Border Protection broker license.

Federal Trade Commission • www.ftc.gov
This is the online location of the federal government agency whose mission it is to protect the consumer by preventing deceptive, fraudulent, and unfair business practices, while also providing access to accurate information.

Harmonized Tariff Schedule of the United States
http://hts.usitc.gov
This schedule provides product classification and information on duties for hundreds of thousands of imported products.

KRT Audit Corp • www.krtinspect.com
This company offers shipment inspections, factory audits, and lab testing throughout Asia.

National Customs Brokers and Forwarders
Association of America, Inc. • www.ncbfaa.org
Established in 1897, the NCBFAA represents hundreds of companies in the field of international trade, including freight forwarders and customs brokers.

U.S. Consumer Product Safety Commission • www.cpsc.gov
This is the online location of the federal government's safety watchdog.

U.S. Food and Drug Administration • www.fda.gov
The FDA is a federal agency tasked with protecting the public through regulation of the food supply and medical products.

U.S. Customs and Border Protection • www.cbp.gov
This office's chief function is to protect the borders of the United States while helping to enforce the laws of approximately forty other government agencies.

MARKETING

Cataloglink, Catalogs, Cybercatalogs, Flipseek
www.cataloglink.com • www.catalogs.com • www.cybercatalogs.com
www.flipseek.com
These websites provide links to online catalogs in every conceivable industry, including retail.

Inventor-Mentor • www.inventor-mentor.com
Created by Jack Lander, a contributor to this book, Inventor-Mentor is a reasonably-priced mentoring service for inventors.

Inventors' List • www.inventorslist.com
Created by Bonnie Griffin Kaake, one of this book's contributors, this is a new website that provides information and reviews on providers of services to inventors.

WEBSITES

123RF • www.123rf.com
This website provides royalty-free stock photos to help you develop your website.

CutePDF • www.cutepdf.com/products/cutepdf/writer.asp
CutePDF is a handy tool that converts documents to PDF format.

Eddie Vélez • www.eddievelez.net
Eddie Vélez manages Success by Design. This is Eddie's online presence, which offers marketing, design, and social media services.

Google Docs • https://docs.google.com
This resource allows users to collaborate with each other in real time as they create and edit documents online.

Grammar Girl • www.quickanddirtytips.com/grammar-girl
Although there are many other helpful options online, Grammar Girl, available on the Quick and Dirty Tips website, is a pleasant, easy-to-use free online guide. You can check grammar and punctuation by entering a question or key words into its search engine.

LibreOffice • www.libreoffice.org
LibreOffice is free and open source office software that offers a suite of programs, including a word processor, a presentation program, a spreadsheet app, a database management tool, and more.

Merriam-Webster • www.merriam-webster.com
A division of Encyclopedia Britannica, Merriam-Webster is America's leading dictionary. This online version includes a thesaurus.

PayPal • www.paypal.com
Founded in 1998, PayPal is a leading digital payment processor.

PIXLR • www.pixlr.com/editor
This online tool helps you work with images for your website.

SALES REPS

Contingent • www.contingent.net/maa_agreement
This is a sample Master Agent Agreement.

Don Debelak's One Stop Invention Shop
www.onestopinventionshop.net
Don Debelak has created a website that contains dozens of sales rep lists in connection with numerous industries, offers assistance in finding sales representatives to help you sell your product, posts informative articles on how to seek investments from reps, how to approach sales reps, and how to set up a sales rep network.

RETAILERS

Macy's • www.macysnet.com
This is an example of a retailer's vendor portal—in this case, Macy's.

Retail MBA • www.retailmba.com/training
Karen Waksman offers a free six-part video training series called "How to Sell to Walmart or any Other Chain Store Retailers." She also provides a sample sell sheet from one of her Retail MBA students at www.retailmba.com/sample-sell-sheet.

LICENSING

ACCESSORY BRAINSTORMS, Inc.
www.accessorybrainstorms.com
Owned by Joan Lefkowitz, this company has been licensing fashion and beauty accessories for over thirty years.

America Invents • www.americainvents.com
America Invents is a licensing company with over $1.5 billion dollars in retail sales.

GameBird • www.gamebird.biz
This website is owned by Mary Ellroy, who serves as an agent for toy and game inventors.

Innovative Product Technologies, Inc. • www.inventone.com
Owned by Pamela Riddle Bird, this company assists innovators and entrepreneurs in areas such as marketing, intellectual property, licensing, and funding.

inventRight • www.inventright.com
Cofounded by Stephen Key and Andrew Krauss, inventRight is a licensing firm, offering teaching and coaching assistance to inventors.

Market Launchers • www.marketlaunchers.com
Market Launchers displays inventors' products on its online database of inventions. It also helps inventors with their websites and coaches them through the process of licensing their inventions.

StartupNation • www.startupnation.com
Startup Nation presents information and resources that can help new entrepreneurs start their businesses and foster the growth of already established companies.

PUBLIC RELATIONS

Celebritize Yourself • www.celebritizeyourself.com
Celebritize Yourself is a best-selling book written by Marsha Friedman, who can teach you the many cost-effective ways to generate PR for yourself and for your business.

EMSI Public Relations • www.emsincorporated.com
EMSI Public Relations is a "pay-for-performance" public relations firm with various clients in industries such as writing, health, music, and politics.

Marsha Friedman • www.marshafriedman.com
Author, founder, and CEO of EMSI Public Relations, Marsha Friedman is widely regarded as a pioneer in the PR "pay-for-performance" model.

DIRECT RESPONSE TELEVISION

Distinct Creations • www.yourideastolife.com
Founded in 2012 by Gil Tatarsky, Distinct Creations provides licensing deals in the field of direct response television.

Electronic Retailing Association (ERA) • www.retailing.org
This trade association was founded in 1991 and is now the only group representing companies that use direct response to sell goods and services on radio, television, and online.

HSN, QVC • www.hsn.com, www.qvc.com
These are the two leaders in TV home shopping. HSN began in 1985 as the "Home Shopping Network," and QVC appeared in 1986 as "Quality, Value and Convenience."

The SciMark Report • www.scimark.blogspot.com
This blog was started by Jordan Pine, president of SciMark Corp., and focuses on short-form direct response television.

TRADE SHOWS

ECRM • www.marketgate.com/AboutECRM/TradeCalendar.aspx
This address will take you to ERCM's excellent monthly calendar of
trade shows in every conceivable industry throughout the world.

Javits Center • www.javitscenter.com
The Javits Center is a convention center located in New York City. It is
promoted as the "Marketplace for the World" and hosts leading trade
and consumer shows, conventions, and special events.

Minnesota Inventors Congress
www.minnesotainventorscongress.org
Minnesota Inventors Congress is a nonprofit organization based in
Minnesota. It directs inventors to the right resources and is the sponsor
of the annual Invention Expo held in Minneapolis.

Trade Show News Network • www.tsnn.com
Established in 1996, TSNN is an online resource offering current news
on the exhibition, event, and trade show industries.

About the Contributors

DON DEBELAK

Don Debelak is a new product marketing specialist who has been involved with inventors and inventions for over thirty years. Don has experience working with all types of products, from small novelties to medical innovations. He has also been a columnist for *Entrepreneur*, and has authored several books on the subject of invention. He is a registered patent agent, using his wealth of experience to help his clients with intellectual property protection.

Don Debelak's One Stop Invention Shop is an inventor assistance website dedicated to helping inventors who want to market their own products. It includes additional information on how to best use sales representatives as a marketing tool, and offers for sale lists of sales reps in a variety of industries.

dondebelak34@msn.com
www.onestopinventionshop.net • www.patentsbyDonDebelak.com

MARSHA FRIEDMAN

Marsha Friedman is CEO and founder of EMSI Public Relations, a national agency that has been providing publicity services for twenty-three years. She has helped thousands of entrepreneurs, inventors, professionals, and authors gain exposure and credibility through appearances on radio and TV shows across the country, editorial coverage in newspapers and magazines, and social media. She is the author of the best-selling book *Celebritize Yourself: The Three-Step Method to Increase Your Visibility and Explode Your Business.*

Past clients include Michael Uslan, executive producer of *The Dark Knight Rises* and author of the memoir *The Boy Who Loved Batman;* Irwin Yablans, executive producer and creator of the *Halloween* film series and author of the memoir *The Man Who Created Halloween;* The Temptations; Jim Hoffa, Jr., and Robert McFarlane, former National Security Advisor.

Marsha's clients routinely appear on national TV, from CBS to CNN; on national talk radio shows; and in major publications, from *The New York Times* to *The Washington Post.* She is sought after by journalists writing about public relations issues, and is a popular speaker at regional and national conferences.

info@marshafriedman.com • www.marshafriedman.com

ANDY GIBBS

Andy Gibbs has more than thirty years of technological, corporate, and market development experience. He has founded eight manufacturing and professional service companies, and is an inventor with twenty-five issued and pending patents in the automotive, medical device, electronics, sporting goods, methods of business, and software industry segments. His career experience ranges from startup entrepreneur to Fortune 100 division Executive Vice President.

He is the founder and Chairman of PatentCafe.com, a worldwide provider of patent search and patent portfolio management software, and the publisher of IPFrontline, a leading international IP magazine for patent attorneys, corporate counsel, engineers, and inventors.

Mr. Gibbs has a master's degree in Marketing and Business Administration and a bachelor's degree in Architectural Engineering from Columbia Pacific University, with additional mechanical engineering undergraduate work at Villanova University. Appointed by the United States Secretary of Commerce, Mr. Gibbs served two terms on the United States Patent and Trademark Office Public Patent Advisory Committee (PPAC), which advises the United States Patent and Trademark Office on various labor, budget, legislative, performance and, process operations, and reports annually to the President and the Judiciary Committees.

Mr. Gibbs' product design experience began in 1979 as a codeveloper of many world "firsts," including home satellite TV systems, LCD watches, flat screen color CRTs, 3.5-inch floppy disks, miniature electronics connectors, automotive diagnostic equipment, ink jet printers, UV/ozone water purification systems, and semiconductor testing equipment for companies such as National Semiconductor, Memorex, ADAC Laboratories, ISS Sperry Univac, and System Industries.

His latest startup is ScienceSTYLE, Inc., a new direct response marketing company that builds and sells patented or patent pending high-value consumer products in the fields of fitness and health.

andy@andygibbs.com • www.andygibbs.com

STEVE GREENBERG AND GARY GREENBERG

Steve Greenberg is a product scout, TV personality, and author of *Gadget Nation: A Journey Through the Eccentric World of Invention*. When Steve is not hunting down new products, he routinely appears on *The Dr. Oz. Show* and *The Today Show*. He was also the host of the Food Network's *Invention Hunters*. Each month, Steve can be seen demonstrating innovative products in America's top TV markets, including WGN Chicago, ABC Dallas, NBC Seattle, CBS Houston, and others. Steve has also been a judge for Hammacher Schlemmer's "Search for Invention" contest and the "National School Inventors Challenge" launched by *Popular Science*.

innovationinsider@gmail.com • www.stevegreenberg.tv
twitter.com/stevetv • www.facebook.com/stevetv

Gary Greenberg has designed, negotiated and implemented hundreds of transactions involving M&A, real estate, outsourcing, and partnership agreements. He also has extensive experience managing professional services operations for large companies and has worked as an employee or consultant for several Fortune 100 corporations. As a consultant, Gary assists companies to improve their client relationships, turn around problem situations, and enhance their strategic positions. In recent years, Gary has focused his attention on crowdfunding and the long-term impact this change will have on the financial services and retail industry. Gary is on the Dean's Advisory Board of Rider University, where he also teaches a graduate course. He has also served on the Dean's Advisory Council of the University of Maryland Smith Business School.

garyagreenberg@gmail.com • www.garygreenberg.net

DEB HESS

Deb Hess currently serves as the Program Director of the Minnesota Inventors Congress (MIC). The Minnesota Inventors Congress is a 501(c)(3) nonprofit organization dedicated to stimulating economic development by supporting innovation and inventors at all phases of the invention development process. She learned a great deal about the world of invention while serving as an active volunteer on its Board of Directors for over twenty years before taking the leadership position. She uses her marketing and management experience to teach inventors how to develop marketable products. She is known for the passion she expresses when helping aspiring inventors learn how to make important business decisions regarding their new business ventures. She has been involved in the coordination of the MIC Inventing Success Workshops for thirty years, and is a certified trainer, coach, and facilitator, fostering the creative and innovative spirit of entrepreneurs.

Deb has been invited to speak to numerous groups, including inventors, students, intellectual property law students, entrepreneurs, and manufacturers. On an international level, she has served as a juror for the World Cup of Computer Implemented Inventions in Taipei, Taiwan, and as the US Representative for the Global Sustainability Conference in Bangkok, Thailand.

The co-owner of a microenterprise for the past twenty years, Deb is responsible for the marketing and accounting functions of the family business. Having served as an elected official for Redwood County, she is well versed in consensus building skills and public policy.

deb@minnesotainventorscongress.org
www.minnesotainventorscongress.org

MAUREEN HOWARD

Maureen Howard is a wife, mother of four, and pediatric physical therapist. Maureen's educational background includes a BA in Biology from the University of Delaware. After completing her bachelor's degree, Maureen accepted an invitation to attend Temple University's College of Allied Health Professionals and earned a Master of Physical Therapy degree. She has worked at the renowned Children's Hospital of Philadelphia and Children's Seashore House.

Maureen is the proud mother of two happy little boys and two adorable little girls. After the birth of her first son, Maureen began experimenting with methods to improve the quality and duration of his sleep, which led her to invent the Magic Sleepsuit and start her own company.

All four of her children have used and benefited from the Magic Sleepsuit, and now tens of thousands of babies around the world have, too.
info@magicsleepsuit.com • www.magicsleepsuit.com

BONNIE GRIFFIN KAAKE

Bonnie Griffin Kaake has thirty years of experience working with innovative product-based businesses and inventors. She enjoyed a long career with General Electric, where she was the recipient of many awards for her marketing expertise. She holds a BS in Business Administration, and is a graduate of GE's Technical Marketing and Management Program. She is also the founder of Innovative Consulting Group, Inc., which provides consulting and out-sourced marketing services that accelerate product commercialization.

Bonnie has served as president of the Rocky Mountain Inventors Association, and president of the board of directors and executive director of the United Inventors Association of America. She is a published author, entrepreneur, national speaker, guest lecturer, frequent contributor to forums and blogs, inventor, and inventor's advocate. Recently, she introduced Inventors' List, a website with a growing list of providers of inventor services and reviews of their services.
bgkaake@biz-consult.com
www.icgproductmarketing.com • www.inventorslist.com

JACK LANDER

Jack Lander is a seasoned inventor and mentor to inventors. With thirteen patents, Jack is also a small-business veteran, having founded eleven businesses. He is a past president of the United Inventors Association, and served as Vice President of the Yankee Invention Exposition for fourteen years. He is the founder of DIG, the Danbury (Connecticut) Inventor's Group, and is also a popular speaker around the country. The author of four published books, Jack has also written a column for *Inventors Digest* for the past sixteen years. Jack and his wife, Mary, a retired high school teacher, live in Southbury, Connecticut. He has two grown sons, Jeffrey and Peter, by a previous marriage.

JackL359@aol.com • www.inventor-mentor.com

JOAN LEFKOWITZ

Joan Lefkowitz is the president of ACCESSORY BRAIN-STORMS, Inc., a licensing, sales representation agency, and consultancy for inventions in the fields of fashion, beauty, and intimate apparel; accessories; and lifestyle. Based in New York, it licenses inventors' products to major corporations, and markets to mail-order catalogues, TV shopping programs, and retail outlets. Its products include Topsy Tail and Hairdini.

Specializing in representing unique products and inventions since 1984, ACCESSORY BRAINSTORMS, Inc. is always interested in seeing new products and offers one-on-one consulting to inventors who need guidance. *Accessories* awarded Joan for having the "Most Inventive Products," and also cited her as one of the 100 most important accessories industry "Movers and Shakers."

web@accessorybrainstorms.com • www.accessorybrainstorms.com

LEO MAZUR

Leo Mazur is a former president of the Inventors Society of South Florida and continues to field questions of all types from inventors located all over the world. If he doesn't know the answer to an inventor's question, he will work to find the answer, or show the inventor how to find it. Although Leo makes his own prototypes, does his own research, and has written and prosecuted his own patents, he strongly believes in using a team of experts for a project that warrants one.

mazurelectric@earthlink.net • www.inventorssociety.net

GIL R. TATARSKY

Gil has a wide range of business experience, from developing raw ideas into market opportunities to working with multibillion-dollar global companies. Since 2001, he has been actively involved in the direct response television industry through the creation, introduction, and marketing of several products. Gil formed Distinct Creations in 2011 to help inventors get their ideas to market by structuring licensing deals between inventors and direct marketers. Prior to his work in the DRTV industry, Gil was a senior executive and consultant to various Internet startup companies. As COO of a technology company for Internet recruiting, he helped grow the business by directing the merger of two complementary Internet companies.

Gil is a CPA and a graduate of SUNY Albany's Business School. He has nearly a decade of corporate experience, including work for the world's largest consulting and accounting firm, PricewaterhouseCoopers LLP (PwC). As part of PwC's Entertainment and Media Group, he oversaw large multinational clients such as Viacom, Sony Music, and Reuters. He was also part of the initial implementation team for the launch of Sony's PlayStation.

gil.tatarsky@verizon.net • www.yourideastolife.com

EDDIE VÉLEZ

Eddie Vélez is the founder and CEO of Success by Design, located in Tampa Bay, Florida, and has over twenty years of experience in formulating marketing strategies and implementing the tactics and support material necessary for a synergistic plan. Eddie is a graduate of The School of Art and Design in New York City, with a major in advertising, and has a bachelor's degree in Business Administration. He apprenticed under Neal Martineau of Ogilvy and Mather—a three-time winner of the Ogilvy Award for Advertising Excellence.

Eddie is also a website designer and creative content writer. He creates effective websites with marketing strategy and the client's goals in mind. Success by Design specializes in all aspects of marketing, advertising, and design.

me@eddievelez.net • www.eddievelez.net
www.linkedin.com/in/ successbydesign • twitter.com/edgardovelez
• www.facebook.com/eddie.velez.1840

KAREN WAKSMAN

Karen Waksman is a manufacturer's rep turned author, speaker, and consultant. She has sold millions of units to the world's largest retailers and now teaches her proven sales strategies to thousands of product companies across the country. She is the founder and CEO of Retail MBA, which provides a step-by-step plan on how to approach and pitch to chain store buyers effectively.

karen@retailmba.com • www.retailmba.com

JOSH WALLACE

Award-winning designer Josh Wallace earned his degree in graphic design at the Art Institutes International, Minnesota. He remains in the Twin Cities, where he works on a variety of projects in the fields of graphics, advertising, and illustration, including children's books. His main clients have always been small businesses and proprietorships, for which he manages logos, business cards, brochures, packaging, product illustration, ad design, and more.

joshw@joshwallace.com • www.joshwallace.com

About the Editor

Edith G. Tolchin, "The Sourcing Lady," has over thirty-five years of international trade experience and has worked exclusively with factories in China and Taiwan since 1990. She created EGT Global Trading in 1997, with a goal to link U.S. inventors with Asian manufacturers, and to provide an exclusive import service for sourcing, quality control, production testing and safety issues, manufacturing, international financing, air and ocean shipping, customs clearance arrangements, and dock-to-door delivery. EGT Global Trading specializes in offshore manufacturing services for inventions of textiles and sewn items, bags, baby and fashion accessories, unique arts and crafts items, and household goods.

Ms. Tolchin began her career in import and international trade fresh out of New York University, with a New York City importer of frozen fish and bicycles, and has dealt with both large and small importers, handling all sorts of commodities, including salted nuts, chemicals, waxes, apparel, and toys. She holds a U.S. Customs Broker License and has extensive experience with U.S. Customs and customs brokers of various products and issues, including binding rulings, duty protests, and drawbacks. She is an expert in the Consumer Product Safety Improvement Act's requirements for product safety, the General Certificate of Conformity, and tracking labels.

Along with Don and Eric Debelak, Ms. Tolchin is a coauthor of

Sourcing Smarts: Keeping it SIMPLE and SAFE with China Sourcing and Manufacturing. She is also a contributing editor and freelance writer for *Inventors Digest* magazine. She regularly provides pro bono presentations for inventors' organizations and trade shows throughout the United States on topics such as importing basics, offshore manufacturing, and the Consumer Product Safety Improvement Act.

www.egtglobaltrading.com • www.edietolchin.com • EGT@egtglobaltrading.com • twitter.com/QueenWrites • www.facebook.com/QueenWrites

Index

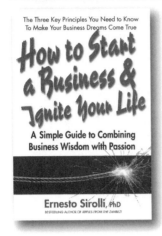

HOW TO START A BUSINESS & IGNITE YOUR LIFE

A Simple Guide to Combining Business Wisdom with Passion

Ernesto Sirolli, PhD

Starting a business from scratch can be a huge undertaking, and even the best have been known to fail because they didn't know a few simple but essential rules. In *How to Start a Business & Ignite Your Life*, world-renowned business consultant Ernesto Sirolli offers an easy-to-follow formula for success that allows you to discover your strengths while surrounding yourself with people who have complementary skills. Using this team approach, you can avoid common pitfalls and make your business dreams come true.

$16.95 • 144 pages • 6 x 9-inch quality paperback • ISBN 978-0-7570-0374-5

DO THIS, GET RICH!

12 Things You Can Do Now to Gain Financial Freedom

Jim Britt

Do This. Get Rich! is a straightforward guide that offers twelve simple yet powerful tools for achieving financial success by awaking the entrepreneur within. You will not only gain the skills needed to build and succeed in your own business, but you will win a new sense of direction and confidence that will guide you in reaching your most ambitious goals. You will also have a practical framework from which to handle everyday personal and business challenges, as well as strategies needed in today's business world.

$25.95 • 216 pages • 6 x 9-inch hardback • ISBN 978-0-7570-0241-0

THE PATENT WRITER

How to Write Successful Patent Applications

Bob DeMatteis, Andy Gibbs,
and Michael Neustel

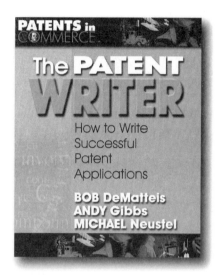

Every year, thousands of inventors and product developers waste their time and money in the pursuit of worthless patents. Why worthless? Because unless you have a clear understanding of the basics of patent writing, your application may be rejected, or—if accepted—may fail to provide you with the protection your invention needs and deserves.

The good news is that you *can* create a powerful patent application that will support and protect your product in any court of law. This book will show you how it's done. In simple layman's terms, *The Patent Writer* provides step-by-step instructions for writing successful patent applications. The authors first help you pinpoint your invention's patentable subject matter, and offer extensive information on identifying claims—an essential step in defining the scope of your patent. They clarify pertinent patent laws and facts, discuss superior word usage, and explore the methodologies required to ensure that your patent cannot be exploited by others. Most important, they take you through each stage of filing a sample application, covering everything from filing fees to international filing rights.

Whether you're a first-time inventor or someone with a pile of patented products, *The Patent Writer* will help avoid the consequences of poorly written patents, guard against infringement-related issues, and save you thousands in lawyer's fees. Endorsed by leading inventors, patent attorneys, and government agencies, this book takes the mystery out of writing patents.

$18.95 • 248 pages • 7.5 x 9-inch quality paperback • ISBN 978-0-7570-0176-5

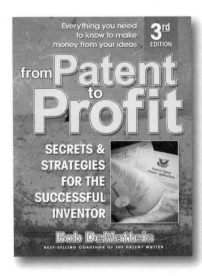

FROM PATENT TO PROFIT

THIRD EDITION

Secrets & Strategies for the Successful Inventor

Bob DeMatteis

Having a novel idea and turning that idea into cash is not quite as simple as it sounds. In today's highly complex and competitive world of business, not knowing what to expect and what to do will almost always guarantee failure. To help innovative individuals learn to navigate around the many pitfalls of inventing, Bob DeMatteis has written this up-to-date guide.

Bob DeMatteis has been directly involved in every phase of the inventing process—creation, patenting, licensing, manufacturing, and marketing. He has enjoyed tremendous successes and has also made his share of mistakes; he has also learned from all of his experiences. Now he has taken his accumulated knowledge and turned it into a well-organized handbook for inventors. The information, forms, insights, and advice found in this book are reliable and easy to understand, and the guidance will allow any individual with a creative streak to sail around potential problems and set a course towards a successful launch.

Whether you are a professional inventor, a part-time dabbler, or just a clever daydreamer, *From Patent to Profit* can help make your dreams a reality.

$29.95 • 432 pages • 8.5 x 11-inch quality paperback • ISBN 978-0-7570-0140-6